# Jewish Identity in Contemporary Architecture
## Jüdische Identität in der zeitgenössischen Architektur

# Jewish Identity in Contemporary Architecture
## Jüdische Identität in der zeitgenössischen Architektur

Edited by | herausgegeben von **Angeli Sachs, Edward van Voolen**

With an introduction by | mit einer Einführung von **Angeli Sachs, Edward van Voolen**

Essays by | von **Samuel D. Gruber, Michael Levin, Edward van Voolen, James E. Young**

and contributions by | und Beiträgen von **Aaron Betsky, Stephen Fox, Ruth Hanisch, Roman Hollenstein, Hans Ibelings, Rudolf Klein, Mordechai Omer, Wolfgang Pehnt, Danette Riddle, Angeli Sachs, Anna Teut, Heinrich Wefing**

Prestel
München · Berlin · London · New York

**Museums | Museen**

## Preface

Is architecture capable of lending form to Jewish identity? The present international survey of contemporary architecture for Jewish institutions, totaling sixteen projects, illustrates key architectural approaches and their relationship to their cultural environment. We hope that the topics addressed and the material presented in the exhibition and catalogue, *Jewish Identity in Contemporary Architecture,* will encourage a more profound discussion on the potential and tasks of contemporary architecture for Jewish institutions, and on the issue of the expression of Jewish identity through architecture.

The exhibition was initiated and organized by the Joods Historisch Museum, Amsterdam. This is no coincidence. Amsterdam is the city where, in the Golden Age of Holland in the seventeenth and eighteenth centuries, Portuguese and Ashkenazi synagogues attested with pride to a flourishing Jewish identity. Admittedly, such striking synagogues were built there, as elsewhere, only when Jews felt at home in their environment or when it gave them a feeling of being welcome. The decision to erect such buildings emerged from a long-term perspective—the ability to say "we live here"—which in Jewish history was sometimes associated with the decision to remain in the Diaspora rather than emigrating to Israel. The present exhibition offers the opportunity to experience the motivation behind present-day decisions to erect such charismatic structures as the Jewish Museum in Berlin or the Dresden Synagogue.

A great number of people and institutions have contributed to making this exhibition and book a reality. Our thanks go first to Edward van Voolen, curator at Joods Historisch Museum, and Angeli Sachs, guest curator and editor-in-chief for architecture and design at Prestel Publishing. With great expertise, persuasiveness, and persistence these two developed the conception, organized the exhibition tour, and undertook the scholarly supervision of both project and catalogue. We are also grateful to their assistant, Sabine Schmid, who mastered the many obstacles involved in collecting the material, and the exhibition team at Joods Historisch Museum, with Bernadette van Woerkom,

## Geleitwort

Kann Architektur der jüdischen Identität Form verleihen? Dieser internationale Überblick über zeitgenössische Architektur für jüdische Institutionen zeigt an 16 Projekten die wichtigsten Architekturhaltungen und ihre Beziehung zum kulturellen Umfeld. Wir hoffen, die Ausstellung und das Katalogbuch *Jewish Identity in Contemporary Architecture* tragen mit den Themen, die sie ansprechen, und dem Material, das sie zu deren Illustration zeigen, zu einer vertieften Diskussion über die Möglichkeiten und Aufgaben der zeitgenössischen Architektur für jüdische Institutionen und die Frage nach dem Ausdruck jüdischer Identität in der Architektur bei.

Initiiert und organisiert wurde diese Ausstellung vom Joods Historisch Museum Amsterdam. Das ist kein Zufall. Amsterdam ist die Stadt, in der im 17. und 18. Jahrhundert, dem Goldenen Zeitalter Hollands, die portugiesischen und aschkenasischen Synagogen mit Stolz von einer starken jüdischen Identität zeugten. Allerdings wurden im Lauf der Jahrhunderte dort und überall sonst nur dann Aufsehen erregende Synagogen gebaut, wenn Juden sich zu Hause fühlten oder ihnen durch ihre Umgebung ein Heimatgefühl vermittelt wurde. Die Entscheidung für diese Bauten hing mit einer langfristigen Perspektive zusammen: Wir leben hier – was manchmal in der jüdischen Geschichte mit der Wahl verbunden war, in der Diaspora zu bleiben und nicht nach Israel auszuwandern. In dieser Ausstellung werden Sie erfahren, was gegenwärtig die Entscheidungen motiviert, Gebäude mit solch großer Ausstrahlungskraft wie das Jüdische Museum in Berlin oder die Dresdner Synagoge zu realisieren.

Viele verschiedene Personen und Institutionen haben zum Gelingen der Ausstellung und des Buches beigetragen. Unser Dank richtet sich zuallererst an Edward van Voolen, Kurator des Joods Historisch Museum, und Angeli Sachs, Gastkuratorin und Cheflektorin für Architektur und Design im Prestel Verlag. Beide haben mit großer fachlicher Kompetenz, Überzeugungskraft und Ausdauer die Konzeption entwickelt, die Ausstellungstournee organisiert und die wissenschaftliche Betreuung des Projekts sowie des Katalogs übernommen. Der Dank gilt weiterhin ihrer Assistentin Sabine Schmid, die mit großer Präzision die oft schwierige Beschaffung des notwendigen Materials leistete, und dem Ausstellungs-

Ischa Mulder and Michèle Jacobs, who professionally handled the extensive organizational problems involved. Our special thanks go to Mark de Jong, of Kossmann.dejong, for the innovative exhibition architecture he designed for Amsterdam. We thank Joram ten Brink for making a documentary on the subject.

The exhibition and catalogue could never have become a reality without the trust, cooperation, and support of the contributing architects and their staffs, the photographers, and other lenders who made material available for the presentation and catalogue. The curators wish to thank the contributing architects for conversations that inspired the project, and their colleagues in the field who accompanied it with interest and their ideas. The exhibition tour was facilitated by the willingness of the guest museums in Osnabrück, Warsaw, Berlin, Vienna, Munich, and London to enter, with the Joods Historisch Museum in Amsterdam, on this journey of several years. The result is a truly European project that does justice to current aspects of the issue of Jewish identity in architecture. Without the aid of numerous sponsors in the different countries, to whom we wish to convey our cordial thanks, we could never have realized this important exhibition.

The editors were able to gain the support of internationally distinguished authors for the book. Each of them has faced the challenge of shedding light on fundamental issues raised by forms of Jewish identity, and of analyzing these contemporary projects in terms of the multifarious aspects of their architects' stance combined with the cultural and urban context. Prestel Publishing, with project director Angeli Sachs, has supported the production of this book with great commitment. We appreciate the demanding work of the translators, John Gabriel, Bram Opstelten, and Annette Wiethüchter, the copyeditor Charles Heard, editorial assistant Sabine Schmid, and Cilly Klotz, who provided the compelling book design.

We wish you an interesting and exciting experience with the exhibition and book.

team des Joods Historisch Museum mit Bernadette van Woerkom, Ischa Mulder und Michèle Jacobs, die sich um die umfangreiche Organisation der Ausstellung kümmerten. Ganz besonders möchten wir uns auch bei Mark de Jong von Kossmann.dejong für seine innovative Ausstellungsarchitektur in Amsterdam bedanken. Wir danken Joram ten Brink für seine Dokumentation zum Thema.

Ausstellung und Katalog wären nicht möglich ohne das Vertrauen, die Mitarbeit und Unterstützung der beteiligten Architekten und ihrer Mitarbeiter, der Fotografen und anderer Leihgeber, die uns das Material für die Präsentation und den Katalog zur Verfügung gestellt haben. Die Kuratoren danken den Architekten für Gespräche, die das Projekt inspiriert haben, ebenso den Fachkollegen, die sie mit ihrem Interesse und ihren Ideen begleitet haben. Die Ausstellungstournee wird möglich durch die Bereitschaft der Gastmuseen in Osnabrück, Warschau, Berlin, Wien, München und London, sich mit dem Joods Historisch Museum Amsterdam auf diese mehrjährige Reise einzulassen – so ist ein wahrhaft europäisches Projekt entstanden, das den aktuellen Dimensionen der Fragestellung gerecht wird. Ohne die Hilfe der zahlreichen Sponsoren in den verschiedenen Ländern, denen wir an dieser Stelle besonders herzlich danken möchten, hätten wir diese Ausstellung nicht realisieren können.

Für das Buch konnten die Herausgeber international angesehene Autoren gewinnen. Alle haben sich der Herausforderung gestellt, in ihren Essays die grundlegenden Fragestellungen der Formen jüdischer Identität zu analysieren und die zeitgenössischen Projekte unter den vielfältigen Aspekten der architektonischen Haltung ihrer Architekten sowie Fragen des kulturellen und urbanen Kontexts differenziert darzustellen. Der Prestel Verlag und die Projektleiterin Angeli Sachs haben die Entstehung dieses Buches mit großem Engagement unterstützt. Unser Dank gilt der anspruchsvollen Arbeit der Übersetzer John Gabriel, Bram Opstelten und Annette Wiethüchter, des Lektors Charles Heard, der Lektoratsassistentin Sabine Schmid sowie Cilly Klotz für ihre überzeugende Buchgestaltung.

Wir wünschen Ihnen mit der Ausstellung und dem Buch eine anregende und interessante Zeit.

| | |
|---|---|
| Joel Cahen | Joods Historisch Museum, Amsterdam |
| Inge Jaehner | Felix-Nussbaum-Haus, Osnabrück |
| Jerzy Halbersztadt | Museum of the History of Polish Jews, Warsaw \| |
| | Museum für die Geschichte der polnischen Juden, Warschau |
| W. Michael Blumenthal | Jüdisches Museum Berlin |
| Karl Albrecht-Weinberger | Jüdisches Museum Wien |
| Wolfgang Till | Münchner Stadtmuseum |
| Richard Aronowitz-Mercer | Ben Uri Gallery, The London Jewish Museum of Art |

## Introduction

Building for Jewish institutions means building for Jewish identity. Buildings such as museums, synagogues, community centers, and schools are not merely accommodations for the activities of Jewish communities or attempts to give shape to the history of Jewish life or the Holocaust. Being public buildings, they are also an external expression of Jewish identity. This identity is shaped not only by Jewish culture and religion but also by the dislocations in Jewish history, particularly in the twentieth century. There is a tension between Jewish life as an ongoing or re-emerging entity and the extinction of Jewish life and Jewish culture during the Nazi era that is ever-present in personal experience or memory.

The situation varies, of course, fundamentally from country to country. Continuity and adoption of regional traditions contrast with the search for new, appropriate forms of expression in architecture. In the USA, the architecture of Jewish institutions looks back on a long history of uninterrupted development, but important new buildings are sporadic and reflect the general range of architectural concepts. Examples are Ralph Appelbaum's Holocaust Museum in Houston, Will Bruder's community center in Scottsdale, or Mehrdad Yazdani's school in Los Angeles. In Israel, a building style has developed since the beginning of the twentieth century—most prominently since the great wave of immigration from 1933 on—that has adopted not only international modernism but also elements of Mediterranean architectural traditions. Mario Botta's synagogue in Tel Aviv, Moshe Safdie's new Holocaust Museum for Yad Vashem, and Al Mansfeld's school in Ramat Alon are excellent examples of this architectural tradition. In Europe, especially Germany, the situation is quite different again. At the end of World War II, Jewish culture had been largely destroyed and Jewish communities were infinitesimal in comparison with prewar times. Their architectural presence was correspondingly inconspicuous. This situation changed with new waves of immigration. But whereas the influx of North African Jews into France did not trigger any noteworthy building activity, the immigration of Russian Jews into Germany after nearly seventy years of oppression in the former Soviet Union led to a radical change, i.e., an unanticipated growth in Jewish communities and to a number of innovative projects by leading architects—which gave shape to this development.

It was initially buildings for Jewish and Holocaust museums that gave expression to an altered Jewish self-awareness. The starting point was to break the silence and anchor Jewish life and Jewish history—including the history of destruction—conspicuously in society and the urban landscape. At first, existing buildings were converted into the first major Jewish museums. These were followed by relatively traditional new buildings like the Holocaust Memorial Museum in Washington. They manifested architectural significance mainly in the interiors of the structures, in the display architecture. But by the time Daniel Libeskind came to design the Jewish Museum in Berlin, things had changed. In Berlin, worldwide attention focused on an architecture whose external form and inner structure is a clear expression of the memory of Jewish life in Germany and its extinction during the Nazi era. And the consequence has been that buildings for Jewish communities and schools now assert a more pronounced architectonic character in the European

## Einführung

Bauen für jüdische Institutionen bedeutet Bauen für die jüdische Identität. Denn Bauaufgaben wie Museen, Synagogen, Gemeindezentren oder Schulen sind nicht nur Behausungen für die Aktivitäten einer jüdischen Gemeinde oder der Versuch, der Geschichte jüdischen Lebens und des Holocaust Form zu verleihen, sondern als öffentliche Bauten auch Ausdruck des jüdischen Selbstverständnisses nach außen. Dieses ist sowohl von der jüdischen Kultur und Religion als auch von den Brüchen innerhalb der jüdischen Geschichte, besonders im 20. Jahrhundert, bestimmt. Es besteht eine Spannung zwischen den Polen fortdauernden oder wiedererwachenden jüdischen Lebens und der in der persönlichen Erfahrung oder Erinnerung stets anwesenden Auslöschung jüdischen Lebens und jüdischer Kultur während des Nationalsozialismus.

Dabei unterscheiden sich die Situationen in den verschiedenen Ländern grundlegend. Kontinuität und Aufgreifen regionaler Traditionen stehen im Kontrast zu der Suche nach neuen, angemessenen Ausdrucksmöglichkeiten in der Architektur. In den USA kann die Architektur für jüdische Institutionen auf eine lange Geschichte ungestörter Entwicklung zurückblicken, in der jetzt nur noch punktuell bedeutende Neubauten entstehen, die von unterschiedlichen architektonischen Haltungen geprägt sind. Beispiele sind Ralph Appelbaums Holocaust Museum in Houston, Will Bruders Gemeindezentrum in Scottsdale oder Mehrdad Yazdanis Schule in Los Angeles. In Israel entwickelte sich seit Beginn des 20. Jahrhunderts, aber vor allem mit der großen Einwanderungswelle ab 1933 ein Baustil, der neben der internationalen Moderne Elemente mediterraner architektonischer Traditionen aufgreift. Mario Bottas Synagoge in Tel Aviv, Moshe Safdies neues Holocaust Museum für Yad Vashem und Al Mansfelds Schule in Ramat Alon sind besonders qualitätvolle Beispiele dafür. Ganz anders verhält sich dagegen die Situation in Europa, vor allem in Deutschland, wo die jüdische Kultur nach dem Ende des Zweiten Weltkrieges weitgehend zerstört und die jüdischen Gemeinden im Gegensatz zur Vorkriegszeit verschwindend klein waren. Entsprechend unauffällig war ihre architektonische Präsenz. Verändert wurde diese Situation durch neue Einwanderungsbewegungen. Doch während der Zuzug nordafrikanischer Juden nach Frankreich keine nennenswerte Bauaktivität auslöste, führte in Deutschland die Immigration der russischen Juden nach fast siebzig Jahren Unterdrückung in der ehemaligen Sowjetunion zu einer radikalen Veränderung der Situation, zu einem ungeahnten Wachstum der jüdischen Gemeinden und damit zu innovativen Projekten bedeutender Architekten, die dieser Entwicklung Raum geben.

Es waren zuerst die Bauten für jüdische Museen und Holocaust-Museen, die einem veränderten jüdischen Selbstverständnis Ausdruck verliehen. Der Ausgangspunkt war, das Schweigen zu brechen und das eigene Leben und die eigene Geschichte, aber auch die Geschichte ihrer Vernichtung unübersehbar in der Gesellschaft und in der urbanen Landschaft zu verankern. Am Beginn standen die Umnutzung vorhandener Gebäude als erste größere jüdische Museen. Darauf folgten relativ traditionelle Neubauten wie das United States Holocaust Memorial Museum in Washington. Sie entfalteten mit architektonischen Mitteln Bedeutsamkeit vor allem im Inneren des Baus, in der Ausstellungsarchitektur. Diese Situation hat sich spätestens mit Daniel Libeskinds Berliner Jüdischem Museum geändert. Die weltweite Aufmerksamkeit gilt einer Architektur, die in ihrer äußeren Form und inneren Struktur deutlicher Ausdruck der Erinnerung an

Diaspora. The new community center by Zvi Hecker in Duisburg not only occupies a prominent location in the city, but its vaulting structure attracts attention as an ambitious, even conspicuous work. But this can be achieved as well through other architectural languages which convey presence and confidence in ways that are apparently all too obvious. In our selection, this is the case for the entrance building of Kamp Vught by Claus en Kaan, the schools of Adolf Krischanitz in Vienna, and the synagogues and community centers by Wandel Hoefer Lorch + Hirsch in Dresden and Munich.

At the same time, there has been an international exchange of architectural ideas. The Swiss architect Mario Botta has built in Israel. Likewise, the American architect Frank O. Gehry, with the Jerusalem Museum of Tolerance, is building his first Jewish structure. Architects like Zvi Hecker and Moshe Safdie have worked in Israel, Europe, and the USA. Daniel Libeskind has made the transition from Germany to America not only with his design for the new World Trade Center, but also with the project for the new Jewish Museum in San Francisco.

Our intention is to provide an international overview of the contemporary architecture of Jewish institutions in the late twentieth and early twenty-first centuries. A key consideration was the observation that the major publications and exhibitions on these subjects only covered the period up to the 1980s, and since that time a number of buildings have been constructed that have aroused interest worldwide. Indeed, a trend is emerging that, to a certain extent, can be described as "Jewish avant-garde." But this itself is a rather nebulous notion because many Jewish architects like Richard Meier, and until recently Frank O. Gehry, built neither in a Jewish style nor for Jewish institutions. On the other hand, non-Jewish architects such as Mario Botta and Will Bruder have built outstanding buildings for Jewish institutions. The term is most readily applicable where Jewish culture and religion, symbols or Hebrew script have been taken on board in the architectural design as in Daniel Libeskind's idea for the Jewish Museum in San Francisco. To some extent, these avant-garde projects are linked to the architectural idiom of deconstructivism, which appears particularly suited to expressing in concrete terms the discontinuity of history, its fractures, caesuras, and deformations. But it is only one of many possibilities.

Popular interest in Jewish life and culture has increased dramatically in recent years. A project at whose center contains the question of the forms of Jewish identity in architecture, helps to explain the concerns of Jews as well as that which remains incomprehensible to non-Jews. In addition to presenting these outstanding contemporary architectural projects, we also aim to initiate a dialogue about creating structures for different religions which do justice to their own particular identity in a society which is becoming increasingly pluralistic. It is hoped that mutual understanding and tolerance will develop on the basis of this exchange.

Angeli Sachs and Edward van Voolen

die jüdische Geschichte Deutschlands und ihrer Auslöschung während des Nationalsozialismus ist. Und in der Folge künden auch Bauten für jüdische Gemeinden und Schulen von einer stärkeren jüdischen Präsenz in der europäischen Diaspora. Das neue Gemeindezentrum von Zvi Hecker in Duisburg ist nicht nur an einem prominenten städtischen Ort entstanden, sondern mit seiner ausgreifenden Struktur ein Aufmerksamkeit beanspruchendes, ja unübersehbares Bauwerk. Aber dies lässt sich auch durch andere Architektursprachen erreichen, die Präsenz und Selbstbewusstsein durch das scheinbar Selbstverständliche zum Ausdruck bringen. Dies gilt für das Eingangsgebäude von Claus en Kaan in Kamp Vught, die Schulen von Adolf Krischanitz in Wien und die Synagogen und Gemeindezentren von Wandel Hoefer Lorch + Hirsch in Dresden und München.

Gleichzeitig findet ein internationaler Architekturaustausch statt: Der Tessiner Architekt Mario Botta baut in Israel, ebenso der amerikanische Architekt Frank O. Gehry, dessen Jerusalem Museum of Tolerance sein erster jüdischer Bauauftrag ist. Architekten wie Zvi Hecker und Moshe Safdie arbeiten sowohl in Israel wie in Europa und den USA, und Daniel Libeskind hat sich nicht nur mit seinem Entwurf für das World Trade Center, sondern auch mit dem Projekt des Jüdischen Museums in San Francisco von deutschem auf amerikanischen Boden begeben.

Unser Ziel ist ein internationaler Überblick über die zeitgenössische Architektur für jüdische Institutionen am Ende des 20. Jahrhunderts bis in die ersten Jahre des 21. Jahrhunderts. Ausschlaggebend war die Beobachtung, dass die wichtigen umfassenderen Publikationen und Ausstellungen zu diesen Themen nur den Zeitraum bis in die 1980er Jahre darstellen, seitdem aber etliche Bauten entstanden sind, die weltweit Beachtung gefunden haben, und sich eine Entwicklung abzeichnet, die teilweise als »jüdische Avantgarde« betrachtet wird. Dies ist schon deshalb ein unscharfer Begriff, weil viele jüdische Architekten wie Richard Meier und bis vor kurzem Frank O. Gehry weder in irgendeiner Form jüdisch noch für jüdische Institutionen bauen. Andererseits haben nichtjüdische Architekten wie Mario Botta oder Will Bruder herausragende Bauten für jüdische Institutionen realisiert. Worauf dieser Begriff am ehesten anwendbar ist, ist die Berücksichtigung jüdischer Kultur und Religion, Symbole oder der hebräischen Schrift im architektonischen Entwurf, wie es zum Beispiel in Daniel Libeskinds Ideen für das Jüdische Museum in San Francisco einfließt. Zum Teil sind diese avantgardistischen Projekte mit der Architektursprache des Dekonstruktivismus verbunden, die besonders geeignet scheint, die Diskontinuität der Geschichte, ihre Brüche, Einschnitte und Deformationen anschaulich auszudrücken. Aber sie ist nur eine unter vielen Möglichkeiten.

Das öffentliche Interesse an jüdischem Leben und jüdischer Kultur hat in den letzten Jahren stark zugenommen. Ein Projekt, in dessen Zentrum die Frage nach den Formen jüdischer Identität in der Architektur steht, hilft vieles verstehen, was Juden beschäftigt und Nichtjuden sonst häufig unverständlich bleibt. Neben der Vorstellung dieser herausragenden zeitgenössischen Architekturprojekte ist es unser Anliegen, ein Gespräch über die Gestaltung unterschiedlicher religiöser und kultureller Identitäten in einer zunehmend pluralistischen Gesellschaft anzuregen. Auf der Basis dieses Austauschs werden sich gegenseitiges Verständnis und Toleranz hoffentlich weiter entwickeln.

Angeli Sachs und Edward van Voolen

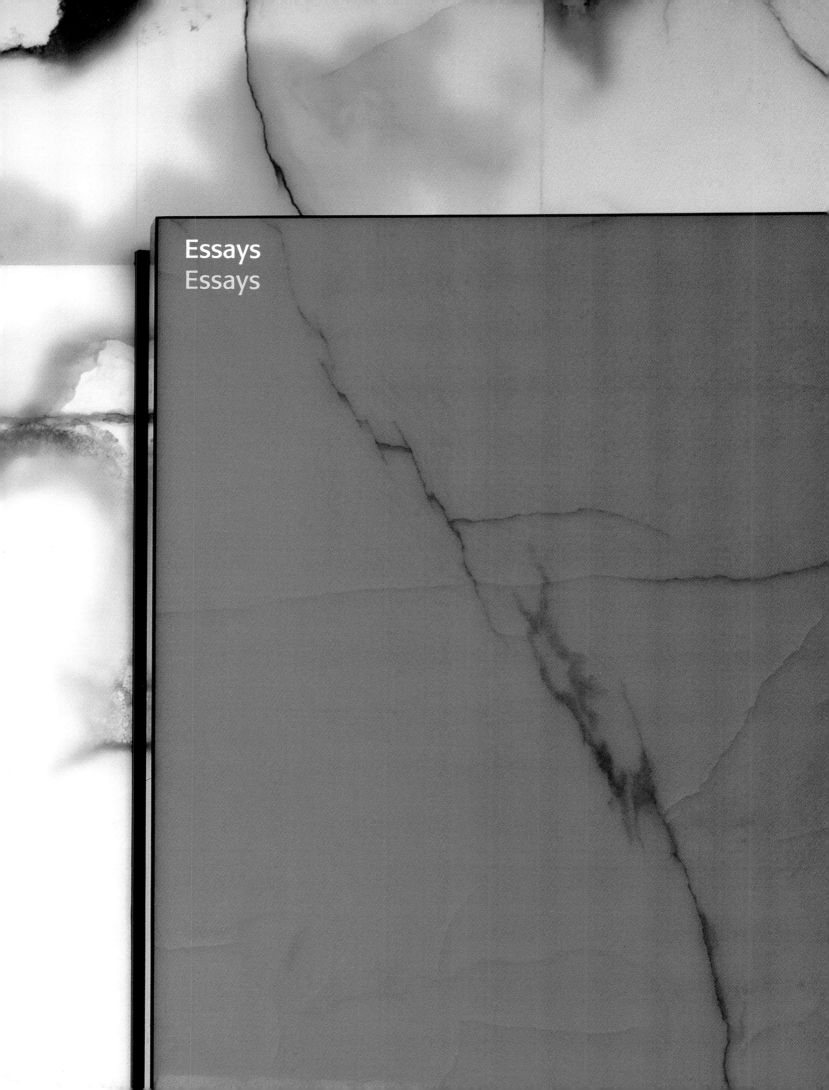

Essays
Essays

Edward van Voolen

## From Time to Place
## Shaping Memory in Judaism

From their earliest origins over four millennia ago, Jews have been dealing with and living through the tension between Diaspora and home. Most of their existence was a wandering one—living in Israel, the Promised Land, was the exception. Their only sanctuary and most glorious building, the Temple in Jerusalem (founded three thousand years ago), was destroyed for the first time in 586 BCE and once more two millennia ago in the year 70 CE. In the Diaspora that followed, remains of Jewish material culture, apart from its writings, are few and far between.

For Jews, a little sanctuary in the form of a modest building would suffice for prayer, study, and gatherings. The earliest examples go back some two millennia. Mostly inconspicuous and small, synagogue architecture prospered in the following centuries wherever the Jewish minority lived securely.

Model of the Second Temple in Jerusalem. Germany, ca. 1920    Modell des Zweiten Tempels in Jerusalem. Deutschland, ca. 1920

The two essential requirements for a synagogue have remained the same. The first is the Ark, the Hebrew name of which (*aron ha-kodesh*) recalls of the Ark in the Holy of Holies in the Tabernacle and Temple. This shrine, placed in a niche directed toward Jerusalem, contains the holiest and most precious object Jews possess—one or more handwritten parchment scrolls with the text of the Pentateuch (*Torah*). Each scroll, with the text of the first five books of the Hebrew bible, is carefully dressed in protective textiles and decorative silver. The Ark is the

Edward van Voolen

## Von Zeit zu Ort.
## Wie Erinnerung im Judentum Form annimmt

Seit Anbeginn ihrer Existenz vor über 4 000 Jahren mussten die Juden mit einem Leben im Spannungsfeld zwischen Diaspora und Heimat umgehen. Die meiste Zeit waren sie ein Volk auf Wanderschaft – Leben in Israel, dem Gelobten Land, war die Ausnahme. Ihr einziges Heiligtum und prächtigstes Gebäude, der vor 3 000 Jahren erbaute Tempel in Jerusalem, wurde zum ersten Mal im Jahr 586 vor unserer Zeitrechnung zerstört und ein zweites Mal im Jahr 70 unserer Zeit. Aus der darauf folgenden Periode des Exils, der Diaspora, sind, abgesehen von Schriften, nur wenige Beispiele jüdischer Kultur erhalten geblieben.

Den Juden sollte von nun an ein kleines Heiligtum in Form eines bescheidenen Gebäudes für Gebet, Studium und Versammlungen genügen. Die frühesten erhaltenen Beispiele sind etwa 2000 Jahre alt. Die meist unauffällige und in ihren Ausmaßen bescheidene Synagogenarchitektur erlebte in den folgenden Jahrhunderten ihre Blüte überall da, wo jüdische Minderheiten in Sicherheit lebten.

Die zwei unerlässlichen Elemente einer Synagoge sind bis heute dieselben geblieben: Das erste ist der Thoraschrein, dessen hebräischer Name Aron ha-Kodesch auf den Schrein für das Allerheiligste im Tabernakel und im Tempel hinweist. Dieser Schrein in einer nach Jerusalem ausgerichteten Wandnische nimmt die heiligsten und kostbarsten Gegenstände auf, die Juden besitzen: eine oder mehrere handbeschriebene Pergamentrollen mit den Texten des Pentateuchs – die Thora. Jede Rolle dieser fünf Bücher Mose, der ersten fünf Abschnitte der hebräischen Bibel, wird mit Stoff und Silberschmuck bekleidet. Der Thoraschrein ist der heilige Raum der Synagoge und traditionell die Stelle, an der diese Kultgegenstände aufbewahrt, gesammelt und sorgsam erhalten wurden – Hunderte von Jahren, bevor jüdische Museen diese Aufgabe übernahmen und zu Hauptaufbewahrungsorten dieser zeremoniellen Objekte wurden.

Ebenso unerlässlich ist in jeder Synagoge das Lesepult (Bima) für Lesungen aus der Thora und die Auslegung der Textstellen. Die Bima befindet sich meistens in der Mitte des Saals, oft aber auch vor der Rückwand oder direkt vor dem Thoraschrein. In prämodernen und heute in traditionellen Synagogen sitzen die Frauen von den Männern getrennt im hinteren Teil des Raums oder auf einer Empore. Synagogen gehören häufig zu einem Gebäudekomplex, der eine Schule, ein Ritualbad, eine Bibliothek, ein Restaurant und eine Empfangshalle umfasst – ein Gemeindezentrum im modernen Sinn.

Die Synagoge ist der Ort, wo die Thora in einem jährlichen Zyklus jede Woche vorgelesen und von Gelehrten (Rabbinern) ausgelegt wird, die ihre Geschichten und Instruktionen auf das heutige jüdische Leben übertragen. Der liturgische Kalender mit seinen wöchentlichen Sabbat-Tagen und saisonalen Festen, mit Predigten, liturgischen Dichtungen, Ritualen und Bräuchen wurde zum Hauptvehikel jüdischer Geschichte und jüdi-

Pages    Seiten 10/11
Detail of Mario Botta's Cymbalista Synagogue    Detail aus Mario Bottas Cymbalista-Synagoge

synagogue's sacred space. It is traditionally the place where these ritual objects are stored, collected, and carefully preserved—centuries before Jewish museums would take over that role, becoming the chief receptacle for ceremonial objects.

Equally important in the synagogue is the presence of a platform (*bimah*), from which the Torah can be read and expounded. The bimah is often situated the middle of the building, but can also be found towards the rear, or right in front of the Ark. In pre-modern synagogues and traditional synagogues today, women sit separately in the back or on a gallery. As a building, the synagogue is often part of a complex including a school, ritual bath, library, restaurant, and reception hall— a community center in the modern sense of the word.

The synagogue is the place where the Torah is read every week in a yearly cycle and explained by scholars (rabbis) who apply its stories and instructions to contemporary Jewish living. The liturgical calendar with its weekly Sabbaths and seasonal festivals, with its sermons, liturgical poetry, rituals, and customs became the main vehicles of Jewish history and Jewish memory, as Yosef Yerushalmi has pointed out in his classic study *Zakhor*.[1] In the synagogue, Jewish collective memory materialized and was kept alive, long before Jewish museums would attempt to take over that function for secularized Jews in the late nineteenth century. For additional historical information, Jews relied on communal record books (*pinkassim*) and memorial lists (*memorbooks*). Chronological accounts and histories in the modern sense appeared occasionally in the Renaissance before becoming common in the nineteenth century.

Jews cared about scripture and books, particularly about the holy book, the Torah, which they could carry wherever they went. The temporality of the synagogue, the place where the memory of the past is kept alive and applied to the present situation, is accentuated by an unfinished piece of wall, as a reminder of the destruction of the Temple (*zekher le-churban*), or for that matter, of any possible destruction.

In the beginning there was exile, as several modern Jewish historians and thinkers have pointed out.[2] Most of Jewish history has taken place in exile; exile is the essence of the Jewish people. The biblical drama begins with the expulsion of Adam and Eve from Paradise.[3] From Abraham onward (who was himself born in exile), Jewish history moves between exile and home with all its heroes continually wandering between various places in the ancient Near East, between Mesopotamia, Canaan, and Egypt. Equally, the Pentateuch's core events take place outside the land: The exodus starts from Egypt, and the giving of the Torah—the constitution—takes place during the wanderings through the desert.

The memory of slavery in the Egyptian Diaspora was to impress itself indelibly on Jewish conscience and would influence the celebration of all festivals and lifecycle events. Three seasonal festivals—Passover, the Festival of Weeks, and Tabernacles—celebrate and commemorate the exodus, the giving of the constitution, and the desert wanderings respectively. Only the High Holidays in autumn solemnly recall the service at a long since destroyed Temple in Jerusalem. Purim, the Feast of Lots, recollects how Jews were saved from physical extinction in the Persian Diaspora, somewhere in the fifth century BCE. Hanukah, which celebrates the rededication of the Jerusalem Temple in the second century BCE, has, from the time of its inception, shifted the focus from a military victory to the miracle of the spiritual survival of Jews wherever they live. Significantly, no festival exists to mark the entry into the bib-

Curtain for Torah Ark with attributes of the Tabernacle, framed by two twisted columns Jachin and Boaz as in the Temple of Solomon, the Netherlands, 1830, 1876
Vorhang für den Thoraschrein mit Attributen des Tabernakels, eingerahmt von zwei gedrehten Säulen Jachin und Boaz, wie in Salomons Tempel. Niederlande, 1830, 1876

scher Erinnerung, wie Yosef Yerushalmi in seiner klassischen Studie *Zachor*[1] festgestellt hat. In der Synagoge materialisierte sich das kollektive jüdische Gedächtnis und wurde wachgehalten, lange bevor jüdische Museen den Versuch unternahmen, für die säkularisierten Juden im ausgehenden 19. Jahrhundert diese Funktion zu übernehmen. Bei der Beschaffung zusätzlicher historischer Informationen verließen sich die Juden auf Gemeinderegister (Pinkassim) und die Listen der Verstorbenen (Memorbücher). Chroniken und Geschichtsbücher im modernen Sinn kamen vereinzelt in der Renaissance auf, bevor sie im 19. Jahrhundert üblich wurden.

Für Juden waren Schriften und Bücher von besonderer Bedeutung, besonders aber das Heilige Buch, die Thora, die sie mit sich tragen konnten, wo immer sie hinzogen. Die Zeitlichkeit der Synagoge als des Ortes, an dem die Erinnerungen an die Vergangenheit wachgehalten und auf das Leben in der Gegenwart übertragen werden, wird durch ein unvollendetes Wandstück betont, das an die Zerstörung des Tempels (Secher le-Churban) erinnern soll – und im Übrigen an jede Art von Vernichtung.

Am Anfang war das Exil, wie einige moderne jüdische Historiker und Philosophen ausgeführt haben.[2] Der Großteil der jüdischen Geschichte hat im Exil stattgefunden; das Exil bildet die Substanz des Volkes Israel. Das biblische Drama beginnt mit Adams und Evas Vertreibung aus dem Paradies.[3] Seit Abraham (der selbst im Exil zur Welt kam) hat sich die jüdische Geschichte stets zwischen Diaspora und Heimat abgespielt, und ihre Helden zogen im Nahen Osten der Antike zwischen Mesopotamien, Kanaan und Ägypten von Ort zu Ort. Auch die im Pentateuch beschriebenen Hauptereignisse fanden fern der Heimat statt: Der Exodus ging von Ägypten aus, und die Thora – die Gesetze – erhielt das Volk Israel auf seiner Wanderschaft in der Wüste.

Die Erinnerung an die Sklaverei in der ägyptischen Diaspora sollte sich dem jüdischen Bewusstsein unauslöschlich einprägen und die Feiern sämtlicher Feste und markanter Ereignisse des Lebenszyklus prägen. Drei jahreszeitliche Feiertage – Pessach, Wochenfest und Laubhüttenfest – erinnern an den Auszug aus Ägypten, die Übergabe der Gesetze und die Wanderschaft in der Wüste. Nur die Hohen Feiertage im Herbst erinnern

lical land. However, the destruction of the First and Second Temple, marking Exile, is commemorated by way of a fast day.

The cyclical structure of the Jewish year enables Jews to relive their past and can be applied to all following Jewish experiences in the course of time. After the Temple's destruction, all festivals were reinterpreted by the rabbis from sacrificial services in Jerusalem to celebrations at home and in the synagogue, wherever these were erected. Since His house was destroyed, even God Himself was now perceived as having gone into exile, His divine presence accompanying His people during their wanderings. Protected by the divine presence (shechinah), each Jew in every generation could imagine himself as if he went out of Egypt. This ancient rabbinic metaphor for the communal celebration during the Passover meal was aptly applied to all festivals of the year.

Somewhat deviating from this pattern is, interestingly enough, the day on which the mass destruction of European Jewry during the Second World War is remembered, the Holocaust (a word meaning whole burnt offering). Rather than being associated with the fast days commemorating the (beginning of) the destruction of the Temple, the Shoa (this preferred Hebrew word means destruction) is remembered on the twenty-seventh of the month of Nissan, a day close to the start of the Warsaw Ghetto Uprising in April 1943. This time of year coincides with the destruction of many Jewish communities by the Crusaders, who are seen as forefathers of the Nazis. The day is officially called Yom Hashoa Vehagevurah (Day of Destruction and Heroism), the latter term countering the popular myth of Jewish passivity in the Diaspora and addressing the "shame" of victims and survivors. In the calendar, Yom Hashoa falls right after Passover which celebrates the liberation from Egyptian bondage, and before Israel's Independence Day which marks the proclamation of the state in 1948 and a new dignity for the survivors.[4]

The major pre-modern disaster, the expulsion from Spain in 1492, led to the birth of a new "creation myth" in mystic circles, a myth that became popular thanks to eighteenth century Hassidism and a growing influence during the last few decades due to translations. Whereas classical rabbinic thinking postulated that exile and destruction are ultimately caused by the sinful behavior of Jews themselves, sixteenth century Kabbalists in their response to the Spanish expulsion explained evil by claiming that an endlessly perfect God had to withdraw part of Himself in order to make the creation of the world possible. In the creative process that followed, divine sparks, stuck to vessels that had broken in the course of events and were trapped in lower space, needed to be mended again. In this concept, the primary human task became the process of restoring the sparks to the divine world and thus mending and completing the creation. In other words, Exile was the essence of God Himself, and brokenness is the condition of the world.

This Kabbalist myth, with its awareness of divine withdrawal (tsimtsum) in the primordial stages of creation and emphasis on the human responsibility to restore the divine wholeness, would influence modern artists like Barnett Newman in his design for a never realized synagogue and architects like Moshe Safdie in his new plans for a museum in Yad Vashem.

Over all these thousands of years, almost up to today, time, interpreted and actualized, prevailed over place. The Bible never specified on exactly which mountain in Sinai Moses received the Torah (the

feierlich an den Gottesdienst in einem vor langer Zeit zerstörten Tempel in Jerusalem. Purim, das Losfest, gedenkt der Rettung der Juden vor der Vernichtung in der persischen Diaspora irgendwann im 5. Jahrhundert vor der heutigen Zeitrechnung. Chanukka, das Lichterfest, erinnert an die Wiedereinweihung des Tempels in Jerusalem im 2. Jahrhundert vor unserer Zeit und hat sich von der Feier eines militärischen Siegs zum Wunder des spirituellen Überlebens der Juden, wo auch immer sie sich aufhalten, entwickelt. Interessanterweise gibt es keinen Feiertag zur Ankunft im Land der Bibel. Der Zerstörung des ersten und des zweiten Tempels, die das Volk Israel ins Exil trieb, wird mit einem Fastentag gedacht.

Die zyklische Gliederung des jüdischen Jahres ermöglicht es den Juden, ihre Geschichte nachzuerleben, und lässt sich auf alle darauf folgenden Erfahrungen der Juden im Lauf der Jahrhunderte übertragen. Nach der Zerstörung des Tempels wurden sämtliche Feste von den Rabbinern neu interpretiert – von Opfergottesdiensten in Jerusalem bis zu religiösen Feiern im eigenen Heim oder in der Synagoge, wo immer diese errichtet wurde. Infolge der Zerstörung seines Hauses war nach Auffassung der Juden Gott selbst ins Exil gegangen und begleitete sein Volk auf der Wanderschaft mit seiner göttlichen Gegenwart (Schechina). Unter dem Schutz der Schechina konnte jeder Jude in jeder Generation sich in die Lage versetzen, als ob er selbst aus Ägypten ausgezogen wäre. Diese alte rabbinische Metapher zur Begründung der gemeinschaftlichen Feier während des Pessachmahls gilt entsprechend auch für alle weiteren Feste des jüdischen Jahres.

Der Tag, der an die Massenvernichtung der europäischen Juden im Zweiten Weltkrieg – den Holocaust (das Wort bedeutet Ganz- oder Brandopfer) – erinnert, weicht interessanterweise von diesem Muster ab. Statt in Verbindung mit den Fastentagen zum Gedenken an den Beginn der Zerstörung des Tempels wird der Shoah (dieses heute bevorzugte Wort bedeutet Katastrophe) am 27. Tag des Nissan gedacht, einem Tag im jüdischen Kalender, der dem Beginn des Aufstands im Warschauer Ghetto vom April 1943 nahe ist. In diese Jahreszeit fallen auch die Zerstörung vieler jüdischer Ortschaften und Gemeinden durch die Kreuzfahrer, die als Vorläufer der Nationalsozialisten betrachtet werden. Offiziell heißt der Gedenktag Jom ha-Shoah Wehagewura, ›Tag der Katastrophe und des Heldentums‹ – ›des Heldentums‹, um die weit verbreitete Legende von der jüdischen Passivität in der Diaspora zu widerlegen und die den Opfern und Überlebenden angetane ›Schmach‹ anzusprechen. Jom ha-Shoah wird unmittelbar nach dem an die Befreiung aus der ägyptischen Sklaverei erinnernden Pessachfest und vor dem israelischen Unabhängigkeitstag begangen, der an den Tag der Proklamation des Staates Israel im Jahr 1948 erinnert, der den Holocaust-Überlebenden neue Würde gegeben hat.[4]

Das einschneidendste Ereignis in der prämodernen Geschichte der Juden – die Vertreibung aus Spanien im Jahr 1492 – führte in Mystikerkreisen zum Entstehen eines neuen ›Schöpfungsmythos‹, den die Chassidim des 18. Jahrhunderts populär machten und der seit einigen Jahrzehnten durch Neuübersetzungen wieder an Einfluss gewinnt. Während die klassische rabbinische Auslegung davon ausgeht, dass die Vertreibung und Vernichtung des Volkes Israel letztlich durch das sündige Verhalten der Juden selbst verursacht wurde, erklärten die Kabbalisten des 16. Jahrhunderts – als Reaktion auf die Vertreibung aus Spanien – die Natur des Bösen, indem sie behaupteten, ein ewig vollkommener Gott hätte sich teilweise in sich selbst zurückziehen müssen, um die Erschaffung der Welt zu ermöglichen. In dem darauf folgenden schöpferischen Prozess seien die göttlichen Funken an im Verlauf der Ereignisse zerbrochenen Gefäßen

Barnett Newman, Design
for a synagogue, 1963
Barnett Newman, Entwurf
einer Synagoge, 1963

The Western ("Wailing")
Wall is the only remnant
of the Second Temple.
Photo on calendar
designed by Fré Cohen.
Amsterdam, 1941
Die westliche (›Klage-‹)
Mauer ist der einzige
Überrest des Zweiten
Tempels. Foto in einem
Kalender von Fré Cohen.
Amsterdam, 1941

present monastery was founded in early Christian times). Equally, the Pentateuch stresses we don't know the burial place of Moses, the founding father of Judaism. The Temple Mount stands in Jerusalem, but exactly where the Temple stood is unknown. Before present-day Israel's conquest of the eastern part of Jerusalem in 1967, its remaining outside western "wailing" wall, located in a narrow alley in Jerusalem's Old City, was a place visited only by pious Jewish pilgrims. The importance of the space itself, with its enormous square and an open air synagogue with separation between men and women, is a rather recent phenomenon. The same applies to the tombs of Rachel in Bethlehem and of rabbinical scholars in Safed and Tiberias; whereas, the tombs of the patriarchs in Hebron now have become a real bone of religious and political contention. In Exile, Holy Land and Holy City Jerusalem were, in the spirit of Psalm 137, not forgotten but constantly symbolically present not only at all festivals, but also at lifecycle events as well as in daily prayer, at meals, at home, and the synagogue. Prayer is directed towards Jerusalem. Though there are numerous references to the land of Israel, the city of Jerusalem, and the Temple in the Bible, rabbinic texts, and the liturgy, the rabbis managed to maintain a careful balance between the ideological centrality of the Holy Land and the reality of Diaspora. From the European Middle Ages till well into the nineteenth century, they de-emphasized the significance of Israel in favor of Jewish life outside the land. In other words, "home" could be virtually realized in Exile.[5]

### Emancipation

Returning to the land, originally just a pious hope dependant upon the arrival of the Messiah or Messianic Age, only became a real theme in the nineteenth century. Jews received civil rights, first in the United States (1776), then in France (1791), the Netherlands (1796), and in the course of the nineteenth and early twentieth centuries in all European states. Historically subjected to a variety of often discriminatory laws, they now became equal citizens. At the same time, Jews entered the general historic and political arena. Jews were no longer considered a separate nation within a nation, but individual adherents of

haften geblieben und nun mit diesen in den Niederungen des Weltalls gefangen, wo sie restauriert werden müssten. In dieser gedanklichen Konstruktion besteht die Hauptaufgabe des Menschen darin, die Funken zu befreien, in die göttliche Welt zurückzutransferieren und dadurch die Schöpfung wiederherzustellen und zu vollenden. In anderen Worten: Exil ist das Wesen Gottes und Gebrochenheit der Zustand der Welt.

Dieser kabbalistische Mythos mit seinem Bewusstsein des göttlichen Rückzugs in sich selbst (Zimzum) zu Beginn der Schöpfung und seiner Betonung der Verantwortung des Menschen für die Wiederherstellung der göttlichen Einheit der Welt sollte in der Folge auch moderne Künstler beeinflussen, so zum Beispiel Barnett Newman bei seinem Entwurf einer nie ausgeführten Synagoge oder Moshe Safdie bei seinen neuen Plänen für ein Museum in Yad Vashem.

In all diesen Jahrtausenden war und ist fast bis zum heutigen Tag die Zeit – gedeutet und aktualisiert – wichtiger als der Ort. Die Bibel macht keine exakten Angaben, auf welchem Berg im Sinai Moses die Thora erhielt (das bestehende Kloster wurde erst in frühchristlicher Zeit gegründet). Ebenso wenig verrät uns der Pentateuch den Ort der Grabstätte von Moses, dem Gründervater des Judentums. Der Tempelberg befindet sich in Jerusalem; wo genau aber der Tempel stand, ist nicht bekannt. Vor der Eroberung des Ostteils von Jerusalem durch das heutige Israel im Jahr 1967 wurde der Überrest seiner Westmauer, der ›Klagemauer‹, in einer

the Jewish religion, which became matter of personal choice. In the footsteps of Spinoza, Moses Mendelssohn (1729–1786) had already argued that religious authorities had no right to coercion, religion being a private, personal matter. With real political power limited to biblical times and to the pre-modern, semi-autonomous Jewish minority in Europe, Jews should now be loyal to the state. Jerusalem and the biblical state were considered of minor importance; Jews if anything could be "a light unto the nations," as both modern Orthodox and Reform Jewish thinkers consistently emphasized. References to Zion and the Temple in liturgy were deleted by Reform and reinterpreted by the modern Orthodox rabbis.

Jews, who from Biblical times onward, had always been involved in the arts—as commissioners or creators—were now for the first time able to express themselves fully in art and architecture, unhampered by any official restrictions.[6] The style in which they chose to build their synagogues, reflected their desire to belong to their respective country: Romanesque, to stress their centuries-old presence in Europe; or Oriental (Moorish), which referred to the Jewish Golden Age in medieval Spain while simultaneously stressing their difference, i.e., their historical origin in the Orient. The wish to belong went hand in hand with the search for an identity. Building commissions and their architects frantically looked for the proper architectural style, until early twentieth century modernism created more neutral ground. The Jews, who up to the Emancipation had only rarely possessed impressive architecture, had, in the words of the philosopher Heschel,[7] through Sabbath and festivals created "cathedrals in time" and not in space. Only now did they start to build the actual equivalents of cathedrals. Looking back at what survived the destruction by the Nazis in Europe, one may say that mid and late nineteenth century synagogues like the ones in Berlin, Budapest, Brussels, and Paris indeed radiate the self-awareness and optimism of a recently integrated Jewish bourgeoisie.

The return to Zion, once a dream which rabbis carefully avoided realizing in practice, became a serious political option for those Jews who were confronted with the winds of anti-Semitism and nationalism in nineteenth century Europe. Palestine was no longer a destination for Christian pilgrims only, but for Jews as well, this time as pioneers. The new medium of photography and a veritable souvenir industry spoke to the sentiment of even those Jews who had no intention to emigrate.

Those who did not flee the Russian pogroms in the 1880s but stayed home and kept believing in the idea of progress despite anti-Semitic scandals like the Dreyfus affair, started to construct a new orientation to their past history and culture to justify themselves and their place in society. On the one hand, a romantic nostalgia for the past became part of the Jewish conscience for both religion, as one imagined it used to be, and for the Orient. From the third quarter of the nineteenth century onward, Jewish exhibitions and museums started to present Jewish religion, history, and material culture to a secularizing Jewish bourgeoisie. Jewish museums, soon present in most larger European cities, emphasized the glorious past, like the Golden Age of Spanish Jewry before the expulsion and Spanish-Portuguese Jews in Amsterdam. Publications proudly presented Jewish ceremonial artifacts and newly discovered illuminated Jewish manuscripts from the Middle Ages. Jewish travelers began to visit places in Europe which reflected a glorious Jewish history, such as the Iberian peninsula, where Jewish courtiers, poets, and politicians like Maimonides lived; the romantic ghetto of Venice and Prague, home of the Golem; the Jewish

schmalen Gasse der Altstadt nur von frommen jüdischen Pilgern aufgesucht. Die Bedeutung dieses Ortes, nun mit großem Vorplatz und einer in Männer- und Frauenbereiche unterteilten Freilicht-Synagoge, ist ein relativ neues Phänomen. Das gleiche gilt für Rachels Grab in Bethlehem und die Gräber gelehrter Rabbiner in Safed und Tiberias, während die Grabstätten der Patriarchen in Hebron inzwischen zu religiösen und politischen Zankäpfeln geworden sind. Im Exil waren das Heilige Land und die Heilige Stadt Jerusalem im Geiste des Psalms 137 nicht vergessen, sondern ständig symbolisch präsent – nicht nur an den Feiertagen, sondern auch bei allen wichtigen Ereignissen im Leben der Menschen, beim täglichen Gebet, bei den Mahlzeiten, im eigenen Heim und in der Synagoge. Gebete werden in Richtung auf Jerusalem gesprochen. So zahlreich die Hinweise auf das Land Israel, die Stadt Jerusalem und den Tempel in der Bibel, in rabbinischen Texten und der Liturgie aber auch sind, den Rabbinern gelang es stets, das Gleichgewicht zwischen der zentralen ideologischen Bedeutung des Heiligen Landes und der Realität der Diaspora herzustellen. Vom Mittelalter bis weit ins 19. Jahrhundert hinein spielten sie die Bedeutung Israels zugunsten des jüdischen Lebens außerhalb des Landes herunter. Damit sagten sie: Heimat ließ sich praktisch auch im Exil herstellen.[5]

### Emanzipation

Die Rückkehr in das Heilige Land – ursprünglich nur eine fromme Hoffnung, die sich an die Ankunft des Messias und den Anbruch des Messianischen Zeitalters knüpfte – wurde im 19. Jahrhundert zum konkreten Anliegen. Die Juden erhielten die Bürgerrechte, zuerst in den Vereinigten Staaten (1776), dann in Frankreich (1791), den Niederlanden (1796) und im Verlauf des 19. und zu Beginn des 20. Jahrhunderts in allen europäischen Ländern. Früher einer Vielzahl häufig diskriminierender Gesetze unterworfen, wurden sie nun zu gleichberechtigten Bürgern. Gleichzeitig betraten Juden die allgemeine geschichtliche und politische Arena. Sie galten nicht länger als separates Volk innerhalb einer Nation, sondern als Einzelpersonen jüdischen Glaubens, der nun zur Frage ihrer persönlichen Entscheidung wurde. Sozusagen in Spinozas Fußstapfen hatte schon Moses Mendelssohn (1729–86) argumentiert, die religiöse Obrigkeit habe nicht das Recht, Zwang auszuüben, da der Glaube eine private, persönliche Angelegenheit sei. Nachdem die Ausübung politischer Macht sich für Juden zeitlich auf die biblische Periode und in Europa im Mittelalter auf die halb autonome Führung der jüdischen Minderheit beschränkt hatte, sollten sie nun dem Staat gegenüber loyal sein. Jerusalem und der biblische Staat galten dabei als zweitrangig. Wenn es irgendetwas gab, was Juden sein konnten, dann »ein Licht unter den Völkern«, wie moderne orthodoxe und liberale jüdische Denker beharrlich betonten. Das liberale Judentum löschte Hinweise auf Zion und den Tempel aus der Liturgie, die von modernen orthodoxen Rabbinern neu interpretiert wurde.

Die Juden, die sich seit biblischer Zeit als Mäzene oder Kunstschaffende stets in den Künsten engagiert hatten, konnten sich nun zum ersten Mal frei von offiziellen Beschränkungen umfassend in jeder Form von Kunst und Architektur ausdrücken.[6] Der Baustil, den sie für ihre Synagogen wählten, spiegelte ihren Wunsch nach Zugehörigkeit zum jeweiligen Land: romanisch, um ihre jahrhundertelange Anwesenheit in Europa zu betonen, oder orientalisch (maurisch) als Hinweis auf das Goldene Zeitalter der Juden im mittelalterlichen Spanien und zugleich als Betonung ihrer Herkunft aus dem Orient. Der Wunsch nach Zugehörigkeit ging mit der Identitätssuche Hand in Hand. Auftraggeber und die von ihnen beauf-

quarter of Amsterdam, where Rembrandt once lived next to the Jews; or Budapest and Vienna, two cities close to the *Ostjuden* who, however negatively perceived as immediate neighbors, did still possess the very religiosity lacking in Western Europe.[8]

### The present situation

After the Holocaust, Jewish museums in Europe reopened, but their impact remained limited till the 1970s. In the United States, the Jewish Museum of New York (founded in 1904) opened in new premises on Fifth Avenue in 1947 and would soon develop an innovative exhibition program. In the past decade, the number of Jewish museums has vastly increased. In the United States, synagogue museums were officially accredited while in metropolitan areas like Los Angeles, New York, Chicago and Wahington, Jewish museums were either expanded or newly built; whereas in Europe, museums were founded, sometimes even in countries and places where Jews had been or became numerically marginal, or were murdered outright. Museums also arose in deserted synagogues in cities where reminders of a onetime Jewish presence had almost completely been destroyed.[9] How embarrassing

Moshe Safdie, Skirball Cultural Center, Los Angeles, 1995
Moshe Safdie, Skirball Cultural Center, Los Angeles, 1995

some exhibitions in these often well-meaning museums can be, needs no comment.

Compared to their modest size and well-meaning but amateurish contents, a real change occurred in the late 1980s when Jews decided to take charge of their history themselves or, at the same time, when national or local governments for political reasons chose to pay prominent attention to the fate of Jews in their society. Museums of an unsurpassed size and impressive museological quality, located in prime locations (and soon attracting large crowds), opened their doors one after the other: Amsterdam (1987), Frankfurt am Main (1988), Vienna (1993), Paris (1998), and as a climax for the time being Berlin (2001). In contrast to those housed in restored synagogues (Amsterdam) or upper middle-class bourgeois palaces (Frankfurt, Vienna, Paris), the Berlin Jewish Museum was built *as* a museum and explicitly in a form that could not be overseen by anyone. The Jewish Museum, once a modest receptacle for the religious and historical remains of an almost extinct people, became a major tourist attraction and a Jewish pilgrimage destination. Most European capitals and major cities now possess or will shortly have Jewish museums of some size and importance, like

tragen Architekten suchten intensiv nach dem passenden Baustil, bis die frühe Moderne des 20. Jahrhunderts ihnen neutralere Gestaltungsmöglichkeiten eröffnete. In den Worten des Philosophen Abraham Heschel haben die Juden – die bis zur Emanzipation nur vereinzelt über eindrucksvolle Architektur verfügten – in der Feier des Sabbats und ihrer religiösen Feste »Kathedralen in der Zeit« und nicht im Raum errichtet.[7] Erst danach begannen sie in Entsprechung christlicher Kathedralen große Synagogen zu bauen. Wenn man die europäischen Synagogen aus der Zeit des mittleren und späteren 19. Jahrhunderts zum Beispiel in Berlin, Budapest, Brüssel und Paris betrachtet, die der Zerstörung durch die Nationalsozialisten entgangen sind, so strahlen sie tatsächlich das Selbstbewusstsein und den Optimismus des gerade erst integrierten jüdischen Bürgertums aus.

Die Rückkehr nach Zion, einst ein Traum, den die Rabbiner mit Bedacht in der Praxis zu verwirklichen vermieden, wurde für diejenigen Juden zu einer ernsthaften politischen Option, denen im 19. Jahrhundert der scharfe Wind des europäischen Antisemitismus und Nationalismus ins Gesicht blies. Palästina war nicht länger nur das Ziel christlicher Pilger, sondern auch von Juden, diesmal als Pioniere. Das neue Medium der Fotografie und eine regelrechte Andenken-Industrie appellierten sogar an die Emotionen derjenigen Juden, die gar nicht auswandern wollten.

Juden, die nicht vor den russischen Pogromen der 1880er Jahre flohen, sondern im Land blieben und trotz skandalöser antisemitischer Vorfälle wie der französischen Dreyfus-Affäre noch immer an die Idee des Fortschritts glaubten, legten sich eine neue Auffassung der eigenen Geschichte und Kultur zurecht, um sich selbst und ihre gesellschaftliche Stellung zu rechtfertigen. Eine romantische Nostalgie in Bezug auf die Vergangenheit wurde Teil des jüdischen Bewusstseins; sie betraf einerseits das religiöse Leben, wie man es sich im Nachhinein vorstellte, und andererseits den Orient. Nach 1850 begannen jüdische Ausstellungen und Museen damit, einem zunehmend säkularisierten jüdischen Bürgertum die eigene Religion, Geschichte und Kultur nahezubringen. Jüdische Museen, bald in den meisten europäischen Großstädten präsent, betonten die glanzvollen Epochen, zum Beispiel das Goldene Zeitalter des spanischen Judentums vor der Vertreibung und der spanisch-portugiesischen Juden in Amsterdam. In Publikationen wurden mit Stolz jüdische zeremonielle Objekte und wiederentdeckte illuminierte jüdische Handschriften des Mittelalters abgebildet. Jüdische Reisende besuchten Orte in Europa, die für eine ruhmvolle jüdische Geschichte standen, wie die Iberische Halbinsel, wo jüdische Höflinge, Dichter und Politiker wie Maimonides gelebt hatten, die malerischen Ghettobezirke von Venedig und Prag, Heimat des Golem, das jüdische Viertel von Amsterdam, wo Rembrandt Seite an Seite mit Juden gewohnt hatte, oder Budapest und Wien mit ihrer Nähe zu den Ostjuden, die, wie negativ man sie als unmittelbare Nachbarn auch immer empfinden mochte, immer noch die tiefe Religiosität besaßen, die in Westeuropa verloren gegangen war.[8]

### Die Situation heute

Nach dem Ende des Holocaust wurden die jüdischen Museen in Europa zwar wiedereröffnet, ihr Einfluss blieb bis in die 1970er Jahre jedoch gering. In den Vereinigten Staaten zog das 1904 gegründete Jewish Museum in New York 1947 in sein neues, inzwischen erweitertes Domizil an der Fifth Avenue und entwickelte schon bald ein innovatives Ausstellungsprogramm. In den letzten zehn Jahren ist die Anzahl jüdischer Museen weltweit auf ein Vielfaches angewachsen. In den Vereinigten Staaten wurden viele Synagogen-Museen offiziell anerkannt, während in

The Amsterdam Ashkenazic Synagogues (1671, 1752). On the right, the present Joods Historisch Museum Amsterdam. On the left, the Portuguese Synagogue, 1675
Rechts die Amsterdamer Aschkenasischen Synagogen von 1671 und 1752, heute Sitz des Joods Historisch Museum Amsterdam. Links die Portugiesische Synagoge von 1675

Athens, Bologna, Brussels, Copenhagen, London, Munich, Toledo, Venice, Vilnius, and Warsaw.[10]

Whereas in Europe, Holocaust related sites like the former concentration camps became increasingly professional museums, in the United States and Israel, Holocaust museums and monuments arose for reasons more related to a Jewish need to connect to this dramatic phase of its history. The expansion of Israel's national Holocaust monument and museum Yad Vashem over the last decades into a vast and impressive area, and the establishment of the United States Holocaust Memorial Museum in a vast site at the very center of Washington indicates the prominence of this development.

After World War II, Jewish tourism, primarily from the USA and Israel, extended to the places of destruction: the concentration camps in Eastern Europe, or pilgrimages to the Anne Frank House in Amsterdam. Formerly, the glorious past had been the source of inspiration, connected with a visit by the pious to the tomb of a scholar. Now the places of denigration had to bring redemption by connecting the visit to the camps with a pilgrimage to the Holy Land. Europe was literally the dead end: The course of European Jewish history with its emancipation, integration and assimilation, was perceived to lead directly to the extermination camps.[11]

Jewish memory has become fully secularized; history is presented in chronological and not cyclical order, as Jews used to do for centuries in their synagogues. Place has fully taken over from time, in the same way as history replaces religion. History rather than text, as Yerushalmi has shown, has now become the arbiter, the point of reference for Jews, physical space rather than the cycle of time serving as the vehicle for

Metropolen wie Los Angeles, New York, Chicago und Washington jüdische Museen erweitert oder neu gebaut wurden. In Europa wurden neue Museen gegründet, zum Teil sogar in Ländern und an Orten, wo jüdische Minderheiten entweder schon immer eine Randgruppe gebildet hatten, auf eine solche zusammengeschrumpft oder völlig vernichtet worden waren.[9] Auch in aufgegebenen Synagogengebäuden von Städten, in denen Erinnerungen an einstiges jüdisches Leben fast vollständig ausgelöscht worden waren, wurden jüdische Museen eingerichtet. Wie peinlich manche Ausstellungen in diesen vielfach in bester Absicht eingerichteten Museen sein können, bedarf keines weiteren Kommentars.

Im Vergleich zur der bescheidenen Größe und den wohlmeinend, aber höchst laienhaft zusammengestellten Inhalten dieser Museen zeichnete sich Ende der 1980er Jahre eine deutliche Veränderung ab, als nämlich die Juden beschlossen, die eigene Geschichte selbst in die Hand zu nehmen, und als nationale Regierungen oder Stadtregierungen sich aus politischen Gründen dafür entschieden, dem Schicksal der Juden in ihrer Gesellschaft größere Aufmerksamkeit zu widmen. Museen von bis dahin unerreichter Größe und eindrucksvoller musealer Qualität in bester Lage, die sehr schnell große Besuchermengen anlockten, eröffneten eines nach dem anderen: in Amsterdam (1987), Frankfurt am Main (1988), Wien (1993), Paris (1998) und als bisheriger Höhepunkt in Berlin (2001). Im Gegensatz zu den Sammlungen, die in restaurierten Synagogen (Amsterdam) oder großbürgerlichen Villen (Frankfurt, Wien, Paris) untergebracht wurden, entstand das Berliner Jüdische Museum als Neubau und ganz bewusst in einer Form, die niemand übersehen konnte. Das jüdische Museum, einst ein bescheidener Sammelbehälter für die wenigen noch erhaltenen religiösen und historischen Hinterlassenschaf-

meaning. More Jews visit a museum, Jewish or otherwise, than a synagogue, even on Shabbat. Just as the museum has become the cathedral of the twentieth century for the Gentiles, Jews have equally made the museum their synagogue, where they relate to their past, meet socially, and celebrate secularized festivals and lifecycle events. The memorial reminds them of their tragic past, and leaves them with a determination "never again" or more positively to make a choice for an Israeli or a strong Jewish identity, before an enemy makes a choice for them.

Parallel to the immense popularity of Jewish museums as a point of reference to which secularized Jews return in order to connect with their own roots and at which non-Jews can discover a common if often dramatic past, synagogues, particularly in Europe, fulfill a major role in the integration of the new immigrants. Due to the suppression of Jewish religion, culture, and language during over 70 years of communism, the majority of immigrants not only need basic instruction in the almost lost heritage of their ancestors, they also need to be integrated into their new country. The Jewish community, entrusted by the authorities with this dual task, had to face these challenges by creating, albeit with government support, new community centers and schools. The fact that in so many places well-known and innovative architects were invited to realize projects at prominent spots in the cityscape is a clear indication of the new self-awareness of the Jews. In the United States, this renaissance took place earlier, during the 1950s and 1960s, when

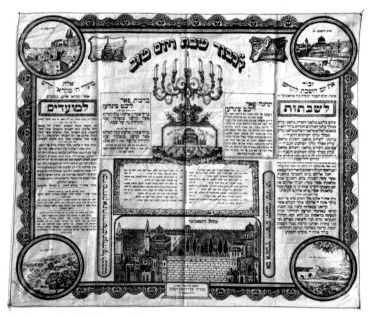

Hallah cover for Sabbath and holidays, made for pious tourists who visited the Holy Land. Depictions of holy sites, Jerusalem, ca. 1900
Challah-Decke für Sabbat und Feiertage, angefertigt für fromme Touristen, die das Heilige Land besuchten, mit Darstellungen der heiligen Stätten. Jerusalem, ca. 1900

the largest and most impressive specimens of synagogue architecture came into being. Currently, the accent in American synagogue architecture lies in multifunctional and flexible use of the available space, and in particular on more intimacy.

In secularized Israel, the urban synagogue is much less of a community center and consequently less prominent than in the Diaspora. Here, the state provides for schools and halls for social meeting. Only

ten eines nahezu untergegangenen Volkes, wurde vielerorts zu einer Haupttouristenattraktion und einem Wallfahrtsort für Juden aus aller Welt. Die meisten europäischen Hauptstädte und Großstädte besitzen heute schon relativ große und bedeutende jüdische Museen oder werden bald eines eröffnen, darunter Athen, Bologna, Brüssel, Kopenhagen, London, München, Toledo, Venedig, Vilnius und Warschau.[10]

Während in Europa die Stätten des Holocaust wie die ehemaligen Konzentrationslager zunehmend professionell zu Museen umgestaltet wurden, entstanden die Holocaust-Museen und -Gedenkstätten in den Vereinigten Staaten und in Israel eher aus dem Bedürfnis der Juden heraus, einen Bezug zu dieser einschneidenden Periode ihrer Geschichte zu finden. Die in den letzten Jahrzehnten erfolgte Erweiterung von Israels nationalem Holocaust-Mahnmal und Museum Yad Vashem zu einer ausgedehnten, eindrucksvollen Anlage und das auf einem riesigen Grundstück im Zentrum von Washington errichtete United States Holocaust Memorial Museum belegen die Bedeutung dieser Entwicklung.

Nach dem Zweiten Weltkrieg erstreckte sich der jüdische Tourismus, hauptsächlich aus den USA und Israel, auch auf die Orte der Vernichtung, die Konzentrationslager in Osteuropa oder Pilgerfahrten zum Anne-Frank-Haus in Amsterdam. Früher war die ruhmreiche Vergangenheit, etwa beim Besuch der Grabstätte eines heiligen Gelehrten, die Inspirationsquelle gewesen. Nun mussten die Orte der Schande Erlösung bringen, wenn ihr Besuch mit einer Pilgerfahrt ins Heilige Land verbunden wurde. Europa wurde buchstäblich als das ›tödliche Ende‹ einer Sackgasse gesehen: Hatte doch der Weg der europäischen jüdischen Geschichte über Emanzipation, Integration und Assimilation direkt in die Vernichtungslager geführt.[11]

Jüdische Erinnerung ist vollkommen säkularisiert worden. Geschichte wird heute in chronologischer Reihenfolge dargestellt und nicht in zyklischer, wie Juden es jahrhundertelang in den Synagogen praktiziert haben. Der Ort hat die Rolle der Zeit übernommen, und genauso hat die Geschichte die Religion ersetzt. Yerushalmi stellt fest, dass die Geschichte und nicht der Text zum Leitfaden geworden ist, zum Bezugspunkt der Juden, wobei der physische Raum und nicht der Zyklus der Zeit als Bedeutungsträger dient. Selbst am Sabbat gehen mehr Juden in ein jüdisches oder anderes Museum als in eine Synagoge. So wie das Museum für Nichtjuden zur Kathedrale des 20. Jahrhunderts geworden ist, so haben auch Juden aus Museen Synagogen gemacht, wo sie Verbindung zu ihrer Geschichte aufnehmen, einander treffen und Familien- und andere nichtreligiöse Feste feiern. Die Gedenkstätte erinnert sie an ihre tragische Vergangenheit und weckt ihre Entschlossenheit des ›Nie wieder‹ oder bestärkt sie, positiv ausgedrückt, in ihrer Entscheidung für eine israelische beziehungsweise eine starke jüdische Identität, bevor ein Feind für sie entscheidet.

Jüdische Museen haben eine große Popularität als Bezugsorte, an die säkularisierte Juden zurückkehren, wenn sie wieder Kontakt zu ihren Wurzeln finden wollen, und in denen ihre nichtjüdischen Mitbürger die gemeinsame, wenn auch oft dramatisch belastete Geschichte entdecken können. Daneben leisten aber auch die Synagogen, besonders in Europa, einen wichtigen Beitrag zur Integration neuer Einwanderer. Infolge der Unterdrückung der jüdischen Religion, Kultur und Sprache während siebzig Jahren kommunistischer Herrschaft muss den meisten Einwanderern aus der ehemaligen Sowjetunion nicht nur Basiswissen über das fast schon verloren gegangene Erbe ihrer Vorfahren vermittelt werden, sie müssen auch ganz praktisch in die Gesellschaft ihrer neuen Heimat integriert werden. Die von den Behörden mit dieser doppelten Aufgabe

at university campuses does the synagogue fulfill the role of a land-mark.

Whether in Israel or in the Diaspora, the search for an identity, for new meaning, and spirituality amongst all currents of modern Judaism have become a new challenge for architects, whether in museums, synagogues, or schools. At the same time, Gentiles identify with this development consciously or unconsciously, since they too are confronted with Diaspora, destruction, and a search for meaning—themes Jews are historically familiar with.

betrauten jüdischen Gemeinden mussten sich dieser Herausforderung stellen und, wenn auch mit öffentlicher Förderung, neue Gemeinde-häuser und Schulen bauen. Die Tatsache, dass vielerorts bekannte und innovativ denkende Architekten dazu aufgefordert wurden, derartige Bau-ten an prominenten Stellen in der jeweiligen Stadtlandschaft zu errichten, ist ein deutlicher Indikator für das neue Selbstbewusstsein der Juden. In den Vereinigten Staaten fand diese Renaissance schon früher statt, in den 1950er und 1960er Jahren, als die größten und eindrucksvollsten Beispiele des Bautyps Synagoge entstanden. Derzeit sind Mehrzweck-charakter, flexible Nutzung des verfügbaren Raums und vor allem mehr Intimität die Hauptintentionen der amerikanischen Synagogenarchitektur.

Im säkularisierten Staat Israel hat die städtische Synagoge als Gemein-dezentrum an Bedeutung verloren und wird daher auch weniger beachtet als in der Diaspora. Hier kümmert sich der Staat um den Bau von Schulen und Versammlungsgebäuden. Nur auf Universitätsgeländen spielt die Synagoge als Wahrzeichen noch eine Rolle.

Ob in Israel oder in der Diaspora – die Suche nach Identität, nach neuer Sinnerfüllung und Spiritualität in allen Strömungen des modernen Judentums ist für die Architekten jüdischer Museen, Schulen und Synago-gen zur neuen Herausforderung geworden. Gleichzeitig identifizieren sich auch Nichtjuden bewusst oder unbewusst mit dieser Entwicklung, weil auch sie verstärkt mit Diaspora, Zerstörung und Sinnsuche konfrontiert werden – Fragen, die den Juden seit jeher vertraut sind.

1 Yosef Haim Yerushalmi, *Zakhor: Jewish History and Jewish Memory,* Seattle 1996 [1982 first edition].

2 See particularly Arnold M. Eisen, *Galuth*: *Modern Jewish Reflections on Home-lessness and Homecoming,* Bloomington 1986, Introduction p. XI. And Y. H. Yerushalmi, "Exil und Vertreibung in der jüdischen Geschichte", in idem, *Ein Feld in Anatot. Versuche über jüdische Geschichte*, Berlin 1993, pp. 21–38. For an excellent introduction to Israel and Diaspora as a historiographical theme see M. Brenner, A. Kauders, G. Reuveni, N. Römer (ed.), *Jüdische Geschichte lesen,* München 2003, pp. 155–160 (German version only).

3 See for a religious perspective on the importance of the exilic experience a lecture by the orthodox philosopher Rabbi Joseph Solovietchik (1903–1993) in1972, published in J. Epstein, *Shiurei Harav: A Conspectus of the Public Lec-tures of Rabbi Joseph B. Soloveitchik*, New York 1974, p. 76.

4 Saul Friedländer, "Memory of the Shoa in Israel," in James E. Young (ed.), *The Art of Memory: Holocaust Memorials in History,* Munich New York 1994, pp. 149–157, esp. 151–153.

5 Marc Saperstein, "The Land of Israel in Pre-Modern Jewish Thought: a History of Two Rabbinic Statements," in Lawrence A. Hoffman (ed.), *The Land of Israel: Jewish Perspectives,* Notre Dame 1986, pp. 188–209, esp. 203.

6 See the fascinating summary of the arguments surrounding the second of the biblical Ten Commandments: Kalman P. Bland, *The Artless Jew: Medieval and Modern Affirmations and Denials of the Visual,* Princeton 2000.

7 Abraham Joshua Heschel, *The Sabbath*, Notre Dame 1951.

8 Richard I. Cohen, *Jewish Icons: Art and Society in Modern Europe,* Berkeley 1998.

9 Ruth Ellen Gruber, *Virtually Jewish: Reinventing Jewish Culture in Europe,* Berkeley 2003.

10 Grace Cohen Grossman, *Jewish Museums of the World,* Westport 2003.

11 See James Young, *The Art of Memory: Holocaust Memorials in History*, Munich New York 1994.

1 Yosef Haim Yerushalmi, *Zakhor*: *Jewish History and Jewish Memory,* Seattle 1996 (Erstausgabe 1982). Deutsche Ausgabe: *Zachor. Erinnere Dich! Jüdische Geschichte und Jüdisches Gedächtnis*, Berlin 1988.

2 Vgl. insbesondere: Arnold M. Eisen, *Galuth. Modern Jewish Reflections on Homelessness and Homecoming,* Bloomington 1986; sowie Y. H. Yerushalmi, *Exil und Vertreibung in der jüdischen Geschichte,* speziell das Kapitel »Ein Feld in Anatot. Versuche über jüdische Geschichte«, Berlin 1993, S. 21–38. Eine ausgezeichnete Einführung in das Thema »Israel und Diaspora als Gegenstand der Geschichtsschreibung« gibt: M. Brenner, A. Kauders, G. Reuveni, N. Römer (Hrsg.), *Jüdische Geschichte lesen,* München 2003, S. 155–160.

3 Zur religiösen Sicht der Bedeutung der Exilerfahrung vgl. den Vortrag des orthodoxen Philosophen Rabbi Joseph Soloveitchik (1903–1993) von 1972, publiziert in: J. Epstein, *Shiurei Harav: a Conspectus of the Public Lectures of Rabbi Joseph B. Soloveitchik,* New York 1974, S. 76.

4 Saul Friedländer, »Memory of the Shoa in Israel«, in: James E. Young (Hrsg.), *The Art of Memory: Holocaust Memorials in History,* München/New York 1994, S. 149–157, insbes. S. 151–153. Deutsche Ausgabe: *Mahnmale des Holo-caust. Motive, Rituale und Stätten des Gedenkens,* München/New York 1994.

5 Marc Saperstein, »The Land of Israel in Pre-Modern Jewish Thought: a History of Two Rabbinic Statements«, in: Lawrence A. Hoffman (Hrsg.), *The Land of Israel: Jewish Perspectives,* Notre Dame 1986, S. 188–209, insbes. S. 203.

6 Vgl. die spannende Zusammenfassung der philosophischen Argumentationen zum zweiten der Zehn Gebote: Kalman P. Bland, *The Artless Jew: Medieval and Modern Affirmations and Denials of the Visual,* Princeton 2000.

7 Abraham Joshua Heschel, *The Sabbath,* Notre Dame 1951.

8 Vgl. Richard I. Cohen, *Jewish Icons: Art and Society in Modern Europe,* Berkeley 1998.

9 Vgl. Ruth Ellen Gruber, *Virtually Jewish. Reinventing Jewish Culture in Europe,* Berkeley 2003.

10 Vgl. Grace Cohen Grossman, *Jewish Museums of the World,* Westport 2003.

11 Vgl. James E. Young (Hrsg.), *The Art of Memory: Holocaust Memorials in History,* München/New York 1994. Deutsche Ausgabe: *Mahnmale des Holo-caust. Motive, Rituale und Stätten des Gedenkens,* München/New York 1994.

Samuel D. Gruber

# Jewish Identity and Modern Synagogue Architecture

Samuel D. Gruber

## Jüdische Identität und moderne Synagogenarchitektur

There are many Jewish architects, but there is no such thing as a "Jewish" architecture. Non-Jews built all European synagogues before the early nineteenth century, and now Jewish architects are building in obviously non-Jewish contexts. Richard Meier recently completed a church in Rome commissioned by the Vatican. But one should not be surprised to find a Jew building a church in Rome. Several decades ago, a Jew (Louis I. Kahn) built the capital city for a Muslim country (Bangladesh).

Do Jewish architects bring anything special to synagogue design or to other designs? As a group, no. We must admit that many of the most banal synagogues have been designed by Jews, and that some of the most spiritually inspiring were built by non-Jews. Yet, Jewish patrons in Europe between the World Wars, and since then particularly in America, have been willing to tread new ground with synagogue design. Even when building in historical styles, as they mostly did through the 1930s, Jewish-American patrons were often willing to engage leading architects or to take risks with younger architects who later came to lead their profession. Thus, even when being traditional—as with the Greek temple style synagogue of Beth Elohim in Charleston, South Carolina (1838)—they broke new ground as it was the first religious building of that type built in Charleston. Similarly, American synagogue patrons and architects were quick to embrace the so-called Moorish style, imported from Europe. They were also among the first to create Roman-Classical style religious buildings (such as Shearith Israel in New York City, 1897) soon after the success of the "White City" of the *Columbian Exposition* in Chicago in 1893. Synagogues were also among the first Byzantine-style buildings in America in the 1920s and among the first Art Deco-style religious buildings in the 1920s and 1930s. Thus, the embrace of modernism for synagogue and Jewish community building design after World War II—popular for many functional, economic, and ideological reasons—was not much of a surprise.

Es gibt viele jüdische Architekten, aber im Prinzip keine ›jüdische‹ Architektur. Bis zum frühen 19. Jahrhundert wurden sämtliche europäischen Synagogen von Nichtjuden errichtet, und heute bauen jüdische Architekten in offenkundig nichtjüdischen Kontexten. Richard Meier hat im Auftrag des Vatikans jüngst eine Kirche in Rom fertiggestellt. Man sollte nicht überrascht sein, dass ein Jude eine Kirche in Rom baut: Vor Jahrzehnten baute ein Jude (Louis I. Kahn) die Hauptstadt eines muslimischen Landes (Bangladesch).

Bringen jüdische Architekten etwas Besonderes in die Architektur von Synagogen oder auch von anderen Gebäuden ein? Als Gruppe, nein. Man muss einräumen, dass die meisten nichtssagenden Synagogenbauten von Juden entworfen wurden, während einige der inspirierendsten Beispiele von Nichtjuden stammen. Dennoch sind jüdische Bauherren in Europa zwischen den Weltkriegen und seitdem in Amerika bereit gewesen, im Synagogenbau neue Wege zu beschreiten. Selbst wenn sie sich, wie überwiegend in den 1930er Jahren, für historische Baustile entschieden, engagierten jüdisch-amerikanische Bauherren vielfach angesehene Architekten oder mit Mut zum Risiko auch jüngere Architekten, die später zu führenden Vertretern des Berufsstands avancierten. Selbst mit einem traditionellen Entwurf betraten sie manchmal Neuland, so zum Beispiel bei der im Stil eines griechischen Tempels errichteten Synagoge Beth Elohim in Charleston, South Carolina (1838), dem ersten Sakralbau dieses Typs in Charleston. Gleichermaßen übernahmen die amerikanischen Bauherren und Architekten von Synagogen schon bald den aus Europa importierten so genannten maurischen Stil. Sie gehörten ebenfalls zu den Ersten, die Synagogen im Stil klassischer römischer Bauten schufen, darunter die Shearith-Israel-Synagoge in New York City (1897), und zwar schon bald nach der erfolgreichen White City auf der *Columbian Exposition* in Chicago (Weltausstellung 1893). Synagogen zählten im Amerika der 1920er Jahre auch zu den ersten Gebäuden, die im byzantinischen Stil errichtet wurden, sowie zu den ersten Sakralbauten der 1920er und 1930er Jahre im Art-Deco-Stil. So war es keine Überraschung, als jüdische Gemeinden sich nach dem Zweiten Weltkrieg beim Bau ihrer Synagogen und Gemeindehäuser der Moderne verschrieben, die aus vielen funktionalen, ökonomischen und ideologischen Gründen populär wurde.

Heute verfügen die meisten Architekten, ob jüdisch oder nicht, nur über geringe Kenntnisse der Traditionen, Rituale, Lehren und Glaubensgrundlagen des Judentums. Jeder Architekt muss etwas darüber lernen, wenn er ein jüdisches Gebäude entwirft. Ein Nichtjude wird ebenso in diesen Lernprozess eintauchen wie ein Jude – vielleicht sogar noch tiefer. Ein Nichtjude wird sich möglicherweise noch mehr anstrengen, es ›richtig zu machen‹. Der amerikanische Architekt Will Bruder, der die in dieser Ausstellung gezeigte Kol-Ami-Synagoge in Scottsdale, Arizona, entwarf, zitiert als einen der Gründe, warum er jüdischen Kollegen vorgezogen wurde, dass er »bereit schien zuzuhören«.[1]

Was lässt sich also über die modernen jüdischen Architekten sagen? Dass sie dazu neigen, ihre Arbeit ernst zu nehmen? Vielleicht haben sie hier eine jüdische Sensibilität geerbt: die Überzeugung, dass es auf die eigene Tätigkeit ankommt, dass die Taten des Einzelnen Auswirkungen auf die Gemeinschaft haben, dass die Errichtung eines Zweckbaus wahrhaft sinnvoll ist. Bauwerke sollten gut sein und müssen ernsthaft sein.

Alfred S. Alschuler, K.A.M. Isaiah Israel Congregation, Chicago, Illinois, 1964
Alfred S. Alschuler, K.A.M. Isaiah Israel Congregation, Chicago, Illinois, 1964

Today, most architects, whether Jewish or not, have little knowledge of the traditions, rituals, teachings, and beliefs of Judaism. Any architect needs to learn something about these things as part of the design process. A non-Jew is just as likely, or perhaps even more likely, to immerse him/herself in this learning process as Jew. A non-Jew may be even more committed to "getting it right." The American architect Will Bruder, who designed Temple Kol Ami in Scottsdale, Arizona, shown in this exhibit, says that one of the reasons he was chosen over Jewish competitors for the commission was that he "seemed willing to listen."[1]

So, what can we say of the modern Jewish architects? That they tend to take their work seriously? Perhaps in this they inherit a Jewish sensibility: that what one does matters, that acts of the individual effect the community, that building a building for use will have real meaning. Buildings should be good and they must be serious.

Many modern American Jews tend to see Judaism as a dynamic religion, one that can stand the blows of history and adapt to a changing world. In America, there are many forms of Judaism, and they are continually evolving. This may be one reason American Jewish architects are also willing to challenge traditions and to welcome change. Israelis see Judaism as almost indistinguishable from national identity; thus, Israeli architecture, as exemplified in this exhibition by the work of Moshe Safdie and Zvi Hecker, is encouraged to push the limits of traditional forms in the process of creating something like the state of Israel—rooted in the past but still entirely new.

Many Jewish architects encourage their buildings to be read like Jewish texts, with many meanings, with hidden messages, with bits and pieces of inchoate form that can even spark the imagination to something profound, something beautiful, something meaningful and good. Architects of contemporary synagogues such as Norman Jaffe (Jewish Center of the Hamptons, Easthampton, New York) and Alex Gorlin (North Shore Hebrew Academy Synagogue, Kings Point, New York) have used Kabbalistic sources as a basis for spatial organization, the use of light, certain phrases, and inscriptions.[2] Daniel Libeskind creates bold forms and then explains them in terms of historic references—as if he was preparing a learned commentary on a Talmudic passage. Richard Meier and Frank Gehry, perhaps the foremost Jewish architects who have not designed much in a Jewish context, remain stalwart formalists. Meier rests firmly in the long tradition of rationalists from Alberti to Terragni, while Gehry, with more baroque forms, creates a fanciful and joyful architecture that, at the same time, has proven quite functional for diverse purposes. Seen from a Jewish perspective, the contrast between these two leading architects recalls the eighteenth and nineteenth century contrast between the intellectual perfectionism of the *Mitnagdim* (Meier) and the exuberant joy of the *Hasidim* (Gehry).[3]

There is no mandated Jewish religious architecture and, with the exception of a few required elements for every synagogue (Ark, *bimah*), there are few constants found in any type of architecture founded, created, or used by Jews. There is, however, architecture conceived for Jewish religious and communal use. Obviously, this can include synagogues, Jewish study houses, cemeteries, certain communal buildings, and Holocaust museums and memorials. At times, this architecture for a Jewish purpose was developed in such a way as to include unique formal and decorative elements that immediately identify the result as serving Jews.

Viele moderne amerikanische Juden sehen das Judentum als eine dynamische Religion, die in der Lage ist, geschichtlichen Schicksalsschlägen standzuhalten und sich einer im Wandel begriffenen Welt anzupassen. In Amerika gibt es viele Ausprägungen des Judentums, die sich alle ständig weiterentwickeln. Das erklärt vielleicht, warum amerikanische jüdische Architekten bereitwillig Traditionen hinterfragen und für Veränderungen offen sind. Für Israelis ist Judentum nahezu identisch mit nationaler Identität, weshalb die israelische Architektur – in dieser Ausstellung beispielhaft vertreten durch Moshe Safdie und Zvi Hecker – sich ermutigt fühlt, die Grenzen der traditionellen Formen wie beim Aufbau des Staates Israel zu sprengen, der seine Wurzeln in der Geschichte hat und doch eine völlige Neuschöpfung ist.

Viele jüdische Architekten tendieren dazu, ihre Bauten wie jüdische Texte lesbar werden zu lassen, mit vielfältigen Bedeutungen, mit versteckten Botschaften, Bruchstücken unfertiger Formen, dazu geeignet, die Fantasie so anzuregen, dass etwas Tiefgründiges, Schönes, Bedeutungsvolles und Gutes dabei herauskommt. Die Architekten zeitgenössischer Synagogen, darunter Norman Jaffe (Jewish Center of the Hamptons, Easthampton, New York), und Alex Gorlin (North Shore Hebrew Academy Synagogue, Kings Point, New York) haben für die räumliche Gliederung, die Lichtplanung sowie für bestimmte Zitate und Inschriften kabbalistische Quellen herangezogen.[2] Daniel Libeskind schafft kühne Formen und erklärt sie mit historischen Bezügen, so als würde er einen gelehrten Kommentar zu einem Abschnitt aus dem Talmud verfassen. Richard Meier und Frank O. Gehry – möglicherweise die bekanntesten jüdischen Architekten, die nur selten in einem jüdischen Kontext gebaut haben – sind unerschütterliche Formalisten. Meier ist immer noch fest in der langjährigen Tradition der Rationalisten von Alberti bis Terragni verwurzelt, während Gehry mit seinen eher barocken Formen eine fantasievolle, heitere Architektur schafft, die sich zugleich für verschiedene Zwecke als durchaus funktional erweist. Aus jüdischer Perspektive erinnert die Gegensätzlichkeit dieser beiden führenden Architekten an den im 18. und 19. Jahrhundert herrschenden Kontrast zwischen dem intellektuellen Perfektionismus der Mitnagdim (Meier) und dem freudigen Überschwang der Chassidim (Gehry).[3]

Vorschriften zur Gestaltung jüdischer Sakralbauten existieren nicht, und bis auf einige für jede Synagoge erforderliche Elemente (Thoraschrein, Bima) finden sich in allen Arten von Gebäuden, die von Juden gegründet, geschaffen oder genutzt werden, nur wenige Konstanten. Allerdings gibt es Architektur, die für jüdisch-religiöse und Gemeindezwecke konzipiert ist. Dazu gehören natürlich Synagogen, jüdische Lehrhäuser, Friedhöfe, bestimmte Einrichtungen der jüdischen Gemeinschaft sowie Holocaust-Museen und Gedenkstätten. Zuweilen wurde die architektonische Gestaltung für jüdische Zwecke in einer Weise entwickelt, dass an ihren einzigartigen formalen und schmückenden Elementen ihre jüdische Identität sofort ablesbar ist.

Einige allgemeine Feststellungen zum Synagogenbau gelten jeweils für bestimmte Orte und Perioden. In Zeiten der Unterdrückung waren die Synagogen bescheidene Gebäude, innen aber vielfach reich geschmückt. Selbst wenn ihnen vorgeschrieben war, die Höhe und den Lichteinfall zu reduzieren, versuchten die Erbauer aus praktischen Erwägungen und Gründen der Symbolik, hohe und gut belichtete Innenräume zu schaffen. Bis in die jüngste Zeit ignorierte die Synagogenarchitektur die weiblichen Gemeindemitglieder oder verwies sie in Nebenräume. Mancherorts und in bestimmten Perioden, so speziell im 18. und 19. Jahrhundert in Polen und während der Zeit der Emanzipation in Frankreich, Deutschland und

A few general statements about synagogues hold true for certain places and certain times. During years of oppression, exteriors were modest, but synagogue interiors were often ornate. Even when told to restrict height and light, builders tried, for practical and symbolic reasons, to have lofty and well-lit interiors. Until recently, synagogue design architecturally ignored women or separated them in ancillary spaces. In a few places and periods Jews did assert themselves architecturally such as in Poland, especially during the eighteenth and nineteenth centuries, and during the period of Emancipation in France, Germany, Austria, and Italy in the nineteenth century. But size, location, and overall ostentation were more important than any particular architectural style. In the nineteenth century, generally known as an age of architectural historicism and eclecticism, individuals would propound this style or that, but there was no accepted norm.

In general terms, architects of synagogues and other buildings for Jewish use have been conscious of the question of Jewish identity and have addressed this in several ways. Most commonly, architects have merely adopted local building methods and design vocabulary, whether high-style or vernacular, to serve Jewish functional needs. It was enough, it seems, to fill a building with Jewish ritual, Jewish objects—and mostly with Jews themselves—to give the place "Jewish" identity. For non-Jews and Jews alike, this was clear. It was the use to which a building was put that conferred identity; a synagogue's sanctity was defined by the presence of the Torah and of acts of prayer and study. The structure had no intrinsic sanctity, nor did it hold symbolic or numinous value.

Jews were discouraged or explicitly forbidden to display identifying markings on their buildings through most of European history. While laws often demanded that Jews wear distinctive clothing or badges, they were, however, to leave their buildings relatively anonymous. While size and site often made this impossible, it is true that the exterior decoration of most European synagogues prior to the eighteenth century was minimal—especially when compared to the often lavish interior decorative displays. Some architectural shapes and forms are more common to synagogues than to other building types. There are also some decorative schemes more common to synagogues, and some decorative elements are almost only found in synagogues or in other Jewish contexts.

When architects have attempted to impose Jewish identity on a building through design and decoration, this was often done in opposition to prevailing Christian forms, rather than through the embodiment of specifically calculated Jewish features or the overall adoption of something recognizable as a Jewish sensibility. Some architectural styles chosen by Christian architects to articulate and essentially isolate Jewish buildings, however, became so widely identified with Jews and Judaism that they were eventually assimilated by Jews themselves, who took them, albeit sometimes awkwardly, to heart. Both the exotic Egyptian and the Moorish styles, and various hybrid expressions of these, became widely recognized by many Jews themselves as appropriate styles of building and design.

A less common way Jewish identity has been addressed in architecture and design has been the conscious consideration, application, and integration of Jewish devices, themes, and other expressions of meaning into a building's design so that to some degree the structure not only has a Jewish function after its completion, but is in fact imbued with Jewish identity during its creation. At least since the Renaissance,

Synagogue Oranienburgerstrasse, Berlin, 1866    Synagoge Oranienburger Straße, Berlin, 1866

Österreich sowie im 19. Jahrhundert in Italien, behaupteten sich die Juden auch architektonisch. Die Größe, Lage und der Gesamteindruck jüdischer Gebäude waren aber stets wichtiger als ein bestimmter architektonischer Stil. Im 19. Jahrhundert, das generell als die Epoche des Historismus und Eklektizismus gilt, vertraten einzelne Architekten diesen oder jenen Stil, es gab aber keine allseits akzeptierte Norm.

Insgesamt gesehen war die Frage der jüdischen Identität den Architekten von Synagogen und anderen von der jüdischen Gemeinschaft genutzten Bauten sehr wohl bewusst, und sie gingen auf unterschiedliche Weise darauf ein. In den meisten Fällen übernahmen sie einfach nur die üblichen lokalen Bauweisen und Gestaltungselemente, ob anspruchsvoll elegant oder volkstümlich, wenn es darum ging, die funktionalen jüdischen Anforderungen zu erfüllen. Es genügte offenbar, ein Gebäude mit jüdischen Ritualen und Objekten anzufüllen – und meistens einfach nur mit jüdischen Menschen –, um ihm eine ›jüdische Identität‹ zu verleihen. Das war allen Nichtjuden und Juden klar. Der Zweck gab dem jeweiligen Bauwerk seine Identität. Die Heiligkeit einer Synagoge definierte sich durch die Anwesenheit der Thora, das Gebet und das Studium der heiligen Schriften. Das Gebäude an sich besaß weder Heiligkeit noch symbolischen oder göttlichen Wert.

Im Verlauf der europäischen Geschichte wurde den Juden die längste Zeit davon abgeraten, ja sogar ausdrücklich verboten, ihre Bauten in irgendeiner Weise als jüdisch zu kennzeichnen. Während Juden vielfach per Gesetz zum Tragen charakteristischer Kleidung oder Abzeichen

many synagogues have referred to the Temple in Jerusalem through the use of paired columns, or exterior turrets, or even to the Temple's destruction by leaving of a patch of wall unfinished.

Beginning in the late eighteenth century, the identification of a synagogue was done simply by applying a Decalogue (Ten Commandments) to the facade. More recently, this might be supplemented by a menorah or six-pointed star. In the twentieth century, many Jewish architects tended to be quite literal with overt inclusion of Biblically-described architectural elements such as Jerusalem wall, or desert tent. Of course, it is sometimes difficult to differentiate amid architects' often-conflicting descriptions and definitions of just which meanings are really intrinsic to the building's design and which meanings have been applied ex post facto.

At the turn of the twentieth century, the spirit of integration was behind much of the new synagogue construction in Europe and America. Distinctive Moorish-style buildings continuing the exotic architectural language first articulated by Gottfried Semper in Dresden (1838–40) continued to be erected, such as the Jerusalem Street Synagogue in Prague (Wilhelm Stiassny and Alois Richter, 1906). Other historic styles such as Romanesque and Gothic (Szeged, Hungary, 1900–03) continued late nineteenth-century traditions. A few distinctive synagogue designs broke with tradition such as Hector Guimard's Art Nouveau Rue Pavée Synagogue in Paris (1911–13), or adapted new traditions such as the synagogue in Subotica, Serbia (Komor and Jakab, 1901) combining Balkan, Hungarian, and Jewish folk architectural traditions. The Prague and Paris architects were not Jewish, those of Szeged and Subotica were. But in none of these buildings is there an overt intent to create a Jewish architecture or even to have the building incontrovertibly identified as Jewish.[4] A strong trend toward classicism, however, especially in America, resulted in notable buildings such as Congregation Shearith Israel, New York (Arnold Brunner, 1897) and Congregation Beth El, Detroit (Albert Kahn, 1903), and scores of similar synagogues. Brunner's small Henry S. Frank Memorial Synagogue in Philadelphia (1901) was the first synagogue to directly refer to archaeological finds of ancient synagogues in Palestine, a motif repeated in his subsequent synagogues such as Temple Society of Concord in Syracuse, New York (1910).

This Classical Revival, which often resulted in synagogues hardly distinguishable from banks, libraries, government, and university buildings evolved into the more distinctive Byzantine-Revival style, particularly popular after World War I. Here, following the lead of Brunner, patrons and architects sometimes justified their designs by linking them to archaeological finds from Palestine, but they also reinvented the distinctive exoticism of the Moorish style. Unlike the Moorish style,

Marcell Komor, Deszo Jakab,
Synagogue in Subotica, 1901
Marcell Komor, Deszo Jakab,
Synagoge in Subotica, 1901

verpflichtet waren, sollten sie ihre Gebäude möglichst anonym belassen. Deren Form und Lage machte das zwar häufig unmöglich, es war aber tatsächlich so, dass der Fassadenschmuck der meisten vor dem 18. Jahrhundert in Europa errichteten Synagogen äußerst sparsam ausfiel, besonders im Vergleich zu den vielfach üppig ornamentierten Innenausstattungen. Bestimmte Bauformen sind bei Synagogen gebräuchlicher als bei anderen Bautypen, ebenso eine Reihe von dekorativen Motiven und Elementen, welche man ausschließlich bei Synagogen oder anderen jüdischen Zweckbauten findet.

Wenn ein Architekt versuchte, einem Gebäude durch architektonische Gestaltung und Dekoration einen jüdischen Stempel aufzudrücken, tat er es eher in Opposition zu den vorherrschenden christlichen Formen statt in einer wohlkalkulierten Umsetzung spezifisch jüdischer Merkmale oder eines ganz allgemein als jüdisch erkennbaren Stils. Einige Stile, die christliche Architekten eigens wählten, um den jüdischen Charakter der von ihnen für Juden errichteten Bauten zu verdeutlichen und diese dadurch von anderen abzusetzen, wurden weithin mit den Juden und dem Judentum derart identifiziert, dass sie schließlich sogar von den Juden selbst angewandt wurden, welche sich diese Gestaltungsweise, wenn auch gelegentlich ungeschickt, zu Eigen machten. Die exotischen Stile – ägyptisch und maurisch – und deren verschiedene Mischformen wurden im Laufe der Zeit von vielen Juden selbst als geeignete Vorbilder für Konstruktion und Gestaltung anerkannt.

Ein seltener beschrittener Weg zur jüdischen Identität in Architektur und Innenarchitektur war die gezielte Berücksichtigung, Anwendung und Integration jüdischer Erfindungen, Themen und anderer sinnstiftender Ausdrucksformen bei der Entwurfsarbeit, so dass der Bau am Ende nicht nur eine jüdische Funktion hatte, sondern auch insgesamt von der ersten Entwurfsidee an von jüdischer Identität durchdrungen war. Spätestens seit der Renaissance wiesen zahlreiche Synagogen mit Säulenpaaren oder turmbewehrten Mauern auf den Tempel in Jerusalem hin oder mit einem unvollendeten Wandstück auf dessen Zerstörung.

Seit dem späten 18. Jahrhundert ließ sich eine Synagoge einfach dadurch kennzeichnen, dass man den Dekalog (Zehn Gebote) an der Fassade anbrachte. In jüngerer Zeit wird er durch eine Menora oder einen sechszackigen Stern ergänzt. Im 20. Jahrhundert pflegten viele jüdische Architekten in der Bibel beschriebene architektonische Elemente direkt in ihre Entwürfe einzubeziehen, zum Beispiel die Mauer in Jerusalem oder das Wüstenzelt. Natürlich ist es manchmal schwierig, aus den häufig widersprüchlichen Erläuterungen und Definitionen der Architekten herauszulesen, welche Bedeutungen tatsächlich integrale Bestandteile des Entwurfs sind und welche einem Bau erst nachträglich zugeschrieben wurden.

Um 1900 basierte die Architektur neuer Synagogen vielfach auf dem Gedanken der Integration der Juden in Europa und Amerika. Es wurden aber auch weiterhin Synagogen im maurischen Stil errichtet, der exotischen architektonischen Formensprache, die Gottfried Semper 1838–40 in Dresden als Erster artikuliert hatte, so die Synagoge in der Jerusalemer Straße in Prag (von Wilhelm Stiassny und Alois Richter, 1906). Andere historische Baustile wie der romanische und gotische (Szeged, Ungarn, 1900–03) setzten die Architekturtradition des ausgehenden 19. Jahrhunderts fort. Einige wenige herausragende Synagogen, darunter Hector Guimards Art-nouveau-Synagoge in der Rue Pavée in Paris (1911–13), brachen mit der Tradition oder adaptierten neue, so etwa die Synagoge in Subotica, Serbien, von Komor und Jakab (1901), die Architekturtraditionen des Balkans und Ungarns sowie jüdische volkstümliche Bauweisen

Gottfried Semper, Synagogue in Dresden, 1838–40
Gottfried Semper, Synagoge in Dresden, 1838–40

Arnold Brunner, Temple Society of Concord, Syracuse, New York, 1910
Arnold Brunner, Temple Society of Concord, Syracuse, New York, 1910

Fritz Landauer, Synagogue in Plauen, 1930
Fritz Landauer, Synagoge in Plauen, 1930

however, the new Byzantine design emphasized plan and massing over decoration.

In Europe and British Palestine during the interwar period, architectural forms prevalent in the nascent modern movement were easily adapted for synagogue design. The synagogue of Zilina, Slovakia by Peter Behrens (1928–30) was, in many ways, a stripped down version of the Byzantine domed synagogue popular in Hungary and the Balkans. In Amsterdam, Jewish architect Harry Elte built the Jacob Obrechtplein Synagogue in a Dutch-cubist style in 1927–28.[5] The building recalls early designs by Frank Lloyd Wright, especially the Unity Temple near Chicago. Amsterdam's Lekstraat Synagogue by A. Elzas (1936–37) is a plain stone box with simple square windows that emphasizes only the Ark and *bimah*. Elzas won a competition among nine Jewish architects for the commission. The simplicity of the building's geometry and white concrete walls is offset slightly by the use of stone on the exterior and the introduction of vast amounts of natural light through large windows.[6] The Osterstrasse Synagogue in Hamburg by Felix Ascher and Robert Friedmann (1931) exhibited a similar blocky form, but followed a traditional Beaux Arts plan. Perhaps the most radical synagogue design of the interwar years was that in Plauen, Germany, designed by Fritz Landauer. The synagogue is conceived as a white box, elevated on stilts at one end. The arrangement of windows differentiates the discreet functions of the building, much as was done in contemporary industrial architecture.[7] Other modern works were built in England, Czechoslovakia, and elsewhere in Germany, as well as in British Palestine, particularly in Tel Aviv. In the Jewish world, modernism appeared in the ascendancy on the eve of destruction.

What might have developed from these innovative modern European synagogue designs if Germany had not embraced Nazism, and then unleashed war and Holocaust, can never be known. Certainly, the prosperity and creativity of Jewish Europe was destroyed, almost to the verge of extinction. And yet, in architectural terms, there was continuity. The aesthetic lessons of prewar Europe, and even many practitioners of modernism, went over to England and America where, in the postwar period, they pioneered a new style of synagogue architecture.

Although all Jewish art and all Jewish life since the Shoah is, at a core level, fundamentally different from what went before, on the surface much seems the same. Despite profound loss, humans are resilient and in within the parameters of life and art certain actions remain virtually constant. After the Holocaust, the formal religious needs

miteinander kombiniert. Die Architekten der Prager und Pariser Bauten waren keine Juden, die von Szeged und Subotica dagegen schon. Keines dieser Gebäude vermittelt die deutliche Absicht, eine jüdische Architektur zu schaffen oder das Gebäude unmissverständlich als jüdisch identifizierbar zu machen.[4] Eine starke klassizistische Strömung brachte allerdings vor allem in Amerika bemerkenswerte Bauten hervor, darunter die Shearith-Israel-Synagoge in New York von Arnold Brunner (1897) und die Beth-El-Synagoge in Detroit von Albert Kahn (1903) sowie Dutzende ähnlicher Beispiele. Brunners kleine Henry-S.-Frank-Memorial-Synagoge in Philadelphia (1901) war die erste Synagoge mit direkten Bezügen zu Tempelresten, die man in Palästina bei archäologischen Grabungen entdeckt hatte, und Brunner verwendete diese Motive bei seinen weiteren Synagogen wie dem Temple Society of Concord in Syracuse, New York (1910).

Der Klassizismus brachte vielfach Synagogen hervor, die sich kaum von Banken, Bibliotheken, Regierungs- und Universitätsgebäuden unterschieden, und mündete dann in den charakteristischeren, nach dem Ersten Weltkrieg besonders beliebten neobyzantinischen Stil. Nach Brunners Vorbild rechtfertigten Bauherren und Architekten ihre Entwürfe zuweilen, indem sie deren Bezüge zu archäologischen Funden in Palästina hervorhoben, sie führten aber auch die besondere Exotik des maurischen Stils wieder ein. Anders als beim maurischen Stil gab der neobyzantinische Stil dem Grundriss und der Gestaltung der Baukörper den Vorzug vor der Ornamentik.

Zwischen den Weltkriegen wurden in Europa und im britischen Mandatsgebiet Palästina die architektonischen Formen der einsetzenden Moderne mühelos auf den Bau von Synagogen übertragen. Die Synagoge in Zilina, Slowakei, von Peter Behrens (1928–30) war in vielerlei Hinsicht eine abgespeckte Version der in Ungarn und auf dem Balkan populären kuppelbedeckten byzantinischen Synagoge. In Amsterdam baute der jüdische Architekt Harry Elte 1927/28 die Synagoge am Jacob Obrechtplein im Stil des holländischen Kubismus.[5] Das Gebäude erinnert an frühe Entwürfe von Frank Lloyd Wright, insbesondere den Unity Temple bei Chicago. Die Synagoge von A. Elzas in der Amsterdamer Lekstraat (1936/37) ist ein schlichter Steinkubus mit einfachen quadratischen Fenstern, in dem nur Thoraschrein und Bima gestalterisch betont sind. Elzas erhielt den Auftrag infolge eines Wettbewerbsverfahrens, an dem neun jüdische Architekten beteiligt waren. Die Strenge der geometrischen Bauform und der weißen Betonmauern wird außen durch Natursteine und innen von dem durch große Fenster reichlich einfallenden Tageslicht

Percival Goodman, Temple Beth El, Providence, Rhode Island, 1954
Percival Goodman, Beth-El-Synagoge, Providence, Rhode Island, 1954

of Judaism at first remained unchanged; thus, we can link synagogue architecture of the post—Holocaust period to what came before. The Holocaust, however, accelerated the acceptance of modern design. In the postwar period, the sincerity of all historical norms and forms was in doubt.

Erich Mendelsohn (1887–1953) and Percival Goodman (1904–1989) were key creative forces in providing a positive and ultimately optimistic connection between the destruction of the Holocaust and the aspiration of Jewish achievement in postwar America. Mendelsohn, in his very person as one of the most visible German-Jewish refugees, created a real connection between past and present, Old World and New. His expressive architecture was emotional, inspirational, and, for America, incredibly new despite his nearly three decades of innovative work in Germany and later in Jewish Palestine. The very act of building his (six) major synagogue designs was a sign of the Jewish phoenix rising from the ashes. Even in 1946, before he had built a single synagogue, Mendelsohn expressed this forward-looking ethos:

> This period demands centers of worship where the spirit of the Bible is not an ancient mirage, but a living truth, where Jehovah is not a desert King, but our Guide and Companion. It demands temples that will bear witness of man's material achievements and, at the same time, symbolize our spiritual renascence. A question no architect can pass upon, but the answer will inevitably be recorded in the pages of history now being written.[8]

The prolific and innovative synagogue architect Percival Goodman said on many occasions that the Holocaust made him a Jew. Recognition of Judaism through the afflictions Jews suffered at the hands of others, instead of by the religious and ethical beliefs and the creative accomplishments of Jews themselves, was common to Goodman's generation of assimilated and secular Jews and continues to dominate discussions of Jewish identity today. As an American without direct connection to the Holocaust, Goodman expressed the link between suffering and survival very differently than Mendelsohn. Goodman's buildings mostly avoided architectural bombast. Even when he created a vaulted space (as in Providence, Rhode Island), he used simple materials and maintained a human scale. His buildings, especially his

etwas gemildert.[6] Die Synagoge in der Hamburger Osterstraße von Felix Ascher und Robert Friedmann (1931) hat eine ähnlich blockhafte Form, dabei aber einen traditionellen Beaux-Arts-Grundriss. Die radikalste moderne Synagoge der Zwischenkriegszeit ist wahrscheinlich die von Fritz Landauer in Plauen. Sie wurde als weißer, an einem Ende auf Stützen ruhender Kasten konzipiert. Die Anordnung der Fenster diente zur Unterscheidung der einzelnen Funktionsbereiche des Gebäudes, wie es damals auch bei Industriebauten üblich war.[7] Weitere moderne Synagogen entstanden in England, der Tschechoslowakei und in anderen deutschen Städten sowie in Britisch-Palästina, vor allem in Tel Aviv. In der jüdischen Welt befand sich die Moderne am Vorabend der Vernichtung also im Aufwind.

Wir werden nie wissen, was aus dieser innovativen modernen Synagogenarchitektur noch geworden wäre, wenn Deutschland sich nicht dem Nationalsozialismus ergeben und dann den Krieg und den Holocaust verursacht hätte. Fest steht, dass der Wohlstand und die Kreativität des jüdischen Europas zerstört und fast völlig vernichtet wurden. Und dennoch gab es in architektonischer Hinsicht auch Kontinuität. Die Gestaltungsprinzipien des Vorkriegs-Europas fanden ihren Weg nach England oder Amerika, ebenso wie viele moderne Architekten, die dort nach dem Krieg eine neue Synagogenarchitektur einführten.

Obwohl sich jüdische Kunst und jüdisches Leben seit der Shoah generell im Kern von allem Vorherigen unterscheiden, erscheint vieles oberflächlich betrachtet gleich geblieben zu sein. Trotz schwerster Verluste sind die Menschen widerstandsfähig, und im Rahmen des Lebens und der Kunst bleiben bestimmte Handlungen nahezu konstant. Nach dem Holocaust blieben die formal-religiösen Bedürfnisse des Judentums zunächst unverändert. Deshalb ist es möglich, den Bezug der Synagogenarchitektur nach dem Holocaust zum Synagogenbau davor herzustellen. Der Holocaust beschleunigte allerdings die Akzeptanz der Moderne. In der Nachkriegszeit wurde die Wahrhaftigkeit aller historischen Normen und Formen in Frage gestellt.

Erich Mendelsohn (1887–1953) und Percival Goodman (1904–89) waren kreative Schlüsselfiguren für die Herstellung einer positiven und letztlich optimistischen Verbindung zwischen den Zerstörungen des Holocaust und den jüdischen Bestrebungen im Amerika der Nachkriegszeit. Als einer der bekanntesten deutsch-jüdischen Flüchtlinge stellte Mendelsohn schon als Person ein reales Bindeglied zwischen der Vergangenheit und der Gegenwart, der alten und der neuen Welt dar. Seine expressive, emotionale, inspirierende Architektur war in Amerika etwas Neues, obwohl er zuvor bereits seit fast drei Jahrzehnten innovative Bauten in Deutschland und später im jüdischen Palästina errichtet hatte. Allein der Bau seiner (sechs) großen Synagogen war ein Signal des aus der Asche aufsteigenden jüdischen Phönix. Schon 1946, noch bevor er auch nur eine einzige Synagoge entworfen hatte, formulierte Mendelsohn seine in die Zukunft schauende Auffassung:

> »Diese Epoche verlangt nach Zentren des Gottesdienstes, wo der Geist der Bibel keine altertümliche Fata Morgana ist, sondern lebendige Wahrheit, wo Jehova kein König der Wüste ist, sondern unser Anführer und Begleiter. Sie verlangt nach Tempeln, die Zeugnis von den materiellen Errungenschaften des Menschen ablegen und zugleich unsere geistliche Wiedergeburt symbolisieren. Eine Frage, die kein Architekt übergehen kann, die Antwort aber wird unweigerlich in der Geschichte verzeichnet sein, die derzeit geschrieben wird.«[8]

Der produktive und innovative Synagogenarchitekt Percival Goodman pflegte zu sagen, dass der Holocaust ihn zum Juden gemacht habe. Diese

early synagogue at Millburn, New Jersey (1949–51), were modern, but modest. But at Millburn, Goodman inserted modern art that symbolically bridged the centuries (Robert Motherwell's mural recalled the Temple period) and also directly addressed recent events.

Within the sanctuary is a memorial niche with two cornerstones from synagogues destroyed by the Nazis in Mannheim, Germany. The inscription reads: "To the heroes and martyrs, the known and the unknown who died for the sanctification of the Divine Name." This reminder of recent horrific events gives the synagogue additional rootedness. Goodman's modernism is also rooted in this past. The awareness of cultural destruction actually frees the architect to embrace a non-historic design. This liberating spirit is explicitly expressed on the exterior of the Millburn synagogue where an abstract sculpture entitled *And the Bush was Not Consumed* is prominently set. In one gesture, Goodman united a very public acknowledgement of the Holocaust, abstract modern art, and a declaration of creative Jewish and spiritual renewal. This combination would be repeated by other architects and artists many times over the next decades. One striking example is the large, sculpted Ark wall by Louise Nevelson at Temple Beth El, in Great Neck, New York (1970). The austere design of architect Armand Bartos vaguely recalls European synagogues of the 1930s, and Nevelson's wall is a memorial specifically called *The White Flame of the Six Million*.

Mendelsohn and Goodman established formal, functional, and symbolic vocabularies that were sustained for decades. Contemporary synagogue architects have moved away from this postwar pattern, but many elements remain inescapable. In Europe, where new synagogues are now being erected in substantial number, Mendelsohn's and Goodman's forms have found new life.

Frank Lloyd Wright, Beth Sholom Synagogue, Elkins Park, Pennsylvania, 1953–59
Frank Lloyd Wright, Beth-Sholom-Synagoge, Elkins Park, Pennsylvania, 1953–59

Influenced by Mendelsohn and Goodman, and continuing with Frank Lloyd Wright's Beth Sholom Synagogue in Elkins Park, Pennsylvania (1953–59), congregations and architects replaced ties to history through the manipulation of form for symbolic association—often favoring building profiles recalling mountains or tents. Frank Lloyd

Haltung war unter seinen assimilierten und säkularisierten jüdischen Zeitgenossen weit verbreitet, die sich aufgrund des Leids, das dem jüdischen Volk von anderen zugefügt wurde, zum Judentum bekannten und nicht etwa aufgrund der religiösen und sittlichen Überzeugungen und kreativen Leistungen der Juden selbst. Sie beherrscht auch heute noch die Diskussion über jüdische Identität. Als Amerikaner, der nicht direkt vom Holocaust betroffen war, drückte Goodman die Verbindung zwischen Leiden und Überleben ganz anders aus als Mendelsohn. Goodmans Bauten vermeiden weitgehend jeden architektonischen Bombast. Selbst für einen überwölbten Raum wie in Providence, Rhode Island, verwendete er einfache Materialien und wahrte ein menschliches Maß. Seine Synagogen, insbesondere seine frühe in Millburn, New Jersey (1949–51), waren modern, aber bescheiden. In Millburn setzte Goodman aber auch moderne Kunst ein, die einen symbolischen Brückenschlag über die Jahrhunderte darstellt (Robert Motherwells Wandbild erinnert an die Tempel-Periode), aber auch auf die jüngsten Ereignisse Bezug nimmt.

Im Innern des Heiligtums befindet sich eine Gedenknische, deren zwei Ecksteine aus Mannheimer Synagogen stammen, die von den Nazis zerstört wurden. Die Inschrift lautet: »Den Helden und Märtyrern, den Bekannten und den Unbekannten, die für die Heiligung des göttlichen Namens starben«. Diese mahnende Erinnerung an die schrecklichen Ereignisse in jüngster Zeit verleiht der Synagoge eine zusätzliche Verwurzelung. Goodmans Moderne wurzelt ebenfalls in der Vergangenheit. Das Bewusstsein der kulturellen Vernichtung gibt dem Architekten tatsächlich die Freiheit, gerade keine historische Gestaltung zu wählen. Dieses befreiende Gefühl lässt sich deutlich am Äußeren der Synagoge von Millburn ablesen, wo gut sichtbar die abstrakte Plastik *And the Bush was not Consumed* platziert ist. In einer Geste vereinte Goodman damit die öffentliche Bestätigung des Holocaust, moderne abstrakte Kunst und die Deklaration der schöpferischen und spirituellen Erneuerung des Judentums. Diese Zusammenstellung sollte in den folgenden Jahrzehnten vielfach von anderen Architekten und Künstlern nachempfunden werden. Ein eindrucksvolles Beispiel hierfür ist die große, von Louise Nevelson plastisch gestaltete Thoraschrein-Wand der Beth-El-Synagoge in Great Neck, New York (1970). Der strenge Bau des Architekten Armand Bartos erinnert vage an europäische Synagogen der 1930er Jahre, und Nevelsons Wand ist ein Mahnmal, das sie bewusst *The White Flame of the Six Million* nannte.

Mendelsohn und Goodman etablierten eine formale, funktionale und symbolische Formensprache, die über Jahrzehnte wirksam blieb. Die heutigen Synagogenarchitekten haben sich zwar von diesem Nachkriegsmuster entfernt, viele seiner Elemente sind dennoch unverzichtbar geblieben. In Europa, wo derzeit eine beachtliche Anzahl neuer Synagogen gebaut wird, hat man Mendelsohns und Goodmans Formen zu neuem Leben erweckt.

Unter dem Einfluss von Mendelsohn und Goodman, gefolgt von Frank Lloyd Wrights Beth-Sholom-Synagoge in Elkins Park, Pennsylvania (1953–59), haben jüdische Gemeinden und ihre Architekten die historischen Bezüge durch die Manipulation von Formen zugunsten einer symbolischen Aussagekraft ersetzt, wobei sie häufig berg- oder zeltförmige Gebäudesilhouetten bevorzugten. Frank Lloyd Wright erklärte seine Absichten für das Innere der Beth-Sholom-Synagoge folgendermaßen: »Wir wollen ein Gebäude schaffen, das den Menschen, die es betreten, das Gefühl gibt, in Gottes Händen geborgen zu sein.« Wright und Rabbi Mortimer Cohen verglichen die Synagoge aber auch mit dem Berg Sinai. Die Konstruktion von Minoru Yamasakis Synagoge Congregation North

Wright expressed his intent for the interior of Beth Sholom: "We want to create the kind of building that people, on entering it, will feel as if they were resting in the very hands of God." But Wright and Rabbi Mortimer Cohen also likened the synagogue to Mt. Sinai. At Congregation North Shore Israel in Glencoe, Illinois (Minoru Yamasaki, 1964) a series of large concrete arches frame the building, but large gaps in the structure fill the sanctuary with filtered light. The interior is spacious, and the use of light, white walls, and sparse ornamentation create a cerebral space. The tall, thin, gilded Ark has been likened to a prayer shawl wrapping the Torah scrolls, but from the sanctuary entrance it also suggests a single flame—a burning bush or eternal light.

In postwar Europe, relatively few new synagogues were erected, and it has taken decades for European Jews to begin to build anew. Of relatively early note, however, is the Ruhrallee Synagogue in Essen, Germany (Dieter Knoblauch and Heinz Heise, 1959). Like Mendelsohn's Park Synagogue in Cleveland, the primary element in Essen is a hemisphere that rises directly from the ground—there is no visible substructure, no drum. The simple unified shape may symbolize the monotheism of Judaism, but it also reflects current trends in architecture which include a search for pure geometric forms. Carol Krinsky aptly describes the contrast between the impression, and perhaps identity of, the pre and postwar synagogue buildings:

> The massive Steelerstrasse building [which still stands], too solid to be blown up, revealed the firm confidence of a community that was in fact to be blown away. The thinner, delicate forms of the postwar construction, with even the concrete hemisphere perched on the ground like an inflatable structure, and made more ephemeral by its light-reflecting copper cladding, hints at the fragile nature of Jewish existence.[9]

The carefully designed, but inherently modest forms and decoration evident in the Essen synagogue have continued to dominate the design of new synagogues in Germany. The many works of Alfred Jacoby, such as the nearly cylindrical synagogue sanctuary in Aachen (1994), which have been subsidized by the German government, derive directly from the architectural forms developed for sacred and communal space in the 1950s. Echoing Krinsky's description, but more judgmental, Jacoby says that:

> The synagogues before the war were bombastic ... they used gold or gold-plated materials and could seat 3,000 people .... There is a rift in the history and the people they represent. You can't go back to early synagogue tradition because it would ignore the terrible historical event called the Holocaust that really changed everything.[10]

The most dramatic postwar European synagogue is in Livorno, Italy, designed by Angelo di Castro (1962), which replaced the famous but totally destroyed Renaissance synagogue. On the outside, the new expressive structure is defined by a series of crooked concrete buttresses connected by concrete walls, appearing to exert intense pressure to keep the building together. This wall allows a large, unimpeded interior sanctuary which, like the Renaissance predecessor, allows for ranges of seats all around. Many have found the building brutal in its appearance. At the time it was built, however, it was seen as a powerful assertion of Jewish perseverance and presence. What some see as ugliness should be viewed in the context of the popular postwar engineering aesthetic in Italy and in view of the widespread adoption of the post-planning principles espoused by Le Corbusier and others. In this light, di

Dieter Knoblauch, Heinz Heise, Ruhrallee Synagogue, Essen, 1959
Dieter Knoblauch, Heinz Heise, Synagoge Ruhrallee, Essen, 1959

Shore Israel in Glencoe, Illinois (1964), wird von einer Reihe großer Betonbögen gebildet, durch deren breite Zwischenräume gefiltertes Tageslicht in das Heiligtum dringt. Der Synagogenraum ist geräumig, und die Lichtgestaltung, die weißen Wände und die sparsame Ornamentik erzeugen eine vergeistigte Atmosphäre. Der hohe, schmale vergoldete Thoraschrein ist mit einem um die Thorarollen gehängten Gebetsschal verglichen worden, vom Eingang her gesehen lässt er aber auch an eine Flamme, einen brennenden Busch oder ewiges Feuer denken.

In Europa entstanden in der Nachkriegszeit nur relativ wenige neue Synagogen, und es verstrichen Jahrzehnte, bevor die europäischen Juden von Neuem bauten. Ein frühes unter den beachtenswerten Beispielen ist die Synagoge in der Ruhrallee in Essen von Dieter Knoblauch und Heinz Heise (1959). Wie Mendelsohns Park Synagogue in Cleveland besteht auch die Synagoge in Essen im Wesentlichen aus einer direkt auf dem Boden aufsitzenden Halbkugel – ohne sichtbaren Unterbau oder Sockelzylinder. Diese schlichte Form symbolisiert möglicherweise das Judentum als monotheistische Religion, reflektiert aber auch die damals aktuellen Architekturströmungen mit ihrer Suche nach reinen geometrischen Körpern. Carol Krinsky hat die Gegensätzlichkeiten im Erscheinungsbild und vielleicht auch in der Identität der vor und nach dem Krieg errichteten Synagogen treffend charakterisiert:

> »Das [erhalten gebliebene] massive Gebäude in der Steelerstraße, zu massiv, um gesprengt zu werden, offenbart die unerschütterliche Zuversicht einer Gemeinde, die [in der Folge] tatsächlich zerstört werden sollte. Die schlankeren, zierlicheren Formen der Nachkriegsbauten, darunter sogar eine Betonhalbkugel, die wie eine pneumatische Konstruktion auf dem Boden hockt und aufgrund ihrer Licht reflektierenden Kupferverkleidung noch ephemerer wirkt, weisen auf die zerbrechliche Natur der jüdischen Existenz.«[9]

Die mit großer Sorgfalt gestalteten, aber grundlegend sparsamen Formen und Dekorationen der Essener Synagoge haben die Architektur neuer Synagogen in Deutschland nachhaltig geprägt. Die zahlreichen mit Bundesmitteln geförderten Synagogen von Alfred Jacoby, zum Beispiel die fast zylindrische in Aachen (1994), leiten sich direkt von den architektonischen Formen ab, die in den 1950er Jahren für Sakralbauten und öffentliche Gebäude entwickelt wurden. Jacoby folgt Krinskys Beschreibung, allerdings in schärferem Ton, wenn er sagt:

> »Vor dem Krieg waren die Synagogen bombastisch ... sie waren verziert mit Gold oder vergoldeten Materialien und konnten 3000 Menschen aufnehmen. [...] Es besteht eine Kluft zwischen der

Castro's Livorno synagogue appears expressive and almost poetic in its unusual form and subtlety-lit interior.

Livorno is an exception. For the most part, the need to remain connected to the past is obviously stronger in Germany and elsewhere where Jewish communities and their synagogues were destroyed. There has been the return of surviving synagogues to religious communities and the adaptation of these buildings for new worship, with occasional conservation of historic features. In Warsaw, Krakow, and Prague the Jewish identity of small "caretaker" communities is enhanced by the visible renewal of older buildings. In Germany, however, many new synagogues have been built. Like Goodman's Millburn Synagogue (or even Nevelson's Ark in Great Neck), they refer to the past, but more explicitly. The Jewish Community Center in Berlin retains a portal from the Fasanenstrasse synagogue (1959) inserted into its modern facade. The synagogue in Dresden, designed by Wolfgang Lorch preserves part of the plan of the destroyed nineteenth century synagogue outlined with glass shards in the new courtyard. Jewish identity is expressed with archaeological precision. Elsewhere, archaeology stands alone. An increasing number of destroyed medieval synagogues have been excavated in recent years, and their exposed remnants are seen to have a meaning parallel to the ruins of the Holocaust.[11]

In Israel similar expressive tendencies are found. The synagogue in Beersheba (1961) nestles under a sweeping concrete vault that covers sanctuary like a turtle's shell. The Israel Goldstein Synagogue on the Givat Ram campus of the Hebrew University (Heinz Rau and David Reznik, 1957) appears ready to float away like a giant balloon; its smooth, white, bulbous form seems to levitate off the ground. And the small synagogue at the army officer training school at Mitzpeh Ramon, an early work of Zvi Hecker (1969–71), is concrete faceted like crystal, creating a complex arrangement of colored shapes and patterns. In Israel, inventiveness for its own sake allowed an extreme distancing from the past. This tendency of Jews to accept unusual architectural forms and materials for synagogues has created a perception of postwar synagogue design as being radical. The numbers clearly do not support this claim (since most synagogues are built and used with little notice),

Geschichte und den Menschen, die sie [die Synagogen] repräsentieren. Man kann nicht zu den frühen Synagogentraditionen zurückkehren, denn das würde das furchtbare historische Ereignis leugnen, das Holocaust genannt wird und wirklich alles verändert hat.«[10]

Die dramatischste Synagoge der Nachkriegszeit steht in Livorno, Italien, und wurde 1962 von Angelo di Castro als Ersatz für die berühmte, aber total zerstörte Renaissancesynagoge gebaut. Die Außenwirkung des expressiven Neubaus beruht auf dem Kranz der durch Betonmauern verbundenen gebogenen Betonstrebepfeiler, die nur scheinbar großen Druck auf die Außenmauer ausüben, um das Gebäude zusammenzuhalten. Diese Konstruktion ermöglichte die Schaffung eines großen stützenfreien Synagogenraums, in dem, wie beim Vorläuferbau aus der Renaissance, die Sitze ringförmig aufgestellt sind. Viele Betrachter haben dieses Gebäude als brutal empfunden. Zur Zeit seiner Fertigstellung galt es jedoch als kraftvolle Bestätigung der Standhaftigkeit und Präsenz der Juden in Livorno. Was einige als hässlich empfinden, muss im Kontext der im Nachkriegs-Italien populären technischen Bauästhetik gesehen werden und im Zusammenhang mit der weit verbreiteten Übernahme der Architekturprinzipien, die Le Corbusier und andere propagierten. In diesem Lichte besehen, erscheint di Castros Synagoge in Livorno mit ihrer ungewöhnlichen Form und ihrem subtil ausgeleuchteten Inneren ausdrucksvoll, ja fast poetisch.

Livorno bildet eine Ausnahme. Größtenteils ist das Bedürfnis nach Verbundenheit mit der Geschichte in Deutschland und anderorts, wo jüdische Gemeinden und ihre Bauten zerstört wurden, natürlich stärker gewesen. Noch erhaltene Synagogengebäude sind den zurückkehrenden religiösen Gemeinschaften zurückgegeben worden, die sie dann als neue Andachtsstätten umbauten, wobei sie gelegentlich auch historische Elemente bewahrten. Die sichtbare Renovierung alter Synagogen in Warschau, Krakau und Prag stärkt die jüdische Identität der dortigen kleinen ›Statthalter-Gemeinden‹. In Deutschland dagegen sind zahlreiche neue Synagogen entstanden. Wie Goodmans Synagoge in Millburn (oder sogar Nevelsons Thoraschrein-Wand in Great Neck) verweisen sie auf die Vergangenheit, aber noch ausdrücklicher. Beim Jüdischen Gemeindehaus in der Berliner Fasanenstraße (1959) wurde ein Portal der alten Synagoge auf diesem Grundstück in die moderne Fassade integriert. Bei seiner Synagoge in Dresden zeichnete Wolfgang Lorch einen Teil des Grundrisses der zerstörten Synagoge aus dem 19. Jahrhundert mit Glasscherben im Boden des neuen Innenhofs nach. Jüdische Identität wird mit archäologischer Akribie ausgedrückt. Anderswo verselbständigt sich die Archäologie. In den vergangenen Jahren wurden immer mehr zerstörte mittelalterliche Synagogen wieder freigelegt; ihren Überresten wird die gleiche Bedeutung zugeschrieben wie denen der Vernichtungslager.[11]

In Israel lassen sich ähnlich expressive Tendenzen ausfindig machen. Die Synagoge in Beersheba (1961) duckt sich unter einem ausgedehnten Betongewölbe, das den Bau wie ein Schildkrötenpanzer bedeckt. Die Israel-Goldstein-Synagoge (1957) von Heinz Rau und David Reznik auf dem Givat-Ram-Campus der Hebräischen Universität sieht mit ihrer glatten, bauchigen weißen Form so aus, als würde sie gleich schwerelos vom Boden abheben und wie ein Riesenballon davonschweben. Und die Fassade der kleinen Synagoge der Offiziersschule in Mitzpeh Ramon, eine frühe Arbeit von Zvi Hecker (1969–71), wirkt mit ihrer Facettenstruktur wie ein Kristall, der eine vielfältige Anordnung von farbigen Formen und Mustern erzeugt. In Israel ermöglichte ein gestalterischer Ideenreichtum als Selbstzweck eine deutliche Distanzierung von der Vergangenheit. Die Neigung der Juden, beim Synagogenbau ungewöhnliche Architektur-

Angelo di Castro, Synagogue in Livorno, 1962    Angelo di Castro, Synagoge in Livorno, 1962

Zvi Hecker, Synagogue at the Military Academy Campus in Mitzpeh Ramon, Negev Desert, 1969–71
Zvi Hecker, Synagoge der Militär-Akademie in Mitzpeh Ramon, Negev Wüste, 1969–71

but the congregational nature of Judaism, especially in America, has certainly allowed greater flexibility and experimentation of design than is usually found in religious architecture.

It took a full generation for a delayed reaction to the Holocaust to destabilize a creative complacency in the Jewish world, where formal and functional considerations had overwhelmed the creative process, and many of the most intellectually and aesthetically challenging architectural projects remained unbuilt. A reevaluation of the Holocaust and recognition that its memory was already fading prompted a movement to create memorials and museums as more explicit reminders than were felt necessary immediately after the event.

An alternative to the language of modernism as expressed in synagogue architecture began to parallel greater recognition of the Holocaust as early as the 1960s. At this time, several buildings referred to the wooden synagogues of Poland, known from recent publications. Congregation Sons of Israel in Lakewood, New Jersey, by Davis, Brody & Wisniewski (1963) recalls Polish plan types and building profile. Louis I. Kahn mixed geometric shapes and volumes at Temple Beth El in Chappaqua, New York (1972), where the central wood-paneled light shaft also recalls Polish wooden sanctuaries. Beginning the late 1970s, postmodern architects designed several historicist, but not Eastern European, prayer halls, like the Perlman Sanctuary at North Shore Congregation Israel in Glencoe, Illinois (Hammond, Beeby & Babka, 1979) and the Sephardic Kol Israel Congregation in Brooklyn, New York (Robert Stern, 1989). Significantly, this growing historicism in synagogue architecture, which is part acknowledgement of the destruction of the Holocaust and also a reaction against it, has been matched by an enormous growth of interest on the popular front in Jewish genealogy, and in academic circles in the increased establishment of university-level Jewish Studies programs.

By 1990, Americans had been searching for an effective, meaningful synagogue style. Unlike new European synagogues that have more in common with American postwar designs and must more immediately and publicly confront the past, the goal of most American congregations is to find greater intimacy and spirituality, often out of the public eye. Modernism has not been rejected, but the gigantism of the postwar period is accepted as counter productive to the creation of a spiri-

formen und Baumaterialien zu akzeptieren, hat dazu geführt, dass die Synagogenarchitektur der Nachkriegszeit als radikal eingestuft wurde. Zahlen stützen diese Behauptung nicht (da die meisten Synagogen gebaut und genutzt werden, ohne große Beachtung zu finden), doch der stark gemeindeorientierte Charakter des Judentums, speziell in Amerika, hat sicherlich eine größere Flexibilität und Experimentierfreudigkeit in der Gestaltung gefördert, als man sie sonst in der Sakralarchitektur findet.

Erst eine ganze Generation später setzte eine verzögerte Reaktion auf den Holocaust ein, welche die jüdische Welt aus ihrer kreativen Selbstzufriedenheit aufrüttelte. Diese äußerte sich darin, dass formale und funktionale Überlegungen den schöpferischen Prozess erstickten und viele der geistig und ästhetisch anspruchsvollsten Bauentwürfe nie ausgeführt wurden. Die Neubewertung des Holocaust und die Erkenntnis, dass die Erinnerung daran im Verblassen begriffen war, führte zum Bau einer ganzen Reihe von Gedenkstätten und Museen als deutlicheren Mahnmalen, als man sie unmittelbar nach den Ereignissen für erforderlich gehalten hatte.

Eine Alternative zur Formensprache der Moderne, die in der Synagogenarchitektur zur Anwendung kam, begann sich schon in den 1960er Jahren parallel zu der zunehmend stärkeren Beachtung der Judenvernichtung zu entwickeln. Damals zitierten mehrere Gebäude die polnischen Synagogenbauten aus Holz, die durch neuere Publikationen bekannt wurden. Die Synagoge der Congregation Sons of Israel in Lakewood, New Jersey, von Davis, Brody & Wisniewski (1963) erinnert an polnische Grundrisstypen und Gebäudesilhouetten. Bei seiner Beth-El-Synagoge in Chappaqua, New York (1972), kombinierte Louis I. Kahn geometrische Flächen und Volumen, und auch der zentrale holzverschalte Lichtschacht lässt an polnische Holzsynagogen denken. Ab den späten 1970er Jahren entwarfen verschiedene postmoderne Architekten eine Reihe von Bethäusern im historistischen, aber nicht osteuropäischen Stil – Hammond, Beeby & Babka zum Beispiel das Perlman Sanctuary der Gemeinde North Shore Congregation Israel in Glencoe, Illinois (1979), und Robert Stern die Synagoge der sephardischen Kol Israel Congregation in Brooklyn, New York (1989). Es ist bezeichnend, dass der für die Synagogenarchitektur an Bedeutung gewinnende Historismus – teilweise in Anerkennung der Zerstörungen des Holocaust, aber auch als Reaktion darauf – seine Ent-

Davis, Brody & Wisniewski, Congregation Sons of Israel, Lakewood, New Jersey, 1963
Davis, Brody & Wisniewski, Congregation Sons of Israel, Lakewood, New Jersey, 1963

tually-aware community. Thus, contemporary architects have adapted many of the expressive features of modernism into a more intimate language conducive to prayer, reflection, and communal bonding with occasional insertion of selected historic references, used symbolically. A new generation of American synagogue builders including architects Will Bruder, Alex Gorlin, Michael Landau, Michael Rosenfeld, and Shinberg/Levinas to name a few, though very different in their aesthetic, seek to distill the essence of traditional form into a contemporary architectural language. Fortunately for them, the architectural and artistic tradition of Judaism is so rich and varied that precedents for every sort of expressive language—subdued or ebullient, classical or modern, vernacular or imperial—can be found. Perhaps it is this very diversity of historic and creative experience that is the real meaning of Jewish identity in the modern world.

1 Author interview with Will Bruder, 22 October 2002.
2 All twentieth century American examples from, Samuel D. Gruber, *American Synagogues: A Century of Architecture and Jewish Community*, New York 2003.
3 Along similar lines, see the comments of Bruno Zevi on these and other contemporary Jewish architects in *L'incidenza ebraica nell'architettura contemporanea, Ebraismo e Architettura,* Firenze 1993, pp. 71–84.
4 Lipot Baumhorn, the prolific Jewish architect of the synagogue Szeged, worked closely with the congregation's learned Rabbi Immmanuel Loew to create an iconographic program related to Jewish thought. See Ruth Ellen Gruber, *Upon the Doorposts of Thy House: Jewish Life in East-Central Europe, Yesterday and Today,* New York 1994, pp. 139–184.
5 On European synagogues see Carol Herselle Krinsky, *The Synagogues of Europe: Architecture, History, Meaning,* New York and Cambridge MA, 1985, pp. 306–07.
6 See Krinsky, *Synagogues of Europe,* p. 400.
7 On Landauer and contemporary Jewish-German architects prior to the Nazi period see Klemens Klemmer, *Jüdische Baumeister in Deutschland: Architektur vor der Shoah,* Stuttgart 1998. Also see the good descriptions on Plauen in Krinsky, *Synagogues of Europe*, pp. 304–5.
8 Quoted in Richard Meier, *Recent American Synagogue Architecture*, The Jewish Museum, New York 1963, p. 24.
9 Krinsky, *Synagogues of Europe*, p. 290.
10 Quoted in B. J. Almond, "Built to heal: German architect builds synagogues to represent life after Holocaust," in *Rice News*, 1, Sept. 20, 2001, p. 5.
11 The archaeology of European synagogues see Samuel Gruber, "Archaeological Remains of Ashkenazic Jewry in Europe: A New Source of Pride and History" in *What Athens has to do with Jerusalem: Essays on Classical, Jewish, and Early Christian Art and Archaeology in Honor of Gideon Foerster,* Paris-Louvain/Dudley MA, 2002, pp. 267–301.

sprechung in einem enorm gestiegenen allgemeinen Interesse der Juden an ihrer Abstammung gefunden hat und in der akademischen Welt in der zunehmenden Anzahl jüdischer Studiengänge auf Hochschulniveau.

Bis 1990 waren die Amerikaner auf der Suche nach einem wirkungs- und bedeutungsvollen Stil für den Synagogenbau. Im Gegensatz zu den neuen europäischen Synagogen, die mehr mit der amerikanischen Nachkriegsarchitektur gemein haben und sich der Vergangenheit direkter und öffentlicher stellen müssen, sind die meisten jüdischen Gemeinden in Amerika bestrebt, in ihren Synagogen für eine intimere und spirituellere Atmosphäre zu sorgen, und vielfach auch, sie vor öffentlichen Einblicken zu schützen. Die Moderne wird zwar nicht abgelehnt, doch die Gigantomanie der Nachkriegszeit wird als kontraproduktiv für den Aufbau einer spirituell lebendigen Gemeinde empfunden. So haben zeitgenössische Architekten zahlreiche expressive Merkmale der Moderne in eine subtilere Formensprache übersetzt, die dem Gebet, der Reflexion und den gemeinschaftlichen Bindungen förderlicher ist, wobei sie durchaus ausgewählte historische Bezüge herstellen und symbolhaft einsetzen. Zur neuen Generation amerikanischer Synagogenarchitekten zählen Will Bruder, Alex Gorlin, Michael Landau, Michael Rosenfeld und Shinberg/Levinas, um nur einige zu nennen. Obwohl sie verschiedene Wege gehen, was ihre ästhetische Haltung angeht, versuchen sie doch alle, das Wesentliche der traditionellen Formen herauszudestillieren und es in eine zeitgemäße Architektursprache zu übertragen. Für sie ist es ein Glück, dass die architektonischen und künstlerischen Traditionen des Judentums so reich und vielfältig sind, dass sich darin Präzedenzfälle für jede Art ausdrucksvoller Gestaltung finden lassen — gedämpft oder überschwänglich, klassisch oder modern, volkstümlich oder majestätisch. Vielleicht liegt die wahre jüdische Identität in der modernen Welt gerade in dieser Vielfältigkeit der historischen und schöpferischen Erfahrung.

1 Gespräch des Verfassers mit Will Bruder am 22. Oktober 2002.
2 Alle zitierten amerikanischen Beispiele des 20. Jahrhunderts sind aufgeführt in: Samuel D. Gruber, *American Synagogues. A Century of Architecture and Jewish Community*, New York 2003.
3 Vgl. auch Bruno Zevis dahingehende Bemerkungen zu diesem und anderen zeitgenössischen jüdischen Architekten in: *L'incidenza ebraica nell'architettura contemporanea, Ebraismo e Architettura,* Florenz 1993, S. 71–84.
4 Lipot Baumhorn, der produktive jüdische Architekt der Synagoge in Szeged, erarbeitete das ikonografische Programm zur Darstellung jüdischen Gedankenguts in enger Zusammenarbeit mit dem gelehrten Rabbiner der Gemeinde, Immanuel Loew. Vgl. Ruth Ellen Gruber, *Upon the Doorposts of Thy House: Jewish Life in East-Central Europe, Yesterday and Today,* New York 1994, S. 139–184.
5 Zu europäischen Synagogen vgl. Carol Herselle Krinsky, *Synagogues of Europe: Architecture, History, Meaning,* Cambridge, MA, 1985. Deutsche Ausgabe: *Europas Synagogen. Architektur, Geschichte, Bedeutung,* Stuttgart 1988.
6 Ebenda, S. 400.
7 Zu Landauer und seinen zeitgenössischen deutsch-jüdischen Kollegen vor dem Dritten Reich vgl.: Klemens Klemmer, *Jüdische Baumeister in Deutschland. Architektur vor der Shoah,* Stuttgart 1998. Vgl. auch die guten Beschreibungen der Stadt Plauen in: Krinsky, wie Anm. 5, S. 304f.
8 Zitiert nach: Richard Meier, *Recent American Synagogue Architecture,* The Jewish Museum, New York 1963, S. 24.
9 Krinsky, wie Anm. 5, S. 290.
10 Zur Archäologie der europäischen Synagogen vgl.: B. J. Almond, »Built to Heal: German Architect Builds Synagogues to Represent Life after Holocaust«, in: *Rice News* 11 (20.9.2001), S. 5.
11 Vgl. Samuel Gruber, »Archaeological Remains of Ashkenazic Jewry in Europe: A New Source of Pride and History«, in: *What Athens has to do with Jerusalem: Essays on Classical, Jewish and Early Christian Art and Archaeology in Honor of Gideon Foerster,* Paris-Louvain/Dudley, MA, 2002, S. 267–301.

Michael Levin

## Jewish Identity in Architecture in Israel

The search for a means of expressing Jewish identity in architecture in Israel during the twentieth and early twenty-first centuries has been characterized by an emphasis on national identity. Beginning in the first half of the twentieth century (the years of the state-in-the-making) and increasingly in the second half (after the establishment of the state) one can observe the quest for unique architectural features. Architecture in Israel was for a population that had gradually become the majority in the country, in contrast to Jewish building in the Diaspora, which was for a Jewish minority in countries with a different religious heritage. The second essential difference regarding Jewish identity in architecture in Israel, as opposed to the Diaspora, was the emphasis on the place itself. Here, architecture was inspired by the "place" and endeavored to harmonize with the local landscape. Architects sometimes attributed a spiritual, religious, and national meaning to the location of their work.

Over the past century, Jewish architects have had a complex relationship with the language of architecture. Five distinct approaches to the Orient can be distinguished in Israeli architecture. These can be classified more or less chronologically, although in some periods architects and society could choose between several simultaneous approaches to the Orient.

The first approach "the Orient as a continuation of tradition" saw builders continuing to build Arab villages unaware that they were perpetuating a unique style. The now destroyed nineteenth century Hurva and Tiferet Yisrael synagogues in the Jewish Quarter of the Old City, whose domes once dominated the Jerusalem skyline, are examples of buildings that pursued the tradition of regional architecture.

The second approach is "the Orient as part of Eclecticism", which was a style that prevailed in the nineteenth century and continued into the twentieth. Oriental elements continued to provide a source of inspiration for synagogues well into the twentieth century.

The third approach "the Orient as a means to develop a local style" is characterized by architects who consciously studied Oriental forms, seeking the essential qualities of a local style befitting the landscape, climate, and history of the place. The Technion in Haifa is an outstanding example of this approach.

The fourth approach "the Orient in Western architecture" reveals the desire of architects possessing both Western training and a Western repertoire of shapes to include a local set of forms or attitudes to sunlight, wind directions, colors, materials, and features of the landscape in their buildings (e.g., the three domes at the entrance to Hadassah University Hospital on Mount Scopus, by Erich Mendelsohn, 1936–1939).

From the end of the 1930s through the 1960s, interest in the Orient waned. Even before 1967, when Israelis once again encountered Arab architecture in Judea and Samaria as well as important monuments in the Old City of Jerusalem, architects built several important buildings that demonstrate a conscious desire to learn from local Oriental architecture in order to strengthen the Jewish identity of their work. The two most important examples are the synagogues on the Givat Ram campus of the Hebrew University of Jerusalem and the Israel Museum.

Michael Levin

## Jüdische Identität in der Architektur Israels

Die Suche nach dem Ausdruck jüdischer Identität der in Israel im 20. und zu Beginn des 21. Jahrhunderts entstandenen Architektur war von der Betonung der nationalen Identität bestimmt. Bereits in der ersten Hälfte des 20. Jahrhunderts (den Jahren, in denen die Gründung des Staates Israel vorbereitet wurde), besonders aber in seiner zweiten Hälfte (nach der Staatsgründung) lässt sich diese Suche nach besonderen architektonischen Merkmalen erkennen. In Israel wurde für eine Bevölkerungsgruppe gebaut, die nach und nach die Mehrheit im Lande bildete, im Gegensatz zur Diaspora, wo für eine jüdische Minderheit in Ländern mit anderem religiösen Erbe gebaut wurde. Der zweite Punkt, in dem sich der Umgang mit jüdischer Identität in der Architektur in Israel wesentlich von dem in der Diaspora unterschied, war die Betonung des Ortes. Er bildete die ausschlaggebende Anregung für die architektonische Gestaltung, die auf den Einklang mit der Umgebung abzielte. In einigen Fällen schrieben Architekten den jeweiligen Standorten ihrer Gebäude spirituelle, religiöse und nationale Bedeutung zu.

Im vergangenen Jahrhundert haben jüdische Architekten einen facettenreichen Umgang mit architektonischen Formensprachen entwickelt. In der israelischen Architektur kann man fünf verschiedene Arten, sich an den Orient anzunähern, ausmachen, die sich mehr oder weniger chronologisch einordnen lassen, wenn auch Architekten und Bauherrn zeitweise zwischen mehreren gleichzeitig wirksamen Möglichkeiten wählen konnten.

Der erste Ansatz repräsentierte die ›Fortsetzung der orientalischen Tradition‹, in der auch weiterhin arabische Dörfer entstanden, deren Erbauer sich jedoch nicht bewusst waren, dass sie einen einzigartigen Stil fortschrieben. Die inzwischen zerstörten Synagogen des 19. Jahrhunderts – Hurva und Tiferet Yisrael – im jüdischen Viertel der Jerusalemer Altstadt, deren Kuppeln einst die Stadtsilhouette beherrschten, sind Beispiele für die regionale Architekturtradition.

Der zweite Ansatz lässt sich als ›orientalischer Eklektizismus‹ umschreiben, als ein Stil also, der im 19. Jahrhundert und darüber hinaus gepflegt wurde. Orientalische Elemente gaben dabei bis weit ins 20. Jahrhundert hinein Anregungen für den Bau von Synagogen.

Den dritten Ansatz – ›der Orient als Weg zu einem ortstypischen Stil‹ – vertraten Architekten, die ganz bewusst orientalische Formen studierten, auf der Suche nach den wesentlichen Merkmalen einer lokalen Bauweise, die sich an die Landschaft, das Klima und die Geschichte des Ortes anpasste. Als hervorragendes Beispiel hierfür ist das Technion in Haifa zu zitieren.

Der vierte Ansatz – ›das Orientalische in der westlichen Architektur‹ – offenbart das Bestreben der im Westen ausgebildeten Architekten mit entsprechend westlichem Formenrepertoire, lokaltypische Elemente oder den in dieser Region altbewährten Umgang mit Sonneneinstrahlung, Windrichtungen, Farben, Materialien und Landschaftsformen in die Gestaltung ihrer Bauten einzubeziehen. Ein Beispiel hierfür sind die drei Kuppeln des Eingangs zum Hadassah-Universitätskrankenhaus am Scopus-Berg von Erich Mendelsohn (1936–39).

Ab Ende der 1930er bis in die 1960er Jahre nahm das Interesse am Orient ab. Noch vor 1967, als die Israelis die arabische Architektur von Judäa und Samarien sowie bedeutende Baudenkmäler der Altstadt Jeru-

Following the first wave, in which architects appropriated what they identified as local figurative elements such as the arch and the dome (which provide a ready device to give an Oriental appearance to buildings whose form and features were based on the principles of modern, Western construction), a second wave arose in which architects used these elements more selectively and in a more serious manner. Whether consciously or not, the 1960s and 1970s saw a return to the motifs and methods of the 1930s.

The fifth approach "a renewed interest in the Orient" is marked by an aspiration to develop local architecture deriving from the concept of critical regionalism, which is more of a planning strategy than an architectural style. Architecture inspired by these ideas takes its repertoire of forms from local architecture—ancient to modern—refraining from sentimentality or kitsch, to create a modern architecture with an affinity

Joseph Berlin, Richard Passovsky, Dome of the synagogue on Shadal Street, Tel Aviv, 1927
Joseph Berlin, Richard Passovsky, Kuppel der Synagoge in der Shadal-Straße, Tel Aviv, 1927

to the place where it develops. The superficial eclecticism of arches, domes, and protruding elements breaking up the mass into smaller parts, acquires a deeper and more critical dimension. Examples include the Valley of Destroyed Communities at Yad Vashem, the Davidson Visitors' Center and Museum at the Western Wall excavations in the Old City of Jerusalem, and the Shalom Hartman Institute in Jerusalem.

When discussing architectural developments in the three types of buildings featured in this book—synagogues, educational institutions, and museums—it becomes clear that each type has a different rate of development. The interest in crystallizing a Jewish identity, the attitude toward historical components typical of that type of building, and the relationship between traditional and modern elements all vary.

## Synagogues

Synagogues have tended to preserve historical patterns more than either educational institutions or museums.[1] The dome, for example, is the most visible element and appeared in the Hurva (1856–64) and

salems wiederentdeckten, realisierten israelische Architekten eine Reihe prominenter Gebäude, an denen sich ihre dezidierte Absicht ablesen lässt, von der örtlichen orientalischen Architektur zu lernen, um die jüdische Identität ihrer Bauten zu stärken. Die beiden Hauptbeispiele hierfür sind die Synagogen auf dem Givat-Ram-Campus der Hebräischen Universität und das Israel-Museum, beide in Jerusalem. Auf die erste Bauwelle, bei der die Architekten sich das zu Eigen machten, was sie als ortstypische Gestaltungselemente identifiziert hatten – etwa den Bogen und die Kuppel (einfache Mittel, um einem ansonsten nach den Prinzipien der westlichen Moderne gestalteten Bau ein orientalisches Aussehen zu verleihen) –, folgte die zweite Welle, bei der Architekten diese Elemente selektiver und auf durchdachtere Weise verwendeten. Ob beabsichtigt oder nicht, die 1960er und 1970er Jahre erlebten die Rückkehr der Motive und Methoden der 1930er Jahre.

Der fünfte Ansatz – ›ein wiedererwachtes Interesse am Orient‹ – zeichnete sich durch das Bestreben aus, eine lokale Architektur nach dem Konzept des kritischen Regionalismus zu entwickeln, was eher einer Planungsstrategie entspricht als einem Baustil. Die dieser Philosophie folgende Architektur bezieht ihr Formenrepertoire aus der – historischen und modernen – lokalen Architektur, verzichtet auf jede Sentimentalität und auf Kitsch, um eine moderne Architektur mit einer Affinität zum Ort ihres Entstehens zu schaffen. Der oberflächliche Eklektizismus aus Bögen, Kuppeln und vorspringenden Fassadenelementen, die die Baumasse auflockern und kleinteiliger gliedern, stößt damit in tiefgründigere, kritischere Dimensionen vor. Zu den Beispielen hierfür zählt das Tal der zerstörten Gemeinden in Yad Vashem, das Davidson-Besucherzentrum und Museum der Ausgrabungsstätte an der Westmauer zur Altstadt Jerusalems und das Shalom-Hartman-Institut in Jerusalem.

Wenn man die architektonische Entwicklung der drei in diesem Buch diskutierten Bautypen untersucht – Synagogen, Bildungsstätten und Museen –, wird deutlich, dass jeder von ihnen unterschiedliche Entwicklungsstadien durchlaufen hat. Das Interesse daran, jüdische Identität herauszuarbeiten, die Einstellung zu den für diese Art von Gebäuden typischen historischen Komponenten und das jeweilige Verhältnis zwischen Tradition und Moderne sind bei allen drei Typen verschieden.

## Synagogen

In stärkerem Maße als bei Bildungsstätten oder Museen neigten die Architekten von Synagogen stets dazu, historischen Vorbildern zu folgen.[1] So wurde zum Beispiel die Kuppel als auffälligstes Bauelement in der Altstadt von Jerusalem sowohl für die Hurva-Synagoge (1856–64) als auch für die Tiferet-Yisrael-Synagoge (1872) verwendet, ebenso bei Yehuda Magidovitchs Großer Synagoge (1925) sowie dem von Joseph Berlin und Richard Passovky 1927 in der Shadal-Straße errichteten jüdischen Gotteshaus (beide in Tel Aviv) und schließlich auch bei Richard Kauffmanns Rechavia-Synagoge (Jerusalem, 1922). Die Kuppel – beliebtes Element

the Tiferet Yisrael synagogues (1872) in the Old City of Jerusalem, the Great Synagogue in Tel Aviv (Yehuda Magidovitch, 1925), the synagogue on Shadal Street also in Tel Aviv (Joseph Berlin and Richard Passovky, 1927), and Richard Kauffmann's project for Rehavia in Jerusalem (1922). The dome, popular in neo-Byzantine synagogues in the Diaspora and a common feature in Oriental architecture, continues to be the dominant element in Israeli synagogues built decades later, such as Hechal Shlomo (Alexander Friedman,1953) as well as the synagogue designed by Heinz Rau (in partnership with David Reznik) on the Givat Ram campus of the Hebrew University of Jerusalem in 1957.

The radical innovation of Rau's Givat Ram synagogue was the combination of dome and arch in white painted concrete with no stone facing as required by municipal bylaws enacted to preserve the unity of construction in Jerusalem. He combined progressive technology in the spirit of the times, similar to the structures by Pier Luigi Nervi. The use of painted white concrete made the synagogue stand out as a special building on the campus. It must also be noted that the location is an element of considerable importance to the building. Through the arches on the ground floor, one has a view of the center of government and culture in western Jerusalem: the Knesset (Parliament), the Israel Museum and the Shrine of the Book.

In the synagogue at Hebrew Union College (HUC) in Jerusalem built by Rau in the early 1960s, he used sawn stones laid in uneven lines to make clear that the wall was not actually built of stone, but only faced with it. By employing this design element, Rau was able to conform to the spirit of the municipal bylaws while challenging the letter. He also incorporated white concrete pergolas into the structure, an element which plays a role in later expansions. Further, Rau refrained from any adornment on the synagogue or college. Visitors who climbed the stairs leading from King David Street to the entrance of the synagogue and college, used to have a panoramic view of the Old City that could not be seen from the sidewalk. The view, reflected in the glass-sided entrance pavilion covered by a pergola, was the highlight of the visit. When Moshe Safdie expanded HUC in 1986, the view was blocked, but he maintained the idea of looking towards the Old City by continuing the pergola along the roofs of the buildings.

In synagogues from the second half of the twentieth century, Jewish and non-Jewish architects alike have created a variety of designs which allow natural light to contribute to both the aesthetic and spiritual requirements of these structures. At Givat Ram, the floor of the prayer hall is not attached to the exterior walls, but rests on eight pillars. Natural light filters through the gap between the outer edge of the floor and the exterior shell. At HUC, narrow windows in the walls and low, semi-transparent arches in the roof allow natural light in. The synagogue at the Technion (Aharon Kashtan, 1969) provides another imaginative solution to the problem of illumination. The roof, which is shaped like an inverted ziggurat, is not supported by the walls but by exposed concrete pillars creating a space between the ceiling and the walls through which natural light permeates, contributing considerably to the atmosphere in the synagogue.

Between 1968 and 1974, the visionary architect Louis I. Kahn planned several alternatives for the Hurva synagogue in the Old City on the site of the original, destroyed in 1948. He planned a building whose repertoire of shapes departs significantly from his other buildings and is unlike other synagogues. His sketches and models for this project

Heinz Rau, David Reznik, Synagogue on the Givat Ram Campus, Jerusalem, 1957
Heinz Rau, David Reznik, Synagoge auf dem Givat-Ram-Campus, Jerusalem, 1957

neobyzantinischer jüdischer Gotteshäuser in der Diaspora und in der orientalischen Architektur weit verbreitet – beherrscht auch noch in den folgenden Jahrzehnten die in Israel gebauten Synagogen, unter anderem Hechal Shlomo (Alexander Friedman, 1953) oder die von Heinz Rau (mit David Reznik) auf dem Givat-Ram-Campus der Hebräischen Universität Jerusalem gebaute Synagoge (1957).

Raus Entwurf für Givat Ram stellte eine architektonische Revolution dar: Er kombinierte Kuppel und Bögen aus weiß getünchtem Beton ohne die vom Stadtbauamt geforderten Steinverblendungen, die dem einheitlichen Erscheinungsbild der Jerusalemer Bauten dienen sollten. Ähnlich wie Pier Luigi Nervi kombinierte Rau im Geist seiner Zeit verschiedene fortschrittliche Bautechniken miteinander. Die weiß gestrichenen Betonfassaden heben die Synagoge aus der Masse der Campus-Gebäude heraus. Anzumerken ist auch, dass der Standort für ihre Gestaltung von beträchtlicher Bedeutung war. Durch ihre Fassadenbögen im Erdgeschoss hat man Ausblick auf das Zentrum der Regierung und Kultur in West-Jerusalem: die Knesset (Parlament), das Israel-Museum und den Schrein des Buches.

Die Synagoge des Hebrew Union College (HUC) in Jerusalem, die Rau Anfang der 1960er Jahre realisierte, ließ er mit gesägten Natursteinplatten mit unregelmäßigen Fugenlinien verblenden, um deutlich zu machen, dass die Wände nicht aus Stein gemauert, sondern nur damit verkleidet waren. Mit diesem Gestaltungsmittel gelang es Rau, die behördlichen Auflagen dem Sinn nach zu erfüllen, dem Buchstaben des Baugesetzes aber im gleichen Zug zu widersprechen. Rau schuf auch eine Reihe weißer Betonpergolen – Elemente, die bei späteren Erweiterungen eine Rolle spielen sollten. Außerdem verzichtete er auf jede Ornamentierung der Synagoge und des College-Gebäudes. Besucher, die sich über die Treppenstufen von der King-David-Straße dem Eingang zur Synagoge und zum College näherten, konnten von hier aus den Panoramablick über die Altstadt genießen, die vom Bürgersteig aus nicht zu sehen war. Diese sich in den Scheiben der gläsernen Eingangshalle spiegelnde Aussicht bildete den Höhepunkt des Besuchs. Als Moshe Safdie das HUC 1986 erweiterte, versperrte er mit seinem Neubau diese Sicht, bewahrte aber das Konzept des Ausblicks zur Altstadt, indem er die Pergola auf den Dächern seiner Gebäude fortführte.

Jüdische und nichtjüdische Architekten haben in der zweiten Hälfte des 20. Jahrhunderts ganz unterschiedliche Synagogen geschaffen, in denen die natürliche Beleuchtung zur ästhetischen Qualität und sakralen

Louis I. Kahn, Hurva synagogue, Jerusalem, project, 1968–74. Computer simulation
Louis I. Kahn, Hurva-Synagoge, Jerusalem, Projekt, 1968–74. Computersimulation

Aharon Kashtan, Synagogue at the Technion, Haifa, 1969
Aharon Kashtan, Synagoge des Technions, Haifa, 1969

(which was never realized) show how he envisioned the Jerusalem skyline, which is dominated by the golden Dome of the Rock. Some saw echoes of the Temple in the monumental design. Contemplating its size and location, then Mayor Teddy Kollek dubbed Kahn's building a "world synagogue." The "Street of the Prophets," a processional route Kahn planned, would lead from the synagogue to the Western Wall plaza echoing the nearby Via Dolorosa. Again, light played an important role in his monumental, stone-faced building lending it a sense of spirituality and holiness, which can be seen in the computer-imaging model designed by Kent Larson years after Kahn's death.[2]

Light was also meant to play a key role in the Porath Yosef yeshiva and synagogue (1972) designed by Moshe Safdie in the Jewish

Moshe Safdie, Porath Yosef yeshiva and synagogue, Jerusalem, 1972
Moshe Safdie, Porath-Yosef-Yeshiva (-Talmudschule) und -Synagoge, Jerusalem, 1972

Funktion des jeweiligen Bauwerks beiträgt. In Givat Ram wird die Decke des Synagogenraums nicht von den Außenmauern getragen, sondern ruht auf acht Pfeilern. Tageslicht fällt durch die Lücke zwischen Deckenrand und Außenhülle ins Innere. Beim HUC erfüllen schmale Fenster in den Außenwänden und niedrige, halb transparente Bogenkonstruktionen im Dach diese Funktion. Auch die Synagoge des Technions in Haifa (von Aharon Kashtan, 1969) liefert eine einfallsreiche Lösung des Beleuchtungsproblems. Das wie ein hängendes Zackenwerk ausgebildete Dach ruht nicht auf den Außenmauern, sondern auf Sichtbetonpfeilern; durch den Abstandsraum zwischen Decke und Wand fällt natürliches Licht herein und trägt viel zur meditativen Atmosphäre des Synagogenraums bei.

Von 1968 bis 1974 schuf der visionäre Architekt Louis I. Kahn eine Reihe verschiedener Entwürfe für eine neue Synagoge auf dem Grundstück der ersten, 1948 zerstörten Hurva-Synagoge in der Jerusalemer Altstadt. Kahn plante ein Gebäude, dessen Formensprache sich deutlich von der seiner anderen Bauten und von der anderer Synagogen unterscheiden sollte. Seine Skizzen und Modelle für dieses (nie ausgeführte) Bauvorhaben zeigen, wie er sich die neue Jerusalemer Stadtsilhouette vorstellte, die von der goldenen Kuppel des Felsendoms beherrscht wird. Zuweilen wurden in dem monumentalen Entwurf Anklänge an den Tempel gesehen. Angesichts der Größe und des Standortes taufte Bürgermeister Teddy Kollek Kahns Gebäude eine »Weltsynagoge«. Die von Kahn als Prozessionsstraße geplante Straße der Propheten sollte von der Synagoge wie ein Echo auf die nahe gelegene Via Dolorosa zum Platz an der westlichen Mauer des Tempelbergs, der Klagemauer, führen. Auch hier, in diesem monumentalen, mit Naturstein verkleideten Bauwerk war die Beleuchtung von zentraler Bedeutung für die Atmosphäre der Spiritualität und Frömmigkeit, die Kent Larson in seinen Jahre nach Kahns Tod erstellten Computermodellen vermittelt.[2]

Licht sollte auch bei der Porath-Yosef-Yeshiva (-Talmudschule) und -Synagoge eine Schlüsselrolle spielen, die Moshe Safdie 1972 im Jüdischen Viertel von Jerusalem nahe der Klagemauer realisierte. Dieses Beispiel illustriert die allgegenwärtige Spannung zwischen der kreativen, geistigen Vision des Architekten und den praktischen Anforderungen der

Quarter, close to the Western Wall. This example illustrates the ever-present tension between the architect's creative, spiritual vision and the building users' practical concerns. Safdie planned transparent domes, which the yeshiva's rabbis rejected during the final stages of construction on the grounds that it would be impossible to combat the heat in the summer and possibly the rain in winter. Their objections weren't unjustified; however, the transparent domes would have added to the spiritual dimension as well as somewhat offsetting the density of the structure with its impenetrable walls.

The Swiss (non-Jewish) architect Mario Botta, who was commissioned to build a synagogue at the heart of the Tel Aviv University campus, was also inspired by Kahn's synagogue. Botta produced one of the most striking and original usages of light in his Cymbalista Synagogue (1996–98) which was built near the Louis I. Kahn buildings on the campus. The synagogue has two identical, massive towers rising out of an oblong structure on top of which begin as two symmetrical squares that become round near the top. Light penetrates into the chimney-like structure through windows located between the round wall and a concrete square suspended in the center of the circle, reminiscent of a *huppah* (wedding canopy). At night, the lighting inside the building turns the towers into huge lanterns. Here, Botta inverts the paradigm of natural light flowing inward for internal illumination by creating beacons which radiate spiritual energy in the darkness in the form of light. In this one building he also managed to reconcile the irreconcilable: on the one hand the interests of the architect and user; on the other, the requirements and sensibilities of divergent religious perspectives. One of the twin towers is used for Orthodox worshippers and the auditorium in the second tower can be used by Conservative or Reform worshipers, or for meetings and discussions on religious and social topics as well as a synagogue.[3]

On the Mount Scopus campus of Hebrew University (which was designed to be a mega-structure) is a synagogue planned by Ram Karmi (1975–83), located at the center of the facade facing the Old City. Karmi was equally inspired by Louis I. Kahn, and it was his idea to commission Kahn to plan the Hurva synagogue. The large, round windows in the synagogue are reminiscent of Kahn's huge circular elements in the atrium of the library at Philips Exeter Academy in New Hampshire. The synagogue is a separate building set apart from the continuum of faculty buildings and is distinguished by a facade facing the Old City that is not stone-faced but made of glass. It has no dome as is customary in many synagogues. Through a unique design element provided by the landscape, Karmi calls on the congregation to seek another point of reference. Behind the *bimah* (platform), there is a view of the Old City. In the center is the golden Dome of the Rock, located in the middle of the Temple Mount where, according to Jewish tradition, the Binding of Isaac took place and is where the First and Second Temples stood.[4]

### Educational Institutions

The Zionist dream envisioned, from its first formulation by Theodor Herzl, a strong emphasis on education at all levels. Schools of all sorts—for agriculture and crafts, from elementary to university education—were founded by the pioneers long before the foundation of the state, in order to make Jews self sufficient on every level.

Boris Schatz was the driving force behind a movement to create Jewish art and craftsmanship. In 1906 he became the founding director of the Bezalel School of Arts and Crafts in Jerusalem. In the newly

Nutzer. Safdie sah transparente Kuppeln vor, die von den Yeshiva-Rabbis aber gegen Ende der Bauarbeiten abgelehnt wurden mit der Begründung, sie würden weder im Sommer die Hitze noch im Winter den Regen abhalten. Ihre Einwände waren nicht ganz unbegründet; jedoch hätten die transparenten Kuppeln die spirituelle Dimension erweitert und einen gewissen Ausgleich zur Massivität des Gebäudes mit seinen undurchdringlichen Mauern geschaffen.

Der (nichtjüdische) Schweizer Architekt Mario Botta, der mit dem Bau einer Synagoge im Zentrum des Universitätsgeländes von Tel Aviv beauftragt wurde, ließ sich von Kahns Hurva-Synagogenprojekt inspirieren. In seiner Cymbalista-Synagoge (1996–98) schuf er inmitten von Louis I. Kahns Universitätsgebäuden eine äußerst beeindruckende und originelle Lichtinszenierung. Der Bau hat zwei identische massive Türme, die vom Dach eines rechteckigen Baukörpers aufsteigen, am Fuß jeweils quadratisch sind und bis zur Spitze in Zylinder übergehen. Tageslicht fällt durch Oberlichter ins Innere der beiden schornsteinartigen Gebäudeteile ein, die jeweils zwischen der kreisrunden Umfassungsmauer und einem daran eingehängten Betonquadrat (das an den Hochzeitsbaldachin, die Chuppa, erinnert) eingefügt sind. Nachts verwandelt die Innenbeleuchtung die Türme in riesige Leuchtfeuer. Hier kehrt Botta das Paradigma des von außen nach innen einfallenden Lichts um, indem er die beiden Leuchttürme spirituelle Energie in Form von Kunstlicht in die Dunkelheit ausstrahlen lässt. In diesem einen Bauwerk ist es ihm gelungen, das Unvereinbare miteinander zu vereinen, nämlich einerseits die Interessen des Architekten und der Nutzer und andererseits die aus verschiedenen religiösen Perspektiven stammenden Anforderungen und Empfindungen. Einer der beiden Turmaufbauten ist für orthodoxe Gläubige bestimmt, während der Saal im zweiten Turm von Konservativen oder Reformierten für Versammlungen und Podiumsdiskussionen zu religiösen und sozialen Themen oder auch als Bethaus genutzt werden kann.[3]

Auf dem Scopus-Berg-Campus der Hebräischen Universität (die als Megastruktur konzipiert war) steht eine von dem Architekten Ram Karmi errichtete Synagoge (1975–83), und zwar inmitten der zur Altstadt hin orientierten Gebäude. Auch Karmi ließ sich von Louis I. Kahn inspirieren, und es war seine Idee, Kahn mit der Planung der neuen Hurva-Synagoge zu beauftragen. Die großen Rundfenster der Synagoge erinnern an Kahns gewaltige kreisförmige Wandausschnitte im Atrium der Bibliothek der Philips Exeter Academy in New Hampshire. Die Synagoge steht abseits von den verschiedenen Fakultätsgebäuden und unterscheidet sich von ihnen durch ihre zur Altstadt hin orientierte Fassade, die nicht aus Stein, sondern aus Glas besteht. Im Gegensatz zu vielen anderen Synagogen hat sie kein Kuppeldach. Karmi hat die Landschaft der Umgebung als einzigartiges gestalterisches Mittel genutzt: Mit der Glaswand hinter der Kanzel für Lesungen aus der Thora (Bima) fordert er die Gemeinde auf, einen anderen Bezugspunkt zu suchen, denn sie blicken auf die Altstadt mit der goldenen Kuppel des Felsendoms im Zentrum, mitten auf dem Tempelberg – nach jüdischer Überlieferung der Ort von Isaaks Opferung, wo der Erste und der Zweite Tempel standen.[4]

### Bildungseinrichtungen

Der zionistische Traum, wie ihn schon Theodor Herzl formulierte, umfasste schwerpunktmäßig die Bildung des Volkes auf allen Ebenen. Schulen aller Art – von Landwirtschaftsschulen bis zu Ausbildungsstätten des Handwerks, von Volksschulen bis zu Universitäten – betrieben die jüdischen Pioniere schon lange vor der Staatsgründung, um Juden in jeder Hinsicht zu Selbstversorgern zu machen.

founded city of Tel Aviv, he and Joseph Barksy designed the facade of the Herzliyya Gymnasium (1909–10). The monumental structure was the first public institution in Tel Aviv, built in its most prominent location, in a cul-de-sac leading to the school building. In 1912 the cornerstone of a technical university in Haifa, the Technion, was laid. Even before settling in Palestine in 1925 to become the first teacher of architecture at the recently opened Technion, the Berlin-born architect Alexander Baerwald planned a monumental structure with a dominant central arch covered by a dome (1909–24); on either side are symmetrical wings with three rows of windows, a crenellated roof reminiscent of ancient walls, and balconies with stone latticework. Baerwald drew his inspiration from Muslim architecture, particularly the *Madrassehs* (Muslim religious academies) that he had seen on his travels in the Middle East and had learned about in his research and study of professional literature.

Boris Schatz war die treibende Kraft der Bewegung zur Schaffung jüdischer Kunst und jüdischer Handwerkskunst. 1906 wurde er erster Direktor der Bezalel-Schule für Kunst und Kunstgewerbe in Jerusalem. In der neu gegründeten Stadt Tel Aviv gestaltete er zusammen mit Joseph Barksy die Fassade des Herzliyya-Gymnasiums (1909/10). Dieser Monumentalbau war das erste öffentliche Gebäude in Tel Aviv an prominenter Stelle, mit einer Sackgasse zum Schuleingang. 1909 wurde in Haifa der Grundstein für die Technische Hochschule, das Technion, gelegt. Noch bevor er 1925 nach Palästina übersiedelte, um dort als erster Architekturprofessor am kurz zuvor eröffneten Technion zu wirken, hatte der gebürtige Berliner Architekt Alexander Baerwald den von einer Kuppel überwölbten Großbau mit einer dominanten zentralen Bogenkonstruktion entworfen (1909–24); zu beiden Seiten hat das Gebäude symmetrische Flügel mit jeweils drei Fensterreihen, eine zinnenartige Dachkante, die an alte Festungsmauern erinnert, und Balkone mit Gitterwerk aus Stein. Baerwald ließ sich dazu von der muslimischen Architektur anregen, speziell von den Madrassahs (Koranschulen), die er auf seinen Reisen durch den Mittleren Osten besichtigt und anhand der einschlägigen Fachliteratur studiert hatte.

Die offizielle Einweihung der Hebräischen Universität in Jerusalem im Jahr 1925 erfüllte einen weiteren zionistischen Traum. Nach der Grundsteinlegung im Jahr 1918 hatte der Architekt Patrick Geddes das erste Hauptgebäude auf dem Scopus-Berg als internationales geistiges Zentrum in der Gestalt eines gewaltigen Kuppelbaus, ähnlich einer Synagoge, konzipiert (1919). Die Nationalbibliothek, ebenfalls von Geddes, hatte eine Kuppel, die von weitem zu sehen war. Als Motiv für das Steingitterwerk vor dem Hauptfenster verwendete er den Davidstern. Indem sie bei Lehrinstitutionen Gestaltungselemente verwendeten, die normalerweise mit Sakralbauten assoziiert

Alexander Baerwald, Technion, Haifa, 1909–24
Alexander Baerwald, Technion, Haifa, 1909–24

Erich Mendelsohn, Hadassah University Hospital, Jerusalem, 1936–39
Erich Mendelsohn, Hadassah-Universitätskrankenhaus, Jerusalem, 1936–39

The official opening of the Hebrew University in Jerusalem in 1925 meant another fulfillment of a Zionist dream. After its cornerstone had been laid in 1918, the architect Patrick Geddes envisioned the first main structure on Mount Scopus as a world spiritual center (1919); its shape was a giant dome similar to the main element of a synagogue. The National Library, another Geddes building, included a dome that could be seen from far away. He used a Star of David motif for the stone latticework on the main window. By incorporating design elements normally associated with religious structures into the construction of projects intended for academic institutions, architects working in Israel in the first half of the twentieth century sought to ease the often strict line between the spiritual and the scientific. Another primary example is the work of Erich Mendelsohn, who had fled Nazi Germany in the 1930s. He also incorporated three domes in the entrance to Hadassah University Hospital on this campus (1936–39).

In the 1950s, universities developed rapidly. The new campuses in Jerusalem, Tel Aviv, and Haifa were influenced by the various streams of Western architecture, notably that of Le Corbusier. Jerusalem, as the center of higher Jewish learning, has produced several interesting new buildings. One example, the Shalom Hartman Institute of Jewish

werden, versuchten die in der ersten Hälfte des 20. Jahrhunderts in Israel tätigen Architekten, die vielfach strenge Trennlinie zwischen der sakralen Architektur und dem Bauen für Wissenschaft und Bildung zu durchbrechen. Ein weiteres Hauptbeispiel hierfür ist das Werk Erich Mendelsohns, der als Jude 1933 das nationalsozialistische Deutschland verlassen musste. Er schuf die drei Kuppeln des Eingangs zum Hadassah-Universitätskrankenhaus auf dem Campus der Hebräischen Universität (1936–39).

In den 1950er Jahren entstanden in rascher Folge mehrere Universitäten. Die neuen Universitätsbauten in Jerusalem, Tel Aviv und Haifa waren von verschiedenen Strömungen in der westlichen Architektur geprägt, vor allem der Moderne Le Corbusiers. Als Zentrum höherer jüdischer Studien hat Jerusalem eine Reihe interessanter Neubauten aufzuweisen, zum Beispiel das Shalom-Hartman-Institut für jüdische Studien in Jerusalems Deutscher Kolonie, das Lou Gehlerter mit George Hartman und David Smily 1996–99 plante. Der Campus umfasst einen Lesesaal (Beth Midrasch) mit Synagoge, ein Institut für jüdische Studien und eine Sekundarschule. Der symmetrisch angelegte zentrale Hof bietet Ausblick über ein grünes Wohnviertel.

Die Synagoge und das Beth Midrasch mit ihren Mauern aus einem seltenen Naturstein, mit schmalen Fugen zwischen jeder Schicht, bilden

Studies built in Jerusalem's German Colony, was planned by Lou Gehlerter with George Hartman and David Smily (1996–99). The campus includes a *beth midrash* (study hall) and synagogue, an institute for Jewish studies, and a high school. The symmetrical central courtyard has a view of the verdant neighborhood.

The heart of the campus is the synagogue and beth midrash building, which were built in a rare stone with narrow lines between each row. In their search for elements that would give the building a uniquely Jewish symbolism, the architects arranged the windows of one side of the beth midrash in the shape of a nine-branched candelabrum (*menorah*) and planted twelve trees, representing the twelve tribes of Israel. The other walls of the building are opaque.

The rest of the campus is built in conventional stone in the city's building style, with a substantial amount of glass, giving it a feeling of transparency. The roof of the beth midrash and the synagogue is shaped like a gray pyramid with a glazed apex. The pyramid is coated with zinc reminiscent of other holy buildings in Jerusalem coated with metal, for example the Dome of the Rock, the Al-Aqsa Mosque, the Russian churches, and numerous synagogues, but also public buildings such as the dome of the council room at City Hall. It may suggest Rabbi David Hartman's interest in dialogue between the adherents of the three monotheistic religions.

### Museums

Museums fulfill a major role in defining Israel's national identity. The Israel Museum, with a collection spanning several millennia, is a treasure trove covering archaeology, ethnography, Judaica, and Western art. It is in concept, if not in size, comparable to the European and American national institutions like the Louvre in Paris and the Metropolitan Museum in New York. From their inception, the Israel Museum in Jerusalem and the Tel Aviv Museum have collected Jewish art in order to emphasize the longevity of Jewish involvement in the visual arts in the Diaspora and to stress the difference between art in the Diaspora and modern Israeli art. Next to numerous archeological sites, archeological museums provide a vital ideological link between the modern state and its biblical roots. The discovery of the Dead Sea Scrolls has led to the foundation of the Shrine of the Book, located on the site of the Israel Museum. The Holocaust plays an important role as a justification for an independent Jewish state, so it is no wonder that the Yad Vashem Holocaust Martyrs' and Heroes' Remembrance Authority, founded in 1953, became a national monument in Jerusalem.

den Mittelpunkt der Universitätsanlage. In dem Bemühen, dem Gebäude unverwechselbar jüdische Symbolkraft zu verleihen, ordneten die Architekten die Fenster auf der Seite des Beth Midrasch so an, dass sie zusammen einen neunarmigen Leuchter (Menora) darstellen, und pflanzten zwölf Bäume als Symbole für die zwölf Stämme Israels. Die übrigen Mauern des Gebäudes sind opak.

Die anderen Universitätsgebäude wurden im ortstypischen Stein gemauert; ihre großzügigen Verglasungen schaffen den Eindruck von Transparenz. Das gemeinsame Dach des Beth Midrasch und der Synagoge ist als Pyramide mit Glasspitze ausgebildet. Mit graufarbenem Zink verkleidet, erinnert dieser Bau an andere metallverkleidete oder -gedeckte Sakralbauten in Jerusalem, darunter den Felsendom, die Al-Aksa-Moschee, die russischen Kirchen und zahlreiche Synagogen, aber auch an öffentliche Gebäude wie die Kuppel über dem Ratsversammlungssaal des Rathauses. Vielleicht deutet dies auf Rabbi David Hartmans Interesse am Dialog zwischen den Vertretern der drei monotheistischen Weltreligionen hin.

### Museen

Museen spielen bei der Bildung und Förderung von Israels nationaler Identität eine Hauptrolle. Das Israel-Museum mit seinem Bestand an Objekten aus mehreren Jahrtausenden ist eine Schatztruhe voller archäologischer und ethnologischer Funde, Judaika und westlicher Kunst. Seine Konzeption, wenn auch nicht seine Größe, lässt sich mit der europäischer oder amerikanischer Nationalmuseen wie des Pariser Louvre oder des New Yorker Metropolitan Museum vergleichen. Von Anfang an haben das Israel-Museum in Jerusalem und das Tel-Aviv-Museum jüdische Kunst gesammelt, um die Jahrhunderte währende Mitgestaltung der schönen Künste durch die in der Diaspora lebenden Juden zu dokumentieren und den Unterschied zwischen jüdischer Diasporakunst und moderner israelischer Kunst zu verdeutlichen. Neben zahlreichen archäologischen Stätten bilden Museen für Vorgeschichte und die Artefakte der Antike ein wesentliches Bindeglied zwischen dem modernen Staat und seinen biblischen Wurzeln. Der Fund der Qumran-Rollen am Toten Meer gab Anlass zur Errichtung des Schreins des Buches auf dem Grundstück des Israel-Museums. Der Holocaust spielte eine wichtige Rolle als Begründung für die Errichtung eines unabhängigen jüdischen Staates, und es ist daher nicht verwunderlich, dass das 1953 gegründete Yad-Vashem-Zentrum zum Gedenken an die Märtyrer und Helden des Holocaust in Jerusalem zur nationalen Gedenkstätte wurde. In unmittelbarer Nähe des Herzl-Bergs gelegen, wird sie von jedem ausländischen Staatsgast besucht.

Al Mansfeld, Dora Gad, Israel Museum, Jerusalem, 1959–93    Al Mansfeld, Dora Gad, Israel-Museum, Jerusalem, 1959–93

It is located next to Mount Herzl and is visited by every single foreign statesman.

The Israel Museum's precursor, Schatz's Bezalel School (1906), later named the Bezalel National Museum, focused on Jewish ceremonial art and art produced by Jewish artists. The first picture in the collection of the Tel Aviv Museum, founded in 1932, was a painting by Marc Chagall depicting a Jewish man holding a Torah scroll. The museum was housed in the private home of Meir Dizengoff, the first mayor of Tel Aviv. The building was adapted by Carl Rubin, who gave it a modern facade in the spirit of the International Style that characterized and dominated the city in the early 1930s.

The Israel Museum, designed by Al Mansfeld and Dora Gad, who won the commission in a competition in 1959, was inspired by Arab and Mediterranean villages. The buildings are nestled into a mountainside to guarantee that they would have room to grow organically over the years. Since then, the museum has expanded by several times its original size, but this has had a negligible impact on the landscape, greatly contributing to its popularity with the general public. The architects were awarded the Israel Prize for Architecture for their work and the museum was voted the most successful Israeli building in a competition conducted by one of the daily newspapers. From inside the building, one also senses the museum's connection to the landscape. The windows look out onto the Valley of the Cross and the Rehavia neighborhood, which was built as a garden city and has a large concentration of fine International Style buildings, including the Knesset (parliament). From the new pavilions, one can see the Billy Rose Sculpture Garden (designed by Isamu Noguchi) and the Hebrew University campus. The architects sought to emphasize the connection between the entrance plaza, the windows at the entrance to the Bezalel Wing, and the Bronfman Archaeology Wing and the Monastery of the Cross. Mansfeld used the term *genius loci* to explain the importance of the axis between the museum, the valley, the olive trees, and the ancient building in the heart of the valley.[5]

One of the most significant museums (for both aesthetic and cultural reasons) completed in the second half of the twentieth century is the Shrine of the Book by Frederick Kiesler and Armand Bartos. The dome of the building "floats" on a reflecting pool filled by a fountain. The unique shape of the dome has its origins in archeological finds; it is an enlargement of the lids of the containers in which the scrolls were found.

The architects used light in differing degrees of intensity throughout in order to create tension and interest. The alternating light and darkness intensify the visitor's sense that he has undergone an uncommon experience. One can see in the contrast between the white dome and the black vertical walls a visual reference to the war between "light and darkness," between "good and evil." This usage of illumination makes visible an integral part of the beliefs of the ancient people from the Qumran community, who considered themselves to be the "sons of light" and relegated the rest of the world to darkness.

The Davidson Visitor Center, planned by architects Etan Kimmel and Michal Eshkolot in the heart of the Jewish Quarter excavations in the Old City, is eight meters below ground level amidst the excavations. Visitors enter and leave via glass-framed passageways located on different levels. What makes the museum special is that, as visitors walk along a wooden ramp, they can see finds discovered on the site that date from three different periods: the Second Temple period, the

Die Vorgängerinstitution des Israel-Museums war die Bezalel-Schule von Boris Schatz (1906), später umbenannt in Bezalel-Nationalmuseum, die sich auf jüdische sakrale Kunst sowie die Werke jüdischer Maler und Bildhauer konzentrierte. Das erste Gemälde, das in die Sammlung des 1932 gegründeten Tel-Aviv-Museums aufgenommen wurde, war von Marc Chagall. Es zeigt einen Juden, der eine Thorarolle in den Armen hält. Das Museum war zunächst im Privathaus des ersten Bürgermeisters von Tel Aviv, Meir Dizengoff, untergebracht. Später wurde das Haus von Carl Rubin umgebaut, der ihm eine moderne Fassade nach dem Vorbild des Internationalen Stils gab, der Anfang der 1930er Jahre das Stadtbild von Tel Aviv prägte und beherrschte.

Die Architekten Al Mansfeld und Dora Gad ließen sich beim Bau des Israel-Museums, dem Siegerentwurf des 1959 abgehaltenen Wettbewerbs, von arabischen und mediterranen Dörfern inspirieren. Die modularen Gebäudeteile schmiegten sich an einen Hang und waren von vornherein auf späteres organisches Wachstum angelegt. Tatsächlich ist das Museum seither bis zu einem Mehrfachen seiner ursprünglichen Größe erweitert worden, was die Landschaft aber nur unwesentlich beeinträchtigt hat — mit ein wichtiger Grund für die Popularität des Museums. Die Architekten erhielten für diese Arbeit den Israel-Preis für Architektur, und das Museum wurde von den Lesern einer Tageszeitung in einer Umfrage als gelungenstes israelisches Gebäude beurteilt. Auch im Inneren des Gebäudes spürt man seine Verbundenheit mit der Landschaft. Die Fenster bieten Ausblicke ins Tal des Kreuzes und über das als Gartenstadt angelegte Rechavia-Viertel mit seiner großen Zahl von Gebäuden im Stil der internationalen Moderne, darunter das der Knesset (Parlament). Von den neuen Pavillons aus überblickt man den von Isamu Noguchi gestalteten Billy-Rose-Skulpturengarten bis zum Campus der Hebräischen Universität. Die Architekten betonten die Verbindung zwischen dem Platz vor dem Haupteingang, den Fenstern neben dem Eingang zum Bezalel-Trakt, der Bronfman Archäologischen Abteilung und dem Kreuz-Kloster. Mansfeld sprach vom »genius loci«, um die Bedeutung der Achse zwischen dem Museum, dem Tal, den Olivenbäumen und den historischen Bauten im Kernbereich des Tals zu verdeutlichen.[5]

Eines der sowohl in ästhetischer als auch in kultureller Hinsicht bedeutendsten Museen, die in der zweiten Hälfte des 20. Jahrhunderts fertiggestellt wurden, ist der Schrein des Buches von Frederick Kiesler und Armand Bartos. Das Kuppeldach des Bauwerks ›schwebt‹ über einem Wasserbecken mit Fontäne. Die ungewöhnliche Form der Kuppel leitet sich aus archäologischen Funden ab: Sie bildet den Deckel eines Qumran-Rollen-Behälters in vielfacher Vergrößerung nach.

Die Architekten sorgten für unterschiedliche Lichtintensitäten im ganzen Gebäude, um es spannungsvoll und abwechslungsreich wirken zu lassen. Die abwechselnd hellen und dunklen Räume verstärken das Empfinden des Besuchers, hier etwas Ungewöhnliches zu erleben. Der Kontrast zwischen weißer Kuppel und schwarzen Wänden lässt sich als Hinweis auf den Kampf zwischen Licht und Finsternis, zwischen Gut und Böse interpretieren. Diese Art des Umgangs mit der Beleuchtung führt einen integralen Aspekt der religiösen Überzeugungen der Bruderschaft von Qumran vor Augen: Sie verstanden sich selbst als »Söhne des Lichts« und verwiesen den Rest der Welt in die Finsternis.

Das Davidson-Besucherzentrum, entworfen von den Architekten Etan Kimmel und Michal Eshkolot, liegt inmitten der Ausgrabungsorte im Jüdischen Viertel der Jerusalemer Altstadt und ist acht Meter tief in die Erde eingegraben. Man betritt und verlässt das Gebäude auf verschiedenen Ebenen über verglaste Passagen. Das Besondere an diesem Museum ist,

Kimmel Eshkolot, Davidson Visitor's Center, Jerusalem, 2000
Kimmel Eshkolot, Davidson-Besucherzentrum, Jerusalem, 2000

Aryeh El-Chanai, Arieh Sharon, Benjamin Idelson, Hall of Remembrance, Yad Vashem, Jerusalem, 1957
Aryeh El-Chanai, Arieh Sharon, Benjamin Idelson, Gedenkhalle, Yad Vashem, Jerusalem, 1957

Byzantine period, and the remains of a palace from the Umayyad period. In the entrance hall, which has a suspended steel ceiling, visitors can look through a glass "periscope" at the ancient buildings on the Temple Mount and, at the end of their visit, see the Western Wall excavations and the walls of the Temple Mount. This is a late echo of the period when archeology was a "national sport" by means of which it was hoped to create a connection between contemporary Israel and the distant history of the First and Second Temple periods.

The Yad Vashem museum in Jerusalem, which commemorates the Jews who perished in the Holocaust, was built in 1957–61 by Aryeh El-Chanani with Arieh Sharon and Benjamin Idelson. Nissan C'naan's Art Museum (1982) and the International School for Holocaust Studies planned by David Guggenheim, Alex Bloch, and Daniel Mintz were added later (1995–2000). Following the completion of the Children's Memorial (opened 1987) Moshe Safdie was commissioned in 1997 to draft a master plan connecting all the buildings and monuments on the campus. Each of them had been designed in its own right without any comprehensive planning. He was also to add a new building for the visitors' center and historic museum, which would be partially submerged in the ground. Once more light would play a crucial role in establishing both a spiritual and aesthetic atmosphere,

dass seine Besucher auf ihrem Gang über eine Holzrampe die auf dem Grundstück entdeckten archäologischen Fundstücke aus drei Epochen zu sehen bekommen, und zwar aus der Periode des Zweiten Tempels, der byzantinischen Herrschaft sowie die Überreste eines Palastes aus der Zeit der ersten Omajjaden. In der Eingangshalle mit ihrer abgehängten Stahldecke können Besucher sich durch ein Glas-›Periskop‹ die antiken Bauten des Tempelbergs anschauen und am Ende ihres Rundgangs die Ausgrabungen an der Klagemauer und die Mauern des Tempelbezirks besichtigen. Dies ist sozusagen ein spätes Echo auf die Zeit, in der Archäologie als ›Nationalsport‹ betrieben wurde, mittels dessen man eine Verbindung zwischen dem Israel der Gegenwart und dem der fernen Zeit des Ersten und Zweiten Tempels herzustellen hoffte.

Die von 1957–61 in Jerusalem errichtete Yad-Vashem-Gedenkstätte mit Museum erinnert an die während des Holocaust ermordeten Juden und wurde von Aryeh El-Chanani in Zusammenarbeit mit Arieh Sharon und Benjamin Idelson entworfen. Das Kunstmuseum von Nissan C'naan (1982) und die von David Guggenheim, Alex Bloch und Daniel Mintz geplante Internationale Schule für Holocaust-Studien kamen später hinzu (1995–2000). Nach Fertigstellung der 1987 eröffneten Kindergedenkstätte wurde Moshe Safdie 1997 mit der Erstellung eines Generalplans beauftragt, der alle Gedenkstätten und Denkmäler zu einer Gesamtanlage zusammenfassen sollte, denn bis dahin war jedes für sich als Einzelprojekt geplant worden. Der Auftrag umfasste auch den Neubau eines Besucherzentrums und Historischen Museums, das zum Teil in den Erdboden versenkt werden und in dem Licht ebenfalls wesentlich zur Schaffung einer geistig stimulierenden und ästhetisch ansprechenden Atmosphäre beitragen sollte. Licht, das buchstäblich vom Ende eines Tunnels hereinleuchtet, unterstreicht hier die Symbolik des Ortes.

Die ebenfalls von Aryeh El-Chanani mit Arieh Sharon und Benjamin Idelson erbaute Gedenkhalle (Ohel Yiskor) von 1957 war das erste Bauwerk auf dem Gelände und ist vielleicht das bewegendste. Der Besucher betritt es über einen eisernen Steg und geht über eine L-förmige Plattform, die erhöht über einer nicht zugänglichen, mit den Namen sämtlicher Konzentrationslager beschrifteten, geneigten Ebene liegt. Die Halle wird auch für offizielle Gedenkfeiern genutzt und erfüllt somit eine wichtige Funktion. Gestalterische Anregungen lieferte Le Corbusiers Wallfahrtskirche von Ronchamp. Zwar wurde deren gerundetes und geschwungenes Dach hier durch ein quadratisches ersetzt; bei beiden Bauten trennen aber schmale Lichtschlitze das massige Dach von den ebenso massigen

with light entering from the end of a tunnel stressing the symbolism of the site.

Ohel Yizkor (Hall of Remembrance) designed by Aryeh El-Chanai with Arieh Sharon and Benjamin Idelson (1957) was the first building on the site, and is perhaps the most moving. Visitors enter via an iron gate and walk across a raised, L-shaped platform higher than the slanting floor on which are written the names of the extermination camps. It continues to play an important role in official ceremonies today. It was inspired by Le Corbusier's Pilgrims' Chapel at Ronchamp. True, the rounded roof of the latter gave way to the square roof of the former, but in both, narrow ribbons of light separate the heavy mass of the roof and the massive supporting walls. The Pilgrims' Chapel has also been an inspiration to many other architects such as Kahn and Botta. As at Ronchamp, the exposed concrete sculpted roof of the Hall of Remembrance does not rest on the walls. Visitors become aware that the massive wall does not support the heavy ceiling particularly when they enter the building and see the light bursting through the crack and the thin pillars that support the roof.[6] From outside, the concrete cube of the Hall of Remembrance symbolizes the weight of the Holocaust, while inside it becomes a tent, at the center of which is a square opening above the eternal flame.

Finally, the Valley of Destroyed Communities, planned by Lipa Yahalom and Dan Zur (1983–93), derives its inspiration and emotional power from the site as well as from the rocks and the boulders that were brought from distant quarries. The names of the towns and cities in Europe that used to have large Jewish populations before they were destroyed are engraved on the massive stones. The power of the site is found in the sensitive landscaping. The maze of spaces leading into one another is not highly visible from the lower parts of Mount Memorial and only exists for those who take the trouble to go to the site to be with memories of the past in the well-tended natural surroundings.

This site was determined in 1953 by parliamentary decree. The fact that the Hall of Remembrance and Yad Vashem are located adjacent to Mount Herzl, where Theodor Herzl, national leaders, presidents, and prime ministers are buried alongside soldiers who have fallen in battles to establish and defend the state, endows the site with symbolic and emotional value, giving it a special significance in relation to other Holocaust museums and memorial sites all over the world. The connection between the theme of the destruction of Jewry and the founders of the new state conveys an ideological message not available elsewhere in the world.

1   Amiram Harlap, *Synagogues in Israel, From the Ancient to the Modern* (Hebrew), Tel Aviv (n.d.), pp. 13–19; 91–165.
2   Kent Larson, *Louis I. Kahn: Unbuilt Masterworks,* New York 2000, pp. 124–198.
3   Roman Hollenstein, "Citadel of Faith, Mario Botta's Cymbalista Synagogue in Tel Aviv," in *Mario Botta, The Cymbalista Synagogue and Jewish Heritage Center,* Corte Madera and Milan 2001, pp. 25–36. See also project part of this book.
4   Observed by Diana Dolev in her research on the Mount Scopus campus (to be published).
5   Anna Teut, *Al Mansfeld: Architekt in Israel/An Architect in Israel,* Berlin 1999.
6   Michael Levin, "Modern Monumental Architecture–Jerusalem compared with the Capitals of the World," in *Le Carré Bleu,* No. 3–4, 1999, pp. 22–48.

Außenmauern. Le Corbusiers Kirche hat im Übrigen auch viele andere Architekten inspiriert, darunter Kahn und Botta. Wie in Ronchamp entdeckt der Besucher erst, wenn er die Halle betritt, das Licht durch den Schlitz zwischen Wand und Decke einströmen sieht und die schlanken Stützen erblickt, auf denen das Dach ruht, dass die dicken Umfassungsmauern das skulpturale Betondach der Gedenkhalle gar nicht tragen.[6] Von außen gesehen stellt sich der Betonkubus der Gedenkhalle wie ein Symbol für die schwere Last des Holocaust dar, im Innern dagegen wird er zum Zelt mit einer zentralen quadratischen Öffnung an der Spitze, direkt über der ewigen Flamme.

Das Tal der zerstörten Gemeinden schließlich (Valley of Destroyed Communities, Architekten: Lipa Yahalom und Dan Zur, 1983–93) bezieht seine Inspiration und emotionale Ausstrahlungskraft aus dem Ort selbst, aber auch von den gewaltigen Steinen und Felsblöcken aus weit entfernten Steinbrüchen. Die Namen der europäischen Städte und Kommunen mit einem vor dem Holocaust großen jüdischen Bevölkerungsanteil sind in die Felsen eingemeißelt. Die eigentliche Eindrücklichkeit des Tals beruht aber auf der landschaftlichen Gestaltung. Die labyrinthartigen, ineinander fließenden Räume sind von den unteren Abschnitten des Har Hasikaron (Berg des Gedenkens) nur schwer auszumachen und nur erfahrbar von denen, die sich die Mühe machen, hinunterzusteigen und sich inmitten der sorgsam gepflegten natürlichen Umgebung dem Gedenken an die Vergangenheit hinzugeben.

Die Anlage der Yad-Vashem-Gedenkstätte wurde 1953 von der Knesset beschlossen. Die Tatsache, dass die Gedenkhalle (Ohel Yiskor) und Yad Vashem in der Nähe des Herzl-Bergs errichtet wurden, wo Theodor Herzl, viele nationale Führerpersönlichkeiten, Präsidenten und Premierminister neben einfachen Soldaten beerdigt liegen, die im Unabhängigkeitskampf oder bei der Verteidigung des Staates fielen, verleiht dem Ort im Vergleich zu anderen Holocaust-Museen und Gedenkstätten in aller Welt besonderen symbolischen und emotionalen Wert und herausragende Bedeutung. Die Verbindung zwischen dem Thema der Zerstörung des Judentums und den Gründervätern des Staates Israel übermittelt eine ideologische Botschaft, wie sie an keinem anderen Ort möglich wäre.

1   Amiram Harlap, *Synagogues in Israel, From the Ancient to the Modern* (Übersetzung des hebräischen Titels), Tel Aviv (o. J.), S. 13–19, 91–165.
2   Kent Larson, *Louis I. Kahn, Unbuilt Masterworks,* New York 2000, S. 124–198.
3   Roman Hollenstein, »Citadel of Faith, Mario Botta's Cymbalista Synagogue in Tel Aviv«, in: *Mario Botta, The Cymbalista Synagogue and Jewish Heritage Center,* Corte Madera/Mailand 2001, S. 25–36. Siehe auch Projektteil dieses Buches.
4   Von Diana Dolev bei ihren Forschungen zum Mount Scopus Campus beobachtet (Publikation in Vorbereitung).
5   Anna Teut, *Al Mansfeld. Architekt in Israel/An Architect in Israel,* Berlin 1999.
6   Michael Levin, »Modern Monumental Architecture – Jerusalem compared with the Capitals of the World«, in: *Le Carré Bleu,* Nr. 3–4, 1999, S. 22–48.

James E. Young

## Jewish Museums, Holocaust Museums, and Questions of National Identity

James E. Young

## Jüdische Museen, Holocaust-Museen und Fragen der nationalen Identität

The farther events of World War II and the Holocaust recede into time, the more prominent their museums and memorials become. Indeed, there has been a veritable "Holocaust and Jewish museums boom" over the last twenty years, with the establishment around the world of hundreds of museums and institutions dedicated to remembering and telling the history of Nazi Germany's destruction of the European Jews during World War II, as well as dozens more devoted to showing and telling the history of Jewish life and culture before and after the war. Depending on where these museums are built, and by whom, they remember the past according to a variety of national myths, ideals, and political needs. All reflect both the past experiences and current lives of their communities, as well as the state's memory of itself. At a more specific level, these museums reflect the temper of the memory-artists' time, their architects' schools of design, and their physical locations in national memorial landscapes.

Public memory—of Jewish life or mass murder—as found in these museums, is never shaped in a vacuum, its motives never pure. Both

United States Holocaust Memorial Museum, Washington D.C., Tower of Faces
United States Holocaust Memorial Museum, Washington, D.C., Turm der Gesichter

Je weiter sich die Ereignisse des Zweiten Weltkriegs und des Holocaust in den Tiefen der Geschichte verlieren, desto berühmter werden ihre Museen und Gedenkstätten. Tatsächlich hat es in den letzten zwanzig Jahren einen regelrechten Boom an Jüdischen und Holocaust-Museen gegeben: Rund um die Welt sind Hunderte von Museen und Institutionen entstanden, die dem Andenken der von den deutschen Nationalsozialisten während des Zweiten Weltkriegs ermordeten Juden und der Darstellung dieser Ereignisse gewidmet sind. In Dutzenden weiterer Bauten wird das Leben und die Kultur der Juden vor und nach diesem Krieg gezeigt und erzählt. Je nachdem, wo und von wem diese Museen gebaut wurden und werden, erinnern sie an die Vergangenheit in Übereinstimmung mit nationalen Mythen, Idealen und politischen Erfordernissen. Allesamt reflektieren sie die Lebenserfahrung und die gegenwärtige Lebensrealität der Bevölkerung wie auch das historische Selbstverständnis des jeweiligen Staates. Auf der gestalterischen Ebene reflektieren diese Museen die Stimmung der Periode der jeweiligen ›Gedenk-Gestalter‹, die Haltung ihrer Architekten und ihre physische Platzierung in den jeweiligen nationalen ›Denkmallandschaften‹.

Die Form des öffentlichen Erinnerns an jüdisches Leben oder den Massenmord an den Juden, wie man sie in diesen Museen vorfindet, bildet sich niemals aus einem Vakuum heraus, und die der Gestaltung zugrunde liegenden Motive sind niemals eindeutig. Die Gründe für den Bau Jüdischer und Holocaust-Museen und die von ihnen angeregten Arten des Erinnerns sind so vielfältig wie ihre Standorte. Einige entstehen in Befolgung des traditionellen jüdischen Gebots zum Gedenken, andere in Erfüllung eines staatlichen Bedürfnisses, die eigene nationale Vergangenheit zu erklären. Während einige Museen sich die Aufgabe stellen, nachfolgende Generationen zu bilden und in ihnen das Gefühl einer Erfahrungs- und Schicksalsgemeinschaft in Vergangenheit und Zukunft zu wecken, werden andere als Sühnezeichen oder Mittel zur Selbstverherrlichung errichtet. Wieder andere sollen Touristen anlocken. In fast allen Fällen vermischen diese Museen die traditionelle jüdische mit der staatlich-institutionellen Ikonografie und Form des Gedenkens. In Deutschland zum Beispiel wird in Museen und Gedenkstätten bis heute vielfach die von den ermordeten Juden hinterlassene Leere hervorgehoben, in Bezug auf deutsche Opfer dagegen der politische Widerstand. In Polen erinnern Museen in früheren Konzentrationslagern und im ganzen Land an die Vernichtung des ganzen Staates, dargestellt am Beispiel seiner jüdischen Minderheit. In den Museen in Israel wiederum wird der Märtyrer und Helden, erlöst durch die Geburt des jüdischen Staates, gemeinsam gedacht. Jüdische und Holocaust-Museen in Amerika sind ebenso stark von amerikanischen Wertvorstellungen und historischen Erfahrungen wie Freiheit, Pluralismus und Einwanderung geprägt.

Diese Untersuchung von Jüdischen und Holocaust-Museen will ermitteln, wie und zu welchen Zwecken die öffentliche Geschichte des jüdischen Lebens und Sterbens in einer Handvoll Institutionen in aller Welt geformt wird. Statt uns aber auf abgeschlossene oder monolithische Formen der Erinnerung zu konzentrieren, können wir den Prozess der Konstruktion von Geschichtsschreibung und Gedenken betrachten. Wir fragen, wer die Erinnerung unter welchen Bedingungen für welches Publi-

Daniel Libeskind, Jewish Museum Berlin, 1989–99. Old building and new building    Daniel Libeskind, Jüdisches Museum Berlin, 1989–99. Altbau und Neubau

the reasons given for Jewish and Holocaust museums and the kinds of memory they generate are as various as the sites themselves. Some are built in response to traditional Jewish injunctions to remember, others according to a government's need to explain a nation's past to itself. Where the aim of some museums is to educate the next generation and to inculcate in it a sense of shared experience and destiny, others are conceived as expiations of guilt or as self-aggrandizement. Still others are intended to attract tourists. In nearly all cases, these museums mix traditional Jewish memorial iconography with a state's own institutional forms of remembrance. In Germany, for example, museums and memorials to this time often recall Jews by their absence, German victims by their political resistance. In Poland, museums in former death camps and across the countryside commemorate the whole of Polish destruction through the figure of its murdered Jewish part. In Israel's museums, martyrs and heroes are remembered side-by-side, both redeemed by the birth of the state. Jewish and Holocaust museums in America are guided no less by distinctly American ideals and experiences—such as liberty, pluralism, and immigration.

The aim of this inquiry into Jewish and Holocaust museums will be to examine *how* public history of Jewish life and death is being shaped in a handful of museums around the world and to what interpretive ends. Instead of concentrating on finished or monolithic memory, however, we might look at the process by which public history and memory are constructed. We ask who creates this memory, under what circumstances, for which audience? Which events are remembered, which forgotten, and how are they explained? What are these museums' places in national and religious commemorative cycles? What is the

kum erzeugt. Welche Ereignisse werden erinnert, welche vergessen, und wie werden die erinnerten erklärt? Welchen Stellenwert haben diese Museen im jährlichen Zyklus nationaler und religiöser Gedenktage? Welche Rolle spielt der Architekt bei der Formung einer öffentlichen Erinnerung? Welche Auswirkungen haben die Museen auf die jüdische Identität und andere nationale Identitäten? Und schließlich sollten wir bei diesen Überlegungen zu einer kleinen Anzahl von Jüdischen und Holocaust-Museen in den USA, Israel und Deutschland stets die Unterschiede zwischen beiden, ihre etwaigen Überschneidungen und das davon abhängige Entstehen von Identität im Auge behalten.

### Das Jüdische Museum in Berlin

Wie ›behaust‹ eine Stadt wie Berlin die Erinnerung an ein Volk wie die Juden, die hier nicht länger ›zuhause‹ sind? Wie würde Berlin die Juden einladen, in die Geschichte der Deutschen zurückzukehren, nachdem sie auf so mörderische Weise daraus vertrieben wurden? Ein Jüdisches Museum in der Hauptstadt einer Nation, die sich vor gar nicht langer Zeit der Juden fast völlig entledigte und sie zu Fremdlingen in einem Land machte, das ihnen ›Heimat‹ gewesen war, kann der Natur der Sache nach hier nicht ›heimisch‹ sein, sondern muss als ›unheimlich‹ empfunden werden. Das Dilemma, vor dem der Architekt eines solchen Gebäudes steht, drückt sich in der Frage aus: Wie lässt sich dieses Gefühl der Unheimlichkeit in einem Medium wie der Architektur mit ihrer langen Tradition des ›Beheimatens‹ ausdrücken?[1]

Bei ihrem ursprünglichen Konzept einer ›Erweiterung‹ des Berlin-Museums durch ein Jüdisches Museum hofften die Planer nicht nur die Rolle der Juden als Mitgestalter von Berlins Geschichte und Kultur zu

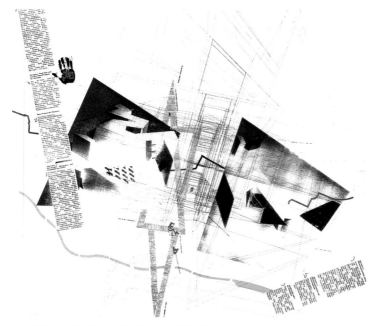

Jewish Museum Berlin. *Star Matrix* by Daniel Libeskind
Jüdisches Museum Berlin. *Star Matrix* von Daniel Libeskind

contemporary architect's role in shaping public memory? What are the consequences of these museums for both Jewish and other national identities? Finally, in these reflections on a small handful of Jewish and Holocaust museums in the United States, Israel, and Germany, we might keep in mind the crucial distinction between Jewish museums and Holocaust museums, when they overlap and when they do not, and the constructions of identity that hang in the balance.

### Berlin's Jewish Museum

How does a city like Berlin "house" the memory of a people like the Jews no longer at "home" there? How would Berlin invite the Jews back into its official past after having driven them so murderously from it? A "Jewish Museum" in the capital city of a nation that not so long ago voided itself of Jews, making them alien strangers in a land they had considered "home," will not by definition be *heimisch* but must be regarded as *unheimlich*—or as our translation would have it, uncanny. The dilemma facing the designer of such a museum thus becomes: How then to embody this sense of *unheimlichkeit*, or uncanniness, in a medium like architecture, which has its own long tradition of being *heimisch*, or homely?[1]

In their initial conception of what they then regarded as a Jewish Museum "extension" to the Berlin Museum, planners hoped to recognize both the role Jews had once played as cocreators of Berlin's history and culture and that the city was fundamentally haunted by its Jewish absence. At the same time, the very notion of an "autonomous" Jewish Museum struck them as problematic: the museum wanted to show the importance and far-reaching effect of Jewish culture on the city's history, to give it the prominence it deserved. But many also feared dividing German from Jewish history, inadvertently recapitulating the Nazis' own segregation of Jewish culture from German. This would have been to reimpose a distinct line between the histories and cultures of Germans and Jews, whose fates had been inextricably mingled for centuries in Berlin.

würdigen, sondern auch darzustellen, dass die Stadt nachhaltig vom nunmehrigen Fehlen der Juden in ihrer Bevölkerung belastet wurde. Gleichzeitig empfanden sie schon allein die Vorstellung eines ›autonomen‹ Jüdischen Museums als problematisch, denn das Museum sollte ja die Bedeutung und die weitreichenden Auswirkungen der jüdischen Kultur auf die gesamte Stadtgeschichte darstellen und den Juden die verdiente Anerkennung zollen. Viele befürchteten aber auch, die Trennung deutscher und jüdischer Geschichte würde versehentlich die von den Nazis betriebene Segregation zwischen jüdischer und deutscher Kultur nachvollziehen. Damit wäre erneut eine klare Trennlinie zwischen der Geschichte und Kultur der Deutschen und der Juden gezogen worden, deren Schicksale doch seit Jahrhunderten in Berlin unauflöslich miteinander verbunden gewesen waren.[2]

Der Zeitpunkt der Eröffnung von Berlins erstem Jüdischen Museum im Jahr 1933, eine Woche vor Hitlers Ernennung zum Reichskanzler, war wirklich katastrophal gewählt. Es wurde in den renovierten Ausstellungsgalerien eines Ensembles in der Oranienburger Straße untergebracht, das bereits die äußerst eindrucksvolle Synagoge mit Gemeindehaus und Bibliothek umfasste. Berlins erstes Jüdisches Museum eröffnete angesichts der wachsenden nationalsozialistischen Bewegung bewusst mit einer Ausstellung der von dem deutsch-jüdischen Künstler Max Liebermann angeführten Berliner Sezession[3], fast so, als hätte das Museum die Tatsache einer unauflöslichen deutsch-jüdischen Kultur institutionalisieren wollen, deren jede Hälfte eine Permutation der anderen darstellte — als eine Art Herausforderung an die nationalsozialistische Annahme einer grundlegenden Feindschaft und Unvereinbarkeit zwischen der deutschen und der jüdischen Kultur.

Selbst damals ist wohl die Vorstellung von der Beschaffenheit eines ›Jüdischen Museums‹ in der Gemeinschaft der Juden umstritten gewesen: Sollte das Museum Kunstwerke zu jüdisch-religiösen Themen von jüdischen und nichtjüdischen Künstlern zeigen? Oder sollte es Kunst von jüdischen Malern und Bildhauern ausstellen? Die Frage nach dem Wesen ›jüdischer Kunst‹ war nun angeschnitten. Tatsächlich untergruben die in den Exponaten des Museums aufscheinenden Fragen nach ›Judentum‹, ›Deutschtum‹ und sogar ›Europäertum‹ nach und nach die Argumente für den Bau eines Jüdischen Museums in Berlin. Der jüdische Kunsthistoriker und damalige Leiter der Berliner Kunstbibliothek, Curt Glaser, wandte sich gegen den Gedanken eines Jüdischen Museums in Berlin und gegen die Annahme, Liebermanns Bilder seien allein aufgrund seiner jüdischen Abstammung irgendwie grundlegend jüdischer Natur, und das obwohl er keinerlei jüdische Themen darstellte.[4] So wurde für das Jüdische Museum in Berlin zunächst zwar ein integrierendes Konzept entworfen, dieses aber schon wenige Tage nach der offiziellen Eröffnung in Frage gestellt. Ob es sich nun den Nazi-Gesetzen anpasste oder nicht — das Museum wurde wie die anderen jüdischen Institutionen im Gebäudekomplex an der Oranienburger Straße und im ganzen Reich beim Pogrom der so genannten Reichskristallnacht vom 9. auf den 10. November 1938 zerstört und ausgeplündert.

Fünfzig Jahre später, nach Jahrzehnten der Diskussion, ob und — wenn ja — wo ein Jüdisches Museum in Berlin eingerichtet werden sollte, erklärte sich der Berliner Senat schließlich bereit, Gelder für eine ›Abteilung Jüdisches Museum‹ bereitzustellen, welche verwaltungstechnisch zwar zum Berlin-Museum im ehemaligen Kollegienhaus in der Lindenstraße gehören, aber einen separaten Bau erhalten sollte. Im Dezember 1988 wurde ein internationaler Wettbewerb für ein Gebäude ausgeschrieben, das sowohl das Berlin-Museum erweitern als auch der ›Abteilung Jüdi-

Indeed, it was with catastrophic timing that Berlin's first Jewish museum opened in January 1933, one week before Adolf Hitler was installed as Chancellor. Housed in a refurbished series of exhibition halls at the Oranienburger Strasse complex already home to the spectacular synagogue there, as well as to the Jewish community center and library, Berlin's first Jewish museum opened quite deliberately in the face of the Nazi rise to power with an exhibition of work by artists of the Berlin Secessionists, led by the German-Jewish artist, Max Liebermann.[2] It is almost as if the museum had hoped to establish the institutional fact of an inextricably linked German-Jewish culture, each a permutation of the other, as a kind of challenge to the Nazis' assumption of an essential hostility between German and Jewish cultures.

But even here, the very notion of what constituted a "Jewish Museum" would be a matter of contention for the community itself: Would the museum show art on Jewish religious themes by both Jewish and non-Jewish artists? Or would it show anything by Jewish artists? The question of what constituted "Jewish art" had now been broached. Indeed, questions of "Jewishness," "Germanness," and even "Europeanness" in art exhibited by the museum began to undercut the case for something called a "Jewish Museum" in Berlin. The Jewish art historian and director of the Berlin Library of Arts, Curt Glaser, attacked both the idea of a "Jewish Museum" in Berlin and the presumption that Liebermann's work was, by dint of his Jewish birth only, somehow essentially Jewish—even though there was nothing thematically Jewish

sches Museum‹ ein eigenes Domizil geben sollte. Die Planer gingen davon aus, dass der jüdische Trakt sowohl autonom als auch integrativ sein müsse, denn die schwierige Aufgabe bestand ja darin, ein Museum für die Geschichte der Stadt und ihrer Menschen mit der Darstellung der menschenverachtenden Behandlung ihrer jüdischen Bürger zu verknüpfen. Die Fragen, die ein solches Museum aufwirft, sind ebenso erschreckend wie potentiell lähmend: Wie realisiert man die Aufgabe in einer Form, die nicht Versöhnung und Kontinuität suggeriert? Wie vereint man Berlin wieder mit seinen jüdischen Bürgern, ohne eine nahtlose Annäherung vorzutäuschen? Wie stellt man jüdische Geschichte und Kultur als Teil der deutschen Geschichte dar, ohne sie dieser vollkommen einzuverleiben? Wie präsentiert man jüdische Kultur einerseits als Teil der deutschen Kultur und andererseits als autonom, ohne die alte Zeitungsente vom besonderen Volk erneut in Umlauf zu bringen? Statt diese schier unlösbaren Fragen zu umgehen, stellten die Planer sich ihnen mutig in dem außergewöhnlichen Ausschreibungstext des Wettbewerbs und machten sie zur Hauptleitlinie für den Entwurfsprozess. Bei der Ausarbeitung dieser Fragen forderte der Ausschreibungstext potentielle Architekten auch dazu auf, die furchtbare Leere anzuerkennen, die dieses Museum erforderlich gemacht hatte. Zum einen bestand die Absicht, die Erinnerung an die Juden und das Gedenken an deren Ermordung in die ansonsten in dieser Hinsicht gleichgültige Berliner Stadtkultur wieder einzuschreiben, zum anderen sollte das Fehlen der Juden in der deutschen Nachkriegskultur offenbart und diese Wiedereinschreibung gefordert werden.

Jewish Museum Berlin. Exhibition space    Jüdisches Museum Berlin. Ausstellungsraum

in the work itself. Thus was an integrationist model for the Jewish Museum in Berlin first proposed and first challenged within days of the museum's official opening. Unfortunately, whether assimilated to Nazi-law or not, like the other Jewish institutions in its complex on Oranienburger Strasse and across the Reich, the Jewish Museum was first damaged, then plundered during the *Kristallnacht* pogrom, 9–10 November 1938.

Fifty years later, after decades of debate over where and whether to reestablish a Jewish museum in Berlin, the Berlin Senate agreed to approve financing for a "Jewish Museum Department" that would remain administratively under the roof of the Berlin Museum at the Collegienhaus on Lindenstrasse, but which would have its own building. A prestigious international competition was called in December 1988 for a building design that would both "extend" the Berlin Museum and give the Jewish Museum Department its own space. According to planners, the Jewish wing would be both autonomous and integrative, the difficulty being to link a museum of civic history with the altogether uncivil treatment of that city's Jews. The questions such a museum raises are as daunting as they are potentially paralyzing: How to do this in a form that would not suggest reconciliation and continuity? How to reunite Berlin and its Jewish part without suggesting a seamless rapprochement? How to show Jewish history and culture as part of German history without subsuming it altogether? How to show Jewish culture as part of and separate from German culture without recirculating all the old canards of "a people apart?" Rather than skirting these impossible questions, the planners confronted them unflinchingly in an extraordinary conceptual brief for the competition that put such questions at the heart of the design process. In elaborating these questions, the conceptual brief also challenged potential designers to acknowledge the terrible void that made this museum necessary. If part of the aim here had been the reinscription of Jewish memory and the memory of the Jews' murder into Berlin's otherwise indifferent civic culture, another part would be to reveal the absence in postwar German culture demanding this reinscription.

Guided by this conceptual brief, city planners issued an open invitation to all architects of the Federal Republic of Germany in December 1988. In addition, they invited another twelve architects from outside Germany, among them the American architect, Daniel Libeskind, then living in Milan. Born in Lodz in 1946 to the survivors of a Polish-Jewish family almost decimated in the Holocaust, Libeskind had long wrestled with many of the brief's questions, finding them nearly insoluble at the architectural level. But having studied at Cooper Union in New York under the tutelage of John Hejduk and Peter Eisenman, two of the founders and practitioners of "deconstructivist architecture," Libeskind was content to propose not so much a solution to the planners' conceptual conundrum as its architectural articulation. Of the 165 designs submitted from around the world for the competition that closed in June 1989, Daniel Libeskind's struck the jury as the most brilliant and complex, possibly as unbuildable. It was awarded first prize and thereby became the first work of Libeskind's ever to be commissioned.[5] Where the other finalists had concerned themselves primarily with the technical feat of reconciling this building to its surroundings in a way that met the IBA's (*Internationale Bauausstellung*) criteria, and to establishing a separate but equal parity between the Berlin Museum and its Jewish Museum Department, Libeskind had devoted himself to the spatial enactment of a philosophical problem.

Mit diesem Auslobungstext forderten die Stadtplaner die Architekten der Bundesrepublik Deutschland im Dezember 1988 zur Teilnahme an einem offenen Wettbewerb auf und luden zusätzlich zwölf ausgesuchte ausländische Architekten ein, darunter den amerikanischen Architekten Daniel Libeskind, der damals in Mailand lebte. Libeskind wurde 1946 in Lodz als Sohn polnischer Juden – Überlebende einer Familie, die im Holocaust ausgelöscht wurde – geboren und hatte sich seit langem mit vielen in der Ausschreibung formulierten Fragen auseinander gesetzt. Bezogen auf die Architektur waren sie ihm nahezu unlösbar erschienen. Da er jedoch unter John Hejduk und Peter Eisenman, zweien der Mitbegründer und Praktiker der dekonstruktivistischen Architektur, an der Cooper Union in New York studiert hatte, beschränkte sich Libeskind darauf, den Auslobern nicht so sehr eine Lösung, sondern vielmehr eine architektonische Formulierung des konzeptionellen Rätsels vorzulegen. Von den 165 Entwürfen aus aller Welt, die bis zur Frist im Juni 1989 eingereicht wurden, erschien Daniel Libeskinds Projekt der Jury als das brillanteste und komplexeste – möglicherweise auch als unbaubar. Es erhielt den 1. Preis und Libeskind den Bauauftrag – seinen ersten überhaupt.[5] Während die anderen Finalisten sich in Übereinstimmung mit den Kriterien der *Internationalen Bauausstellung IBA* überwiegend mit der Technik der ›Versöhnung‹ des Gebäudes mit seiner Umgebung befassten und die Trennung, aber auch Gleichwertigkeit von Berlin-Museum und der Abteilung Jüdisches Museum herzustellen versuchten, hatte sich Libeskind der räumlichen Inszenierung philosophischer Gedankengänge gewidmet.

Seine Zeichnungen des Museums sahen daher eher aus wie Skizzen einer Ruine – als wären die Flügel des Gebäudes infolge der Erschütterungen des Völkermords zerbrochen und dann neu zusammengesetzt worden. Mit diesem Bau fragt Libeskind: Wenn Architektur historische Bedeutungsinhalte verkörpern kann, ist sie dann auch in der Lage, Bedeutungslosigkeit und Sinnsuche auszudrücken? Die Antwort ist ein lang gestreckter, mehrfach gebrochener Baukörper. Die gerade Linie der ›voids‹ (Leerräume) durch das Gebäude tut jedem Raum, den sie durchzieht, Gewalt an und verwandelt ansonsten einheitlich dimensionierte Räume und Säle in missgebildete Anomalien. Einige sind so klein, dass man kaum etwas darin aufstellen kann, andere so schiefwinklig, dass alle Exponate darin wie Fremdkörper wirken. Der ursprüngliche Entwurf sah auch in derart spitzen Winkeln geneigte Wände vor, dass man nichts daran hätte aufhängen können.

Ausgehend von Libeskinds erstem Konzept wurde dem grundlegenden Drama sich gegenseitig ausschließender Ziele und unvereinbarer Mittel vollständig und unerbittlich stattgegeben. Für den Architekten waren die schwierigsten Fragen am wichtigsten: Wie verleiht man einer abwesenden jüdischen Kultur eine Stimme, ohne sich anzumaßen, für sie zu sprechen? Wie überbrückt man die Kluft einer offenen Wunde, ohne sie nahtlos zu schließen? Wie bringt man unter einem Dach ein Spektrum fundamentaler Gegensätze und Widersprüche unter? Mit seinen Zeichnungen erfasste Libeskind nach und nach die wesentlichen Paradoxe im Zentrum des Projekts: Wie gibt man der Leere eine Form, ohne sie aufzufüllen? Wie gibt man dem Formlosen architektonische Gestalt, und wie stellt man sich dem Versuch, solche Erinnerungen zu ›behausen‹?

Die eigentlichen Ausstellungsräume sind zwar geräumig, aber so unregelmäßig gestaltet (von umschlossenen ›voids‹ und Betonträgern durchzogen), dass man nie das Gefühl des ungehinderten Durchgangs hat. Tatsächlich sind es insgesamt sechs ›voids‹, die das Museum horizontal wie vertikal durchschneiden. Von diesen sechs ist nur das letzte für

Jewish Museum Berlin. Last void    Jüdisches Museum Berlin. Letztes ›void‹

His drawings for the museum thus looked more like the sketches of the museum's ruins, a house whose wings have been scrambled and reshaped by the jolt of genocide. In this work, Libeskind asks, if architecture can be representative of historical meaning, can it also represent unmeaning and the search for meaning? The result is an extended building, broken in several places. The straight void-line running through the plan violates every space through which it passes, turning otherwise uniform rooms and halls into misshapen anomalies, some too small to hold anything, others so oblique as to estrange anything housed within them. The original design also included inclining walls, at angles too sharp for hanging exhibitions.

From Libeskind's earliest conceptual brief onward, the essential drama of mutually exclusive aims and irreconcilable means was given full, unapologetic play. For him, it was the impossible questions that mattered most: How to give voice to an absent Jewish culture without presuming to speak for it? How to bridge an open wound without mending it? How to house under a single roof a panoply of essential oppositions and contradictions? He thus allowed his drawings to work through the essential paradoxes at the heart of his project: How to give a void form without filling it in? How to give architectural form to the formless and to challenge the very attempt to house such memory?

The exhibition halls themselves are spacious but so irregular in their shapes (cut through by enclosed voids and concrete trusses) that one never gains a sense of continuous passage. In fact, a total of six voids cut through the museum on both horizontal and vertical planes. Of these six, only the last one is accessible to visitors via the basement. The spaces inside the museum are to be construed as "open narratives," Libeskind said, "which in their architecture seek to provide the museumgoer with new insights into the collection, and in particular, the relation and significance of the Jewish Department to the museum as a whole."[6] Instead of merely housing the collection, this building would, in other words, seek to estrange it from the viewers' own preconceptions. The interior of the building is thus interrupted by smaller, individual structures, shells housing the voids running throughout the structure, each painted graphite–black. They completely alter any sense of continuity or narrative flow and suggest instead architectural, spatial, and thematic gaps in the presentation of Jewish history in Berlin. The absence of Berlin's Jews, as embodied by these voids, is meant to haunt any retrospective presentation of their past here.

By the time the Jewish Museum in Berlin opened its permanent exhibition in September 2001, it had already been visited as an empty shell by hundreds of thousands of visitors, who had come only to experience the building itself. When asked, many of these visitors said they hoped the building would remain empty, and that the building should be designated as the national "memorial to Europe's murdered Jews," a shrine of absence.[7] Indeed, now that the museum is full of artifacts arranged in an exhibition narrative, it is also clear that to some extent the museum's curators have repaired these voids with their exhibition narrative. Now with its thirty connecting bridges, its 7,000 square meters of permanent exhibition space, 450 square meters of temporary exhibition space, and 4,000 square meters of storage, office, and auditorium spaces, the Jewish Museum has roughly three times the space of the former Berlin Museum in the Collegienhaus from which the collection has been removed completely. In any case, all the attention this design has received—both laudatory and skeptical—will generate a final historical irony. Where the city planners had hoped to

Besucher vom Untergeschoss aus zugänglich. Die Innenräume des Museums sind als »offene Erzählungen« konzipiert, so Libeskind, »die mit ihrer Architektur dem Museumsbesucher neue Erkenntnisse über die Sammlung und insbesondere die Bedeutung der Jüdischen Abteilung im und deren Bezug zum Museum als Ganzes vermitteln wollen«.[6] Statt die Sammlung nur zu ›behausen‹, sollte der Bau also — anders gesagt — versuchen, sie den vorgefassten Meinungen der Besucher zu entfremden. Der gesamte Innenraum wird daher von einzelnen kleineren Volumen unterbrochen, von Gehäusen für die den Bau durchziehenden ›voids‹, die sämtlich in dunklem Graphitgrau gestrichen sind. Sie verhindern jedes Gefühl von Kontinuität oder erzählerischem Fluss und suggerieren stattdessen architektonische, räumliche und thematische Lücken in der Präsentation der jüdischen Geschichte in Berlin. Die ›voids‹ verkörpern die von den Berliner Juden hinterlassene Lücke und sollen hier jede retrospektive Präsentation ihrer Geschichte zunichte machen.

Als das Jüdische Museum in Berlin im September 2001 den eigentlichen Museumsbetrieb aufnahm, waren vorher schon Hunderttausende von Besuchern gekommen, um das leere Gebäude selbst zu besichtigen und auf sich wirken zu lassen. Wenn man sie nach ihrer Meinung befragte, äußerten viele, sie hofften, das Gebäude würde leer bleiben, und dass es als nationale ›Gedenkstätte für Europas ermordete Juden‹ – als Schrein der Abwesenden – eingeweiht werden sollte.[7] Tatsächlich wird heute in dem mit Exponaten angefüllten Museum deutlich, dass die Kuratoren die ›voids‹ bis zu einem gewissen Grad mit dem erzählerischen Fluss der Sammlung ›gestopft‹ haben. Mit seinen dreißig Brückenstegen, 7000 m² Ausstellungsflächen für die ständige Sammlung, 450 m² für Sonderausstellungen sowie 4000 m² für Magazin, Büros und Vortragssaal hat das Jüdische Museum heute etwa dreimal so viel Fläche wie das frühere Berlin-Museum im Kollegienhaus, aus dem die Sammlung vollständig entfernt wurde. In jedem Fall wird die große — sowohl bewundernde als auch kritische — Beachtung, die dieser Entwurf gefunden hat, eine letzte historische Ironie beinhalten. Während die Stadtplaner gehofft hatten, die Geschichte der Juden wieder in die Berliner Stadtgeschichte zu integrieren, musste Letztere das von Geistern erfüllte Haus der Erinnerung an die Juden verlassen. Das Jüdische Museum wird fortan ein Prisma bilden, durch das der Rest der Welt Berlins jüdische Vergangenheit kennen lernen wird.

### Israel

Wie jeder Staat erinnert auch Israel seine Geschichte gemäß den eigenen nationalen Mythen und Idealen wie auch den aktuellen politischen Erfordernissen. Zuweilen ambivalent, zuweilen lautstark schwankt die offizielle israelische Haltung zum Gedenken an den Holocaust seit langem zwischen dem Bedürfnis nach Erinnern und Vergessen, zwischen der gewaltigen staatsbildenden Leistung der Gründer und den Gründen für die Errichtung dieses Staates, zwischen den Erinnerungen überlebender Opfer und denen der Widerstandskämpfer. Einerseits betrachteten frühe Staatsangehörige wie David Ben-Gurion den Holocaust als die letzte Konsequenz des jüdischen Lebens in der Fremde. Andererseits erkannten die Staatsangehörigen aber auch, dass sie dem Holocaust auf perverse Weise Dank schuldeten, weil er letzten Endes den Beweis für die zionistische These erbrachte, dass die Juden ohne Staat und ohne die Macht zur Selbstverteidigung im Exil stets potentielle Opfer genau dieser Art von Verfolgung und Vernichtung sein würden.[8]

Ironischerweise haben die Gründer, gerade indem sie die Daseinsberechtigung ihres Staates vom Holocaust ableiteten, die Shoah auch ins

integrate Jewish history into the history of Berlin, the latter has had to leave the haunted house of Jewish memory. The Jewish Museum will now be the prism through which the rest of the world will come to know Berlin's Jewish past.

### Israel

Like any state, Israel also remembers the past according to its national myths and ideals, its current political needs. At times ambivalent, at times strident, the official approach to Holocaust memory in Israel has long been torn between the simultaneous need to remember and to forget, between the early founders' enormous state-building task and the reasons why such a state was necessary, between the survivors' memory of victims and the fighters' memory of resistance. On the one hand, early statists like David Ben-Gurion regarded the Holocaust as the ultimate fruit of Jewish life in exile. On the other hand, the statists also recognized their perverse debt to the Holocaust: it had, after all,

Moshe Safdie, Children's Memorial, Yad Vashem, Jerusalem, 1998
Moshe Safdie, Gedenkstätte für Kinder, Yad Vashem, Jerusalem, 1998

seemed to prove the Zionist dictum that without a state and the power to defend themselves, Jews in exile would always be vulnerable to just this kind of destruction.[8]

Ironically, however, by linking the state's *raison d'etre* to the Holocaust, the early founders also located the Shoah at the center of national identity: Israel would be a nation condemned to defining itself in opposition to that very event that makes it necessary. The question for the early state became: How to negate the Diaspora and put it behind the "new Jews" of Israel while basing the need for new Jews in the memory of Shoah? How to remember the Holocaust in Israel without allowing it to constitute the center of one's Jewish identity? In part, the answer has been a forced distinction between the Israeli and the "*galut* (or exilic) Jew." According to this distinction, the Jew in exile has known only defenselessness and destruction, the Israeli has known fighting and self-preservation. Such a stereotype negates, of course, the early reality of Israel as an immigrant nation whose population in 1948 was over 50% Holocaust survivors. To some extent, this dichotomy is expressed in Israel by the ubiquitous twinning of martyrs and heroes in

Zentrum ihrer nationalen Identität gerückt. In der Folge sollte Israel als Staat dazu verdammt sein, sich selbst im Widerstand gegen ebenjenes Ereignis zu definieren, das seine Gründung überhaupt erst erforderlich gemacht hatte. Die Kernfragen für das frühe Staatswesen wurden: Wie negiert man die Diaspora und lässt sie mit den ›neuen Juden‹ des Staates Israel hinter sich, während man doch das Bedürfnis nach diesen ›neuen Juden‹ mit der Erinnerung an die Shoah begründet? Wie kann man in Israel an den Holocaust erinnern, ohne zuzulassen, dass er zum Kern jüdischer Identität wird? Die Antwort hat zum Teil in der künstlichen Unterscheidung zwischen Israelis und ›galut‹ (Exil)-Juden bestanden, derzufolge der Jude im Exil nur Ohnmacht und Vernichtung erfahren hat, während der Israeli auf Kampf und Selbsterhaltung zurückblickt. Diese stereotype Erklärung leugnet natürlich die Realität der ersten Jahre nach der Gründung Israels als eines Einwandererlandes, dessen Bevölkerung 1948 zu über fünfzig Prozent aus Überlebenden des Holocaust bestand. Bis zu einem gewissen Grad drückt sich diese Dichotomie in Israel durch das Nebeneinander von Märtyrern und Helden in der Ikonografie der Gedenkstätten des Landes aus. In dieser Mischung sind die Opfer vor allem deshalb denkwürdig, weil sie den Bedarf an Kämpfern demonstrieren, an die man ihrerseits wegen ihres Beitrags zur Staatsgründung erinnert. Die Märtyrer sind nicht vergessen, sondern werden als Helden geehrt, als die Ersten, die bei der Verteidigung ihres Landes gefallen sind.

Einerseits scheint die Existenz des Beth Hatefutsoth in Tel Aviv, das man als traditionelles jüdisches Museum beschreiben könnte und das dem Leben der Juden in der Diaspora gewidmet ist, die offizielle israelische Version der in alle Welt zerstreuten Juden als tote oder verkümmerte Zivilisation zu verkörpern. Als Museumsgegenstand wird das Leben in der Diaspora in der Vergangenheitsform dargestellt. Während europäische Mahnmale und Museen — speziell diejenigen an den Standorten der ehemaligen Konzentrationslager — unweigerlich die Vernichtung der Juden fokussieren und das Jahrtausend jüdischen Lebens in Europa bis zum Zweiten Weltkrieg fast völlig ausklammern, stellen die entsprechenden Institutionen in Israel die Ereignisse in ein historisches Kontinuum, das jüdisches Leben vor und nach der Vernichtung umfasst. In israelischen Museen in Kibbuzzim — zum Beispiel in Lohamei Hageta'ot (Ghettokämpfer), Tel Yitzchak, Givat Chaim und Yad Mordechai — wird nicht so sehr der Genozid an den Juden, sondern ihr Leben vor und während des Holocaust hervorgehoben, wobei das Leben nach 1945 überwiegend in Israel stattgefunden hat.

Von allen Gedenkstätten in Israel hat nur die Märtyrer- und Helden-Gedenkstätte in Yad Vashem das offizielle staatliche ›Imprimatur‹ erhalten. Schon zur Zeit der Geburtswehen und der Aufbauphase des Staates Israel eingerichtet, sollte Yad Vashem von Anfang an als integraler Bestandteil der gesellschaftlichen Infrastruktur der Nation angesehen werden. Als einer der Ecksteine der Staatsgründung sollte Yad Vashem die Ideale und das Selbstverständnis des Staates Israel teilen und unterstützen. Mit seiner eklektischen Ansammlung von Monumenten im Freien, Ausstellungshallen und umfangreichen Archiven fungiert Yad Vashem als National-

Israel's memorial iconography. In this mixed figure, the victims are memorable primarily for the ways they demonstrate the need for fighters, who, in turn, are remembered for their part in the state's founding. The martyrs are not forgotten here but are recollected heroically as the first to fall in defense of the state itself.

On the one hand, the very existence of what some might regard as a traditional Jewish Museum in Tel Aviv—Beth Hatefutsoth—dedicated to the Diaspora seems to epitomize the official Israeli view of dispersed Jewry as a dead and withered civilization. As museum object, life in the Diaspora is addressed in the past tense. At the same time, however, where memorials and museums in Europe, especially those located at the sites of destruction, focus relentlessly on the annihilation of Jews and almost totally neglect the millennium of Jewish life in Europe before the war, those in Israel locate events in a historical continuum that includes Jewish life before and after the destruction. In Israeli museums at kibbutzim like Lohamei Hageta'ot (ghetto fighters), Tel Yitzchak, Givat Chaim, and Yad Mordechai, Jewish life before and during the Holocaust is emphasized over the killing itself—and Jewish life after the Holocaust is to be found primarily in Israel.

Of all the memorial centers in Israel, only Yad Vashem Martyrs' and Heroes' Remembrance Authority bears the explicit imprimatur of the state. Conceived in the throes of the state's birth and building, Yad Vashem would be regarded from the outset as an integral part of Israel's civic infrastructure. As one of the state's foundational cornerstones, Yad Vashem would both share and buttress the state's ideals and self-definition. In its eclectic amalgamation of outdoor monuments, exhibition halls, and massive archives, Yad Vashem functions as a national shrine to both Israeli pride in heroism and shame in victimization. The foundation stone for Yad Vashem was thus laid into the hillside just west of the national military cemetery at Mount Herzl on 29 July 1954, in a ceremony that turned this entire area into Har Hazikaron (Memorial Hill).[9] In this way, Yad Vashem would be regarded as a topographical extension of the national cemetery, where Israel's ideological founder, Theodor Herzl, lay alongside Israel's fallen soldiers, including Hannah Senesh, Israel's martyred heroine ideal of the Holocaust.[10] A new historical space would be created, in which events of the Holocaust and the state's founding would quite literally be recalled side by side.

As if trying to keep pace with the state's own growth, Yad Vashem has continued to expand its reservoir of images, sculptures, and exhibitions: as the state and its official memory of the Holocaust evolves, so too has the shape of memory at Yad Vashem.

From the beginning, almost every year has witnessed another unveiling here of a new memorial sculpture or gardens placed around the grounds, including reproductions of memorial sculptures from the Warsaw Ghetto and Dachau. A monument and plaza commemorating Jewish soldiers in the allied forces was added in 1985, a children's memorial in 1988. A memorial sculpture commemorating four martyred women, heroines of the Auschwitz *Sonderkommando* uprising, was dedicated in 1991. A huge project, "The Valley of Destroyed Communities," was completed in 1992. In all cases, however, Yad Vashem concerned itself only with the destruction of Jews during the war—not with other groups murdered en masse by the Nazis. Even so, the construction of memory at Yad Vashem has spanned the entire history of the state itself, paralleling the state's self-construction. For this reason, it seems clear that the building of memorials and new spaces will be

Lippa Yahalom, Dan Zur, Valley of Destroyed Communities, Yad Vashem, Jerusalem, 1992
Lippa Yahalom, Dan Zur, Tal der zerstörten Gemeinden, Yad Vashem, Jerusalem, 1992

heiligtum für den Stolz der Israelis auf ihren Heroismus und zugleich ihre Scham über die Opferrolle ihres Volkes. Am 29. Juli 1954 wurde deshalb der Grundstein für Yad Vashem an einem Hang unmittelbar westlich des nationalen Militärfriedhofs am Mount Herzl gelegt, in einer Feier, die das gesamte Hügelgelände zum Har Hasikaron (Gedenkberg) machte.[9] Auf diese Weise sollte Yad Vashem die topografische Erweiterung des Nationalfriedhofs bilden, auf dem Israels geistiger Gründervater Theodor Herzl inmitten der gefallenen israelischen Soldaten begraben liegt, zu denen auch Hannah Senesh gehört, Israels Nationalheldin und vorbildliche Märtyrerin des Holocaust.[10] Hier sollte ein neuer historischer Ort entstehen, an dem die Ereignisse des Holocaust und der Staatsgründung gleichzeitig in Erinnerung gerufen werden können.

Als hätte die Gedenkstätte mit dem Wachstum des Staates Schritt halten wollen, hat Yad Vashem seinen Fundus an Bildern, Skulpturen und Ausstellungen ständig erweitert. Mit der Entwicklung des Staates und dessen offizieller Erinnerung an den Holocaust haben sich auch Form und Inhalt des Gedenkens in Yad Vashem weiterentwickelt.

never be officially completed, that as the state grows, so too will its memorial undergirding.

Indeed, as the state has begun to recognize the fact of its plural and multiethnic society, and as it recognizes its own debt to globalization, its perception of the Holocaust has also begun to evolve to include other than Jewish victims of the Nazis. With a new generation's mandate in mind, Yad Vashem has thus completely revamped its historical exhibition to reflect a new generation's reasons for remembering such history in the first place. The most significant of the many changes now underway in Yad Vashem's new Historical Museum, therefore, is a narrative that includes not just Jewish victims of the Nazis but also the Gypsies, Jehovah's Witnesses, political prisoners, homosexuals, and even Polish clergy and German victims of the Nazis' early T-4 (euthanasia) program for the mass murder of disabled and handicapped. In a land of immigrants—including Christian Russian spouses of Jewish immigrants from the former Soviet Union and Ethiopian Jews—and in a time when young people are increasingly looking outward at other groups of contemporary victims in the world around them—Yad Vashem also now sees the need to tell the stories of victims other than Jews. With a new-found grasp of itself as a plural, immigrant nation, Israel's national institutions have begun to negate the traditional Zionist negation of the Diaspora.

### America

In 1964, when a group of Jewish-American survivors of the Warsaw Ghetto Uprising submitted a design for a Holocaust memorial to New York City's Arts Commission, they were turned down for three reasons. First, the proposed design by Nathan Rapoport was simply too big and not aesthetically tasteful. Second, such a monument might inspire other "special groups" to be similarly represented on public land— another regrettable precedent. And finally, the city had to ensure that "monuments in the parks … be limited to events of American history."[11] That is, the Holocaust was not an American experience.

For the Jewish survivors of the Holocaust who had immigrated to America after World War II, and who regarded themselves as typical "new Americans," such an answer challenged their very conception of what it meant to be an American in the first place. For the first time in

The 15th Street / Eisenhower Plaza entrance to the United States Holocaust Memorial Museum, Washington D.C. by Pei, Cobb, Freed & Partners, 1986–93
Eingang an der Ecke 15te Straße / Eisenhower Plaza zum United States Holocaust Memorial Museum, Washington, D.C., von Pei, Cobb, Freed & Partners, 1986–93

Von Anfang an hat es hier fast jedes Jahr die feierliche Enthüllung einer neuen Gedenkskulptur gegeben oder die Anlage neuer Gartenbereiche, in denen Repliken der Denkmäler des Warschauer Ghettos und des Konzentrationslagers Dachau aufgestellt wurden. Ein Mahnmal und ein Platz für jüdische Soldaten in den alliierten Truppen wurden 1985 hinzugefügt, eine Gedenkstätte für Kinder 1988. Eine Gedenkskulptur für vier Frauen, Anführerinnen des Sonderkommando-Aufstands in Auschwitz, wurde 1991 eingeweiht und ein Großprojekt, das ›Tal der zerstörten Gemeinden‹, 1992 fertiggestellt. In allen Fällen hat sich Yad Vashem aber ausschließlich der Vernichtung der Juden während des Zweiten Weltkriegs gewidmet und nicht anderen Bevölkerungsgruppen, an denen die Nazis ebenfalls Massenmord verübten. Und dennoch, Yad Vashems Ausprägung des Erinnerns begleitet die Geschichte des Staates Israel parallel zur Entwicklung der staatlichen Identität. Aus diesem Grund erscheint es logisch, dass die Errichtung neuer Denkmäler und Gebäude nie offiziell abgeschlossen werden wird. Im Zuge des staatlichen Wachstums wird auch seine Untermauerung durch Denkmäler zunehmen.

Seit Israel die Tatsache, dass es eine pluralistische und multiethnische Gesellschaft ist, und die eigene Dankesschuld gegenüber der Globalisierung anzuerkennen begonnen hat, hat sich seine Wahrnehmung des Holocaust verändert und berücksichtigt nun tatsächlich auch andere als nur jüdische Opfer. Im Bewusstsein der Voraussetzungen und Erwartungen einer neuen Generation hat Yad Vashem inzwischen seine historische Ausstellung vollständig umgebaut, um jungen Leuten die Gründe nahe zu bringen, warum sie sich überhaupt erinnern sollten. Die bedeutendste aller Veränderungen, die derzeit in Yad Vashems Historischem Museum vollzogen werden, besteht daher in einer geschichtlichen Darstellung, die nicht nur die jüdischen Opfer der Nazis berücksichtigt, sondern auch Sinti und Roma, die Zeugen Jehovas, politische Gefangene, Homosexuelle und sogar polnische Priester und deutsche Opfer des frühen nationalsozialistischen T-4-Programms (Euthanasie), das den Massenmord an geistig und körperlich Behinderten bedeutete. In einem Land voller Immigranten – darunter christlich-russische Ehefrauen jüdischer Einwanderer aus der ehemaligen Sowjetunion sowie äthiopische Juden – und in einer Zeit, in der junge Menschen zunehmend andere Opfergruppen wahrnehmen, die es heute in ihrer Umwelt gibt, spüren die Verantwortlichen von Yad Vashem nun also auch, dass die Geschichte nichtjüdischer Opfer erzählt werden muss. Infolge des neuen nationalen Selbstverständnisses als pluralistisches Einwandererland haben Israels nationale Institutionen damit begonnen, ihrerseits die traditionelle zionistische Leugnung der Diaspora zu leugnen.

### Amerika

1964 legte eine Gruppe amerikanischer Juden, die den Aufstand im Warschauer Ghetto überlebt hatten, dem Kunstausschuss (Fine Arts Commission) der Stadt New York den Entwurf für ein Holocaust-Mahnmal vor, das jedoch aus drei Gründen abgelehnt wurde: Erstens, hieß es, sei der Entwurf von Nathan Rapoport einfach zu groß und ästhetisch nicht sehr ansprechend. Zweitens, so wurde angeführt, würde ein derartiges Denkmal vielleicht andere ›spezielle Gruppen‹ dazu anregen, in ähnlicher Weise im öffentlichen Raum vertreten sein zu wollen, was einen weiteren bedauerlichen Präzedenzfall schaffen würde. Und drittens müsse die Stadt sicherstellen, dass »Denkmäler in den Parks … sich auf Ereignisse der amerikanischen Geschichte beschränken«.[11] Das hieß also: Der Holocaust war kein amerikanisches Ereignis gewesen.

their minds, a distinction had been drawn between "events of American history" and those of "Americans' history." Did American history begin and end within the nation's geographical borders? Or did it, as most of these immigrants believed, begin in the experiences abroad that drove them to America's shores? With the April 1993 dedication of the U.S. Holocaust Memorial Museum in Washington, DC, it could be said that America has finally recognized the survivors' experiences as part of a national experience—and has in this way made the Holocaust part of American history.

Situated adjacent to the National Mall and within view of the Washington Monument to the right and the Jefferson Memorial across the Tidal Basin to the left, the United States Holocaust Memorial

The Hall of Witness at the United States Holocaust Memorial Museum
Die Halle der Zeugen im United States Holocaust Memorial Museum

Museum is a neighbor to the National Museum of American History and the Smithsonian Institute. It has enshrined, by dint of its placement, not just the history of the Holocaust, but American democratic and egalitarian ideals as they counterpoint the Holocaust.

The official American justification for a national Holocaust museum in the nation's capital was provided by President Jimmy Carter in April 1979. Not only would this museum depict the lives of "new Americans," he said, but it would reinforce America's self-idealization as haven for the world's oppressed. It would thus serve as a universal warning against the bigotry and anti-democratic forces underpinning such a catastrophe and call attention to the potential in all other totalitarian systems for such slaughter.[12] In being defined as the ultimate violation of America's Bill of Rights and as the persecution of plural groups, the Holocaust encompasses all the reasons immigrants—past, present and future—ever had for seeking refuge in America.

Yet other levels of meaning can be found in the very design of the museum itself. "It is my view," the museum's architect, James Ingo Freed has said, "that the Holocaust defines a radical ... break with the optimistic conception of continuous social and political improvement

Für die jüdischen Überlebenden des Holocaust, die nach dem Zweiten Weltkrieg nach Amerika emigriert waren und sich nun als typische ›neue Amerikaner‹ betrachteten, bedeutete diese Antwort eine Verletzung der gängigen Erklärung, was einen Amerikaner überhaupt ausmachte. Zum ersten Mal, so empfanden sie, wurde ein Unterschied gemacht zwischen den »Ereignissen der amerikanischen Geschichte« und denen in der »Geschichte von Amerikanern«. Begann und endete denn die Geschichte Amerikas innerhalb der geografischen Grenzen des Landes? Oder nahm sie ihren Anfang nicht doch – wie die meisten dieser Einwanderer glaubten – mit den Erfahrungen, die sie an die Küsten Amerikas getrieben hatten? Mit der Einweihung des United States Holocaust Memorial Museum in Washington, D.C., im April 1993 haben die Vereinigten Staaten die Erfahrungen der Überlebenden endlich als Teil der amerikanischen Geschichte anerkannt – und damit auch den Holocaust selbst.

Das Museum liegt in der Nähe der National Mall – in Sichtweite des Washington Monument zur Rechten und des Jefferson Memorial jenseits des Tidal Basin zur Linken – und ist Nachbar des National Museum of American History und des Smithsonian Institute. Aufgrund dieser Lage würdigt es nicht nur die Geschichte des Holocaust, sondern auch die amerikanischen Ideale der Egalität und Demokratie als Gegengewicht zum Massenmord.

Die offizielle amerikanische Begründung für den Bau eines nationalen Holocaust-Museums in der Hauptstadt lieferte Präsident Jimmy Carter im April 1979. Dieses Museum würde nicht nur die Lebensgeschichten der ›neuen Amerikaner‹ erzählen, so sagte er, sondern auch Amerikas Selbstverständnis als sicherer Hafen für die Unterdrückten der Welt bekräftigen. Es würde daher als universelle Warnung gegen die Bigotterie und die anti-demokratischen Kräfte dienen, die derartige Katastrophen erst ermöglichten, und auf das Potential für derartige Massaker in allen anderen totalitären Systemen aufmerksam machen.[12] Dadurch, dass der Holocaust als entscheidende Verletzung des amerikanischen Grundgesetzes und als Verfolgung mehrerer Bevölkerungsgruppen definiert wurde, repräsentierte er sämtliche Gründe, aus denen Einwanderer in Amerika Zuflucht gesucht haben, gegenwärtig suchen und auch künftig suchen werden.

Es lassen sich aber noch weitere Bedeutungsebenen in der Gestaltung des Museums entdecken. »Meiner Ansicht nach«, so der Architekt James Ingo Freed, »repräsentiert der Holocaust einen radikalen ... Bruch mit der optimistischen Vorstellung fortwährender sozialer und politischer Fortschritte, die der Sachkultur der westlichen Welt zugrunde liegt.«[13] Diese Einschätzung führte zu einem elementaren architektonischen Dilemma: Wie kann man den Holocaust als irreparablen Bruch im Denken des Westens darstellen, ohne die rigoros durchgesetzte architektonische Harmonie der US-Hauptstadt zu stören? Freeds Lösung bestand in einer äußeren Baugestalt, die den strikten Richtlinien des Kunstausschusses entsprach, und einem Inneren, das die Museumsbesucher metaphorisch von der Hauptstadt entfernt. Als Echo der Gebrochenheit, die bereits in traditionellen jüdischen Trauermotiven abgebildet wird, sah Freeds

underlying the material culture of the West."[13] This view led, in turn, to a fundamental architectural dilemma: How to represent the Holocaust as an irreparable breach in the Western mind without violating the strictly enforced architectural harmony of the nation's capital? Freed's answer was an exterior that conformed to the Fine Arts Commission's strict guidelines and an interior that metaphorically removes visitors from the Capital. In an echo of the brokenness already recalled in traditional Jewish mourning motifs, Freed's design includes skewed angles, exposed steel trusses, and broken walls—all to suggest an architectural discontinuity, rawness, and an absence of reassuring forms.[14]

The discontinuity and fragmentation preserved in the museum's interior architectural space cannot, however, be similarly conveyed in the exhibition narrative itself. For like all narrative, that created in the exhibition necessarily depends on the continuous sequence of its telling, the integrative coherence of history's telling. Though housed in a structure reverberating brokenness and the impossibility of repair, the exhibition itself exists solely on the strength of its internal logic, the linear sequence by which events of the Holocaust are ordered in their telling. The exhibition begins with the rise of Nazism and its post–World War I historical context. And then, because the American experience of Nazi Germany in the thirties was necessarily mediated by newsreels, papers, and radio broadcasts, the media-experience itself is recreated in the next part of the permanent exhibition. This is followed by sections on deportation, ghettoization, mass murder, concentration camps, resistance, and rescuers. Finally, like the museum narratives in Israel, where lives were re-built after the Holocaust, this exhibit also ends with the "return to life." For this is the story of an ideal shared by America and Israel: both see themselves as lands of refuge and freedom. What follows is then a story of immigration, the long journey from "old world" D.P. Camps, ravaged towns and anti-Semitism to the "new worlds" of Jewish statehood and American egalitarianism. It is the story of America's absorption of both immigrants and their memories, the gradual integration of Holocaust memory into American civic culture. For at the end, the museum suggests itself as the ultimate triumph of America's absorption of immigrants, the integration of immigrant memory into the topographical heart of American memory.

A similar appreciation for the richness of Jewish life in America is found in New York City's "Museum of Jewish Heritage – A Living Memorial to the Holocaust," located on the Battery in downtown Manhattan, within sight of the Statue of Liberty and Ellis Island, and only blocks removed from Ground Zero of the September 11, 2001 World Trade Center attacks. Though it opened only in September 1997, the Museum of Jewish Heritage is the culmination of what was to be America's first Holocaust memorial. Years of city and state debates over where and how to commemorate the Holocaust in New York combined with numerous competing fundraising agendas to delay the building of what is now one of the city's most prominent memorial institutions. As its name suggests, the Museum of Jewish Heritage integrates the Holocaust into a Jewish past, present and future, locating it in long continuum of Jewish life in Europe before the war and then after the war in Israel and America.

Looking out over New York harbor from the exhibition halls, visitors are able to hold in mind both the time of destruction in Europe and the safety of refuge in America, life before and after the catastrophe. With its much-lauded *Memorial Garden of Stones,* designed by the landscape-artist Andy Goldsworthy (September 2003), the Museum of

Museum of Jewish Heritage, New York, 1997    Museum of Jewish Heritage, New York, 1997

Entwurf schiefe Winkel, unverkleidete Stahlträger und durchbrochene Wände vor, die allesamt architektonische Brechungen, Unfertigkeit und das Fehlen beruhigender Formen suggerieren sollten.[14]

Die in den Innenräumen des Museums konservierte Gebrochenheit und Fragmentierung lässt sich indessen nicht auf die gleiche Weise im erzählerischen Fluss der Ausstellung wiederholen. Wie alle Erzählungen kommt auch die museale hier nicht ohne eine kontinuierliche Sequenz aus, die die integrative Kohärenz jeder geschichtlichen Darstellung bildet. Obwohl sie in einem Gebäude untergebracht ist, das in allen Winkeln von Brüchen und der Unmöglichkeit widerhallt, sie zu heilen, lebt die Ausstellung selbst allein von der Kraft ihrer inneren Logik, der linear angeordneten Folge von Ereignissen der Judenvernichtung. Die Ausstellung beginnt mit dem Aufstieg der Nationalsozialisten und dem historischen Kontext nach dem Ersten Weltkrieg. Im anschließenden Teil der ständigen Ausstellung wird das Erleben der Ereignisse durch die Medien rekonstruiert, weil die amerikanische Wahrnehmung des nationalsozialistischen Deutschlands in den 1930er Jahren natürlich von Wochenschauen, Zeitungsberichten und Radiosendungen geprägt wurde. Die folgende Abteilung dokumentiert die Deportationen, den Aufbau von Ghettos, den Massenmord, die Konzentrationslager, den Widerstand und die Helfer und Retter. Den Abschluss bilden schließlich wie auch in den israelischen Holocaust-Museen Berichte darüber, wie die Überlebenden wieder neu anfingen – über ihre »Rückkehr ins Leben« –, denn dies ist Amerikas und Israels gemeinsame Geschichte: Beide verstehen sich als Länder der Zuflucht und Freiheit. Es folgt die Geschichte der Einwanderung, der langen Reise von den Flüchtlingslagern, zerbombten Städten und dem Antisemitismus der ›alten Welt‹ in die ›neuen Welten‹ des israelischen Staatsbürgertums und der amerikanischen Egalität. Es wird erzählt, wie Amerika sowohl die Einwanderer als auch ihre Erlebnisse und Erfahrungen absorbierte und die Erinnerung an den Holocaust Eingang in die amerikanische Gesellschaft und Kultur fand. Letztlich stellt das Museum selbst den endgültigen Sieg der amerikanischen Einbürgerung von Einwanderern und der Integration ihrer Erinnerungen in das topografische Herz des US-geschichtlichen Gedächtnisses dar.

Eine ähnliche Wertschätzung des reichen jüdischen Lebens in Amerika findet sich im New Yorker Museum of Jewish Heritage mit dem Untertitel »Ein lebendiges Denkmal für den Holocaust« am Battery Park an der Südwestspitze Manhattans, in Sichtweite von Ellis Island und der Freiheitsstatue und nur wenige Straßenblöcke vom ›Ground Zero‹ des am

*Memorial Garden of Stones* by Andy Goldsworthy at the Museum of Jewish Heritage, New York
*Gedenkgarten der Steine* von Andy Goldsworthy im Museum of Jewish Heritage, New York

Jewish Heritage has fully integrated the symbols of universal and Jewish material culture, each now grasped in terms of the other. Sapling trees of life and regeneration now grow out of eighteen boulders to embody the miracle of new life taking hold wherever it can, the indomitable spirit of survivors, and by extension, all immigrants who have been cast voluntarily or involuntarily on America's shore.

In a way, the Museum of Jewish Heritage thus constitutes a bridge between the United States Holocaust Memorial Museum in Washington and America's greatest and most important Jewish Museum, located on Fifth Avenue in New York City. Established in 1904 with a gift of some twenty-six Jewish ceremonial art objects to the Jewish Theological Seminary, The Jewish Museum now houses more than 28,000 artifacts, including painting, sculpture, works on paper, photographs, archaeological artifacts, ceremonial objects, and broadcast media. As described in its mission statement, the Jewish Museum's permanent exhibition, *Culture and Continuity: The Jewish Journey*, uses its collection of art and artifacts to examine "the Jewish experience as it has evolved from antiquity to the present, over 4,000 years, and asks two vital questions: How has Judaism been able to thrive for thousands of years across the globe, often in difficult and even tragic circumstances? What constitutes the essence of Jewish identity?"

The answers proposed by the museum are as multi-faceted and complex as its critically acclaimed exhibitions, which have taken venerated objects, contemporary art, and controversial themes as their points of departure. When the Jewish Museum moved into the Warburg Mansion in 1947, located on what is called New York's "Museum Mile" (which includes the Metropolitan and Guggenheim Museums, among others), its collections and exhibitions came to be regarded by visitors as part and parcel of America's larger composite cultural legacy. As the permanent exhibition has integrated the mass murder of European Jews into a much longer, and still unfolding, narrative of Jewish life around the globe, its rotating schedule of temporary exhibitions alternates among cultural, aesthetic, and social themes, with exhibitions on Holocaust-related themes coming only once every few years. As devastating as it was, the Holocaust is thus viewed at the Jewish Museum through the prism of a 4,000-year journey, as is Jewish identity itself, a constantly changing and adapting negotiation between Jewish life and culture and its national surroundings.

11. September 2001 von Terroristen zerstörten World Trade Center entfernt. Im September 1997 eröffnet, stellt dieses Museum für jüdische Geschichte und Kultur den Kulminationspunkt dessen dar, was Amerikas erste Holocaust-Gedenkstätte werden sollte. Jahrelang war – begleitet von zahlreichen konkurrierenden Spendenwerbekampagnen – auf städtischer und nationaler Ebene darüber diskutiert und gestritten worden, wo und wie in New York an den Holocaust erinnert werden müsse. Das zögerte den Bau eines Museums hinaus, das heute zu den bekanntesten Gedenkstätten der Stadt zählt. Wie der Name schon andeutet, integriert es den Holocaust in die Geschichte, Gegenwart und Zukunft der Juden und platziert ihn in das lange Kontinuum jüdischen Lebens in Europa vor dem Krieg und danach in Israel und Amerika.

Der Blick von den Ausstellungshallen über den Hafen von New York ist dazu angetan, in den Besuchern Gedanken an die Zeit der Vernichtung in Europa und die sichere Zuflucht in Amerika, also an das Leben vor und nach der Katastrophe, zu wecken. Mit dem viel gepriesenen *Gedenkgarten der Steine* des Landschaftskünstlers Andy Goldsworthy (im September 2003 eröffnet) stellt das Museum of Jewish Heritage nun die Symbole der allgemeinen sowie spezifisch jüdischen Kultur als völlig miteinander verwoben und sich gegenseitig prägend dar. Junge Bäume als Symbole des Lebens und der Erneuerung wachsen aus 18 Felsblöcken empor und verkörpern so das Wunder neuen Lebens, das, wo nur immer möglich, aufkeimt, den unbeugsamen Mut der Überlebenden wie auch aller anderen Einwanderer, die freiwillig oder unfreiwillig an Amerikas Küsten landeten.

In gewisser Weise bildet das Museum of Jewish Heritage daher eine Brücke zwischen dem United States Holocaust Memorial Museum in Washington und Amerikas größtem und bedeutendstem Jüdischen Museum an der New Yorker Fifth Avenue. Dessen Sammlung begann 1904 mit der Schenkung von 26 künstlerisch wertvollen jüdischen Kultgegenständen an das Seminar für Jüdische Theologie. Heute besitzt das Museum über 28.000 Artefakte, von Gemälden und Plastiken über Papierarbeiten, Fotografien, archäologischen Fundstücken und sakralen Objekten bis hin zu Filmen und Tonträgern. Wie in seiner Satzung definiert, verwendet die Dauerausstellung des Jüdischen Museums mit dem Titel *Kultur und Kontinuität – Die Jüdische Reise* die Sammlungen von Kunst und Artefakten zur Untersuchung der »jüdischen Erfahrung«, die sich von der Antike bis in die Gegenwart über 4 000 Jahre entwickelt hat, und um zwei entscheidende Fragen zu stellen: »Wie ist es dem Judentum Tausende von Jahren gelungen, in aller Welt zu gedeihen, häufig unter schwierigen und sogar tragischen Bedingungen? Was macht das Wesen jüdischer Identität aus?«

Die vorgeschlagenen Antworten sind so facettenreich und vielfältig wie die kritisch gewürdigten Ausstellungen des Museums zu Kultobjekten, Gegenwartskunst oder einer Reihe von umstrittenen Themen. Nachdem das Jüdische Museum 1947 in das Warburg Mansion an der so genannten New Yorker Museumsmeile (mit unter anderem dem Metropolitan und dem Guggenheim Museum) umgezogen war, betrachteten seine Besucher die Sammlungen und Ausstellungen allmählich als Teil von Amerikas umfassenderem, aus vielen Quellen gespeistem Kulturerbe. Da die ständige Sammlung den Massenmord an den europäischen Juden in die viel ältere und sich weiter fortsetzende Geschichte des jüdischen Lebens rund um den Globus einordnet, werden wechselnde Ausstellungen zu kulturellen, künstlerischen und gesellschaftlichen Themen gezeigt und nur alle paar Jahre einmal solche, die sich mit dem Holocaust befassen. So entsetzlich der Holocaust auch war, im New Yorker Jüdischen

1 This section has been adapted from James E. Young, *At Memory's Edge: After-images of the Holocaust in Contemporary Art and Architecture,* New Haven and London 2000.

2 See Vera Bendt, "Das Jüdische Museum," in *Wegweiser durch das jüdische Berlin: Geschichte und Gegenwart,* Berlin 1987, pp. 200–09.

3 Hermann Simon, "Das Berliner Jüdische Museum in der Oranienburger Strasse," p. 34. Quoted in Martina Weinland and Kurt Winkler, *Das Jüdische Museum im Stadtmuseum Berlin: Eine Dokumentation*, Berlin 1997, p. 10.

4 The issue of what constitutes Jewish art remains as fraught as ever in contemporary discussions of national and ethnic art. Among others, see Joseph Gutmann, "Is There a Jewish Art?" in *The Visual Dimension: Aspects of Jewish Art*, ed. Claire Moore, Boulder CO 1993, pp. 1–20.

5 Though this was Libeskind's first full commission, it was not his first completed building, which is the Felix Nussbaum Museum in Osnabrück. (Refer to Jury Report).

6 *Realisierungswettbewerb*, p. 169.

7 See James E. Young, *At Memory's Edge: After-Images of the Holocaust in Contemporary Art and Architecture,* New Haven and London 2000, in which I tell the entire story of Germany's national *Memorial for the murdered Jews of Europe* proposed for Berlin, including Libeskind's proposed design. In submitting a design for this memorial, the architect made clear that he did not want his museum design for a Jewish Museum to be turned into a Holocaust memorial.

8 In a bulletin prepared for army commanders on Holocaust Remembrance Day in Israel, the meaning of Holocaust memory is made explicit: "The Zionist solution establishing the State of Israel was intended to provide an answer to the problem of the existence of the Jewish people, in view of the fact that all other solutions had failed. The Holocaust proved, in all its horror, that in the twentieth century, the survival of the Jews is not assured as long as they are not masters of their fate and as long as they do not have the power to defend their survival." See "Informational Guidelines to the Commander," as quoted in Charles S. Liebman and Eliezer Don-Yehiya, *Civil Religion in Israel: Traditional Judaism and Political Culture in the Jewish State,* Berkeley and Los Angeles 1983, p. 184.

9 In the words of former prime minister Levi Eshkol, "The very struggle against the adversary [during the Holocaust] and the victory which followed [Israel's War of Independence] laid the foundations for the revival of our national independence. Seen in this light the Jewish fight against the Nazis and the War of Independence were, in fact, a single protracted battle. The geographical proximity between Yad Vashem and Mount Herzl thus expresses far more than mere physical closeness." *Yad Vashem Bulletin,* 16, 1965, p. 62.
Eshkol's words are also cited in an excellent discussion of Yad Vashem's proximity to Mount Herzl by Don Handelman, *Models and Mirrors: Towards an Anthropology of Public Events,* Cambridge and New York 1990, p. 201.

10 For further details, see *Hannah Senesh: Her Life & Diary*, introduction by Abba Eban, New York 1973.

11 Both Platt and Morris are quoted in "City Rejects Park Memorials to Slain Jews," *New York Times*, 11 February 1965, p. 1; and in "2 Jewish Monuments Barred from Park," *New York World Telegram and Sun*, 10 February 1965, p. 1.

12 From an undated press release of the United States Holocaust Memorial Council.

13 James Ingo Freed, *The United States Holocaust Memorial Museum: What Can It Be?,* printed by the United States Holocaust Memorial Museum, Washington DC (no date).

14 For a full-length study of United States Holocaust Memorial Museum, see Edward T. Linenthal, *Preserving Memory: The Struggle to Create America's Holocaust Museum,* New York 1995.

Museum wird er durch das Prisma einer 4000 Jahre währenden Reise betrachtet, ebenso wie die jüdische Identität – ein sich ständig veränderndes Selbstverständnis zwischen jüdischer Tradition und Kultur und der Anpassung an das jeweilige nationale Lebensumfeld.

1 Dieses Kapitel ist eine überarbeitete Fassung von: James E. Young, *At Memory's Edge: After-images of the Holocaust in Contemporary Art and Architecture,* New Haven/London 2000.

2 Vgl. Vera Bendt, »Das Jüdische Museum«, in: *Wegweiser durch das jüdische Berlin: Geschichte und Gegenwart,* Berlin 1987, S. 200–09.

3 Hermann Simon, »Das Berliner Jüdische Museum in der Oranienburger Straße«, S. 34, zitiert in: Martina Weinland, Kurt Winkler, *Das Jüdische Museum im Stadtmuseum Berlin: Eine Dokumentation,* Berlin 1997, S. 10.

4 Die Frage nach den Kriterien, aufgrund derer Kunst als jüdisch eingestuft werden kann, ist in der zeitgenössischen Diskussion nationaler und ethnischer Kunst nach wie vor problematisch. Vgl. u. a.: Joseph Gutmann, »Is There a Jewish Art?«, in: Claire Moore (Hrsg.), *The Visual Dimension: Aspects of Jewish Art,* Boulder 1993, S. 1–20.

5 Dies war zwar Libeskinds erster kompletter Bauauftrag, aber nicht sein erstes vollendetes Gebäude. Das erste war das Felix-Nussbaum-Museum in Osnabrück. Vgl. Jurybericht.

6 Realisierungswettbewerb, S. 169.

7 Vgl. James E. Young, op. cit. (Anm. 1). In dieser Publikation erzähle ich die ganze Geschichte des deutschen *Mahnmals für die ermordeten Juden Europas* in Berlin, einschließlich des von Libeskind vorgelegten Projekts. Als er seinen Entwurf für das Mahnmal vorstellte, erklärte der Architekt, er wolle nicht, dass sein Entwurf für ein Jüdisches Museum zum Holocaust-Mahnmal gemacht würde.

8 In einem für Armeekommandeure verfassten Bulletin zum Holocaust-Gedenktag in Israel wird der Sinn eines Holocaust-Gedenktags erklärt: »Der zionistische Gedanke der Gründung des Staates Israel sollte in Anbetracht der Tatsache, dass alle anderen Lösungen erfolglos geblieben waren, das existentielle Problem des jüdischen Volkes lösen. Mit all seinen Schrecken hat der Holocaust gezeigt, dass das Überleben der Juden im 20. Jahrhundert nicht gesichert ist, solange sie nicht selber Herren ihres Schicksals sind und solange sie nicht die Macht haben, um ihr Überleben zu kämpfen.« Vgl. »Informational Guidelines to the Commander«, zitiert in: Charles S. Liebman, Eliezer Don-Yehiya, *Civil Religion in Israel: Traditional Judaism and Political Culture in the Jewish State*, Berkeley/Los Angeles 1983, S. 184.

9 In den Worten des früheren Premierministers Levi Eshkol: »Der Kampf gegen den Feind [während des Holocaust] und der darauf folgende Sieg [in Israels Freiheitskampf] legten die Grundlagen für die Wiedergewinnung unserer nationalen Freiheit. In diesem Lichte besehen waren der Kampf der Juden gegen die Nazis und der Unabhängigkeitskrieg im Grunde eine einzige in die Länge gezogene Schlacht. Die geografische Nähe zwischen Yad Vashem und Mount Herzl drückt daher viel mehr aus als nur physische Nähe.« *Yad Vashem Bulletin*, 16, 1965, S. 62.
Eshkols Worte werden auch in den hervorragenden Ausführungen Don Handelmans zu Yad Vashems Nähe zum Mount Herzl zitiert: Don Handelman, *Models and Mirrors: Towards an Anthropology of Public Events,* Cambridge/New York 1990, S. 201.

10 Weitere Einzelheiten in: *Hannah Senesh: Her Life and Diary*, Einführung von Abba Eban, New York 1973.

11 Platt und Morris werden beide zitiert in: »City Rejects Park Memorials to Slain Jews«, in: *New York Times,* 11. 2. 1965, S. 1; und: »2 Jewish Monuments Barred from Park«, in: *New York World Telegram and Sun,* 10. 2. 1965, S. 1.

12 Aus einem undatierten Pressebericht des United States Holocaust Memorial Council.

13 James Ingo Freed, *The United States Holocaust Memorial Museum: What Can It Be?*, Druck: United States Holocaust Memorial Museum, Washington, D.C. (o. J.).

14 Zur ausführlichen Untersuchung des United States Holocaust Memorial Museum vgl.: Edward T. Linenthal, *Preserving Memory: The Struggle to Create America's Holocaust Museum,* New York 1995.

Museums
Museen

Ralph Appelbaum

**Holocaust Museum Houston**
Holocaust Museum Houston

Houston, Texas | USA
1993–1996

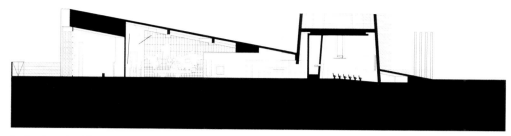

Section through exhibition area and theater    Schnitt durch Ausstellungsbereich und Theater

Ralph Appelbaum (b. 1942) and his firm, Ralph Appelbaum Associates of New York, specialize in interpretive museum installations. They attained wide recognition for their installation design at the United States Holocaust Memorial Museum in Washington, DC (1993). In Houston, Appelbaum Associates designed not just an installation for the Holocaust Museum Houston but the building that contains it, in association with the architect Mark Mucasey. The Houston museum is enigmatic and compelling. It consists of a reinforced concrete wedge that inclines from ground level to a height of nearly forty feet. Protruding from the lower end of the wedge is a thick, truncated cone faced with dark gray brick. An existing one-story, flat-roofed building to which Appelbaum's museum attaches is set back behind the wedge.

The Holocaust Museum Houston is not big. But its geometric shapes, skewed orientation, and blunt scale compel awareness. The design funnels visitors beneath a trabeated canopy of black-painted steel onto a path that winds through the wedge. The museum's high profiled geometry spatializes the historical narrative of the Nationalists Socialists' attempt to exterminate European Jews in the permanent exhibition Appelbaum Associates designed, *Bearing Witness: A Community Remembers*, which emphasizes the stories of Holocaust survivors who eventually made their ways to Houston.

Arriving visitors move between serpentine walls toward the apex of the windowless, spot-lit interior, past installations tracing the origin and dispersion of the Jewish people. A 180° turn reorients visitors and introduces the rise of the Nazis. As visitors proceed, the historical account becomes denser and space compresses beneath the downward slope of the wedge. A sequence of tight, 180° turns are introduced that confront visitors with graphic images of deportation, internment, and extermination before concluding with the liberation of survivors. At the end of the narrative, visitors are routed into the base of the cone, containing the Herzstein Theater (where a film, *Voices*, enables Houston survivors and their families to tell their stories), before being released back into the entrance lobby.

Appelbaum Associates maintain a delicate balance between the disturbing content of the exhibition and the

Ralph Appelbaum (geb. 1942) und die Mitarbeiter seines New Yorker Büros, Ralph Appelbaum Associates, haben sich auf aussagekräftige Museumsarchitektur spezialisiert. Ihre Ausstellungsarchitektur im United States Holocaust Memorial Museum in Washington, D. C. (1993), hat ihnen weithin Anerkennung verschafft. In Houston gestalteten Appelbaum Associates aber nicht nur die Dauerausstellung für das Holocaust Museum, sondern entwarfen in Zusammenarbeit mit dem Architekten Mark Mucasey auch das Gebäude, in dem sie untergebracht ist. Das Museum wirkt geheimnisvoll und zwingend. Der Keil aus Stahlbeton steigt vom Bodenniveau bis zu einer Höhe von etwas über zwölf Metern an. Aus dem unteren Keilende stößt ein mit dunkelgrauen Ziegeln verkleideter Stumpfkegel hervor. Der bestehende eingeschossige Flachbau, an den Appelbaum das Museum angebaut hat, befindet sich hinter dem Keil.

Das Holocaust Museum Houston ist nicht groß. Seine geometrischen Formen, seine Schrägstellung und sein schroffer Maßstab erregen jedoch Aufmerksamkeit. Das Gestaltungskonzept führt die Besucher unter einer Balkenkonstruktion aus schwarz gestrichenem Stahl auf einen Weg, der sich durch den Keil schlängelt. Die markante Geometrie gibt der geschichtlichen Darstellung des Versuchs der Nationalsozialisten, die europäischen Juden auszulöschen, Raum, und zwar in der von Appelbaum Associates gestalteten Dauerausstellung zu dem Thema *Bearing Witness: A Community Remembers* (Zeugnis ablegen. Eine Gemeinschaft erinnert sich), die sich schwerpunktmäßig mit der Geschichte von Holocaust-Überlebenden beschäftigt, die ihren Weg nach Houston fanden.

Der Weg der Besucher durch das Museum verläuft als von Wänden begrenzte, verschlungene Passage bis zum höchsten Punkt des fensterlosen, von Punktstrahlern beleuchteten Innenraums, vorbei an Installationen, die den Ursprung und die Diaspora der Juden darstellen. Nach einer 180-Grad-Wendung wird den Besuchern der Aufstieg der Nationalsozialisten erklärt. In der Folge wird die historische Erzählung dichter und der Raum unter dem sich nach unten abschrägenden Dach der Keilform immer komprimierter. In einer dichten Folge von serpentinenförmig angeordneten Räumen wird der Besucher mit Bildern von Deportation, Einkerkerung und Auslöschung konfrontiert, bevor abschließend die Befreiung der Überlebenden

unobtrusive precision of their installation design. Their treatment of architectural elements—the concrete wedge, the conical theater, the skewed line of steel columns that converges in a walled rear garden—evokes the infrastructure of the "Final Solution" scenographically but with restraint. Their design incorporates not only the existing building (renamed the Morgan Family Center which contains the Mincberg Gallery, the Boniuk Library and Research Center, and staff offices) but also two spaces by other architects. The Lack Memorial Room, a naturally-lit meditation room at the high end of the wedge, contains light-sensitive installations by the Philadelphia artists Patricia and Robert Moss-Vreeland in a setting by Houston architects Murphy Mears. Outside the Lack Room is the Eric Alexander Garden of Hope by the Houston architect Carlos Jiménez (1999). In its clarity and solemnity, Appelbaum Associates' design absorbs these memorials without loss of narrative economy or emotional impact.

The Jewish identity to be construed from the architecture of the Holocaust Museum Houston is layered, historically situated, and complex. It tenuously reclaims urban space as "Jewish" but in a limited, symbolic capacity, signified by being a historical museum among other educational and cultural institutions that aim to represent facets of culture to a general audience. It is engaged in externalizing associations between Houston and Europe that, ostensibly, seem extraneous to Houston. Yet, from the careers of surrounding personalities to the experiences recalled by Houston's European Jewish residents—even the architecture of neighboring buildings—these associations turn out to be embedded in the history of the city. Architecturally it also establishes oppositional relations with selected adjacent buildings to clarify its differences in intent and content. The subliminal geometry of the design for the Holocaust Museum composes likeness, difference, and circumstance into stable forms that contain, store, and represent the consequences for ordinary people when states identify them as extraneous, expendable, and exterminable.

Stephen Fox

gezeigt wird. Am Ende der Dokumentation führt der Besucherweg in den Sockel des Stumpfkegels, das Herzstein-Theater, wo in dem Film *Voices* einige heute in Houston lebende Holocaust-Überlebende und ihre Familien ihre eigene Geschichte erzählen. Danach wird der Besucher wieder in die Eingangshalle entlassen.

Appelbaum Associates haben die heikle Aufgabe gemeistert, eine Balance zwischen dem erschreckenden Inhalt der Ausstellung und der unaufdringlichen Präzision ihrer Ausstellungsarchitektur herzustellen. Ihre Gestaltung der architektonischen Elemente – des Betonkeils, des konischen Theaters, der schrägen Reihe aus Stahlpfeilern, die in dem von Mauern eingefassten rückseitigen Garten zusammenlaufen – erinnert szenografisch, dabei aber zurückhaltend, an die Infrastruktur der ›Endlösung‹. Der Entwurf integriert nicht nur den Altbau (umbenannt in Morgan Family Center mit Mincberg-Galerie, Boniuk-Bibliothek, Forschungszentrum und Büros), sondern auch zwei von anderen Architekten ausgestattete Räume. Der von Murphy und Mears (Houston) gestaltete Lack Memorial Room, ein natürlich beleuchteter Meditationsraum am hohen Keilende, birgt lichtempfindliche Installationen des Künstlerpaars Patricia und Robert Moss-Vreeland aus Philadelphia. Im Außenbereich vor diesem Raum legte der Houstoner Architekt Carlos Jiménez den Eric-Alexander-Garten der Hoffnung an (1999). Mit seiner Klarheit und feierlichen Würde integriert der Entwurf von Appelbaum Associates diese Gedenkräume, ohne an erzählerischem Ausdruck oder emotionaler Wirkung zu verlieren.

Die an der Baugestalt des Holocaust Museum Houston abzulesende jüdische Identität ist vielschichtig, von historischer Bezüglichkeit und komplex. Unaufdringlich nimmt sie den städtischen Raum wieder als ›jüdischen Raum‹ in Anspruch, aber in begrenzter, symbolischer Kapazität als eine von mehreren Bildungs- und Kulturinstitutionen, die einem breiten Publikum unterschiedliche Facetten seiner Kultur und Geschichte nahe zu bringen versuchen. Das jüdische Museum beschäftigt sich damit, Verbindungen zwischen Houston und Europa aufzudecken, die auf den ersten Blick nichts mit Houston zu tun haben, auf den zweiten aber in den Lebensläufen von Personen aus dem Umfeld von Houstons jüdischen Mitbürgern europäischer Herkunft aufscheinen – bis hin zur Architektur der Nachbarbauten. Somit erweisen sich diese Verbindungen als mit der Stadtgeschichte Houstons eng verwoben. Die Architekten des Museums haben auch oppositionelle Beziehungen zu ausgewählten Gebäuden in der Nachbarschaft hergestellt, um mit ihrem Design die Unterschiede in Zweck und Inhalt hervorzuheben. Die unterschwellige Geometrie in der Gestaltung des Holocaust-Museums hat aus Ähnlichkeiten, Unterschieden und der Umgebung des Baus stabile Baukörper abgeleitet, in denen dokumentiert wird, welche Folgen es für Menschen hat, wenn ihr Land sie als Fremde ansieht, sie für überflüssig erklärt und eliminiert.

Stephen Fox

**Building entrance**  Eingang des Gebäudes

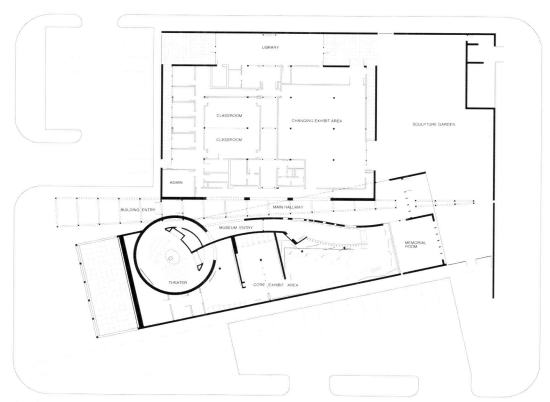

**Floor plan, ground floor**  Grundriss Erdgeschoss

Ralph Appelbaum  **Holocaust Museum Houston**  Holocaust Museum Houston

The construction incorporates elements of concentration camps. Steel columns refer to the six million murdered Jews.
Der Bau nimmt symbolisch Elemente der Konzentrationslager auf. Die Stahlpfeiler verweisen auf die sechs Millionen ermordeter Juden.

**Entrance hall of the exhibition area**
Eingangshalle des Ausstellungsbereichs

Permanent exhibition
Dauerausstellung

Ralph Appelbaum  **Holocaust Museum Houston**  Holocaust Museum Houston

Claus en Kaan

**National Monument
Kamp Vught**
Nationale Gedenkstätte
Kamp Vught

Vught, The Netherlands | Niederlande
2000–2002

Longitudinal section. Left: Memorial room    Längsschnitt. Links der Gedenkraum

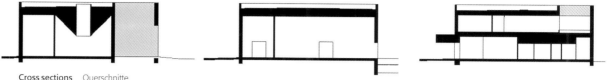

Cross sections    Querschnitte

The Kamp Vught National Monument covers a small part of the former Herzogenbusch SS concentration camp. The camp was in use from January 1943 until September 1944. In that period, more than 31,000 people were detained there. In addition to 12,000 Jews, there were political prisoners, resistance fighters, Sinti and Roma (Gypsies), Jehova's Witnesses, hostages, vagrants, black marketeers, and criminals. For most of the prisoners, Kamp Vught was a transit station on the way to the death camps; however, more than 750 people died from starvation, disease or maltreatment, or were executed here.

The Kamp Vught National Monument first opened in 1990, forty-five years after the end of World War II, on the initiative of a foundation established four years earlier. In 2002, what was left of the camp was restored and one of the barracks was reconstructed. On this occasion, the grounds were discreetly redesigned by Michael van Gessel. Part of the new layout is a large bronze model of the entire camp. That same year, a new entrance pavilion was built based on a design by Claus en Kaan. As a result, the monument, that had been dwarfed by the adjacent penitentiary, has acquired a more emphatic presence. The unpretentious new building testifies to the ability of Claus en Kaan to create dignified and comforting architecture using a timelessly modern idiom, as they had demonstrated previously with their condolatory pavilion at Zorgvlied cemetery in Amsterdam. The entrance pavilion of Kamp Vught eschews any (claim to) monumentality that often burdens this type of charged building project. What distinguishes Felix Claus and Kees Kaan is the extent to which they succeed in lending self-evidence to each of their buildings, be it ordinary housing or offices, or a unique building such as this: their work always looks as if it could have been there for a long time already.

Die Nationale Gedenkstätte Kamp Vught umfasst einen kleinen Teil des ehemaligen SS-Konzentrationslagers Herzogenbusch. Das Lager bestand von Januar 1943 bis September 1944. In dieser Zeit waren dort insgesamt mehr als 31.000 Menschen interniert: neben 12.000 Juden auch politische Gefangene, Widerstandskämpfer, Sinti und Roma, Zeugen Jehovas, Geiseln, Landstreicher, Schwarzhändler und Kriminelle. Für die meisten Gefangenen war Vught ein Durchgangslager auf dem Weg in die Vernichtungslager; mehr als 750 Menschen jedoch kamen hier durch Hunger, Krankheit, Misshandlung oder Exekution ums Leben.

Die Nationale Gedenkstätte Kamp Vught wurde erst 1990, 45 Jahre nach Ende des Zweiten Weltkriegs, auf Initiative einer vier Jahre zuvor gegründeten Stiftung eröffnet. Im Jahr 2002 sind die Teile, die noch vom Lager übrig waren, restauriert und eine der Wohnbaracken rekonstruiert worden. Das Gelände wurde bei dieser Gelegenheit nach einem zurückhaltenden Entwurf von Michael van Gessel neu gestaltet. Teil der neuen Anlage ist ein großes Bronzemodell des gesamten Lagers. Im selben Jahr wurde außerdem ein Eingangsgebäude nach einem Entwurf von Claus en Kaan errichtet. Dadurch hat die Gedenkstätte, die zuvor völlig im Schatten der benachbarten Justizvollzugsanstalt lag, eine nachdrücklichere Präsenz erhalten. Mit dem reduzierten Neubau stellen Claus en Kaan — wie bereits mit ihrem Kondolenzpavillon auf dem Amsterdamer Friedhof Zorgvlied — erneut ihre Fähigkeit unter Beweis, mit einem zeitlos modernen Idiom eine würdige und trostreiche Architektur zu schaffen. Ihr Eingangsgebäude verzichtet auf jeglichen Anspruch auf Monumentalität, die brisante Projekte dieser Art oft belastet. Das Besondere an Felix Claus' und Kees Kaans Arbeiten liegt in der Selbstverständlichkeit, die sie jedem Bauwerk zu verleihen wissen, ob es sich nun um alltäglichen Wohnbau oder Büros handelt oder um ein einzigartiges Gebäude wie dieses: Ihr

**Page** Seite 64
Inner courtyard with memorial plaques from the former execution area
Innenhof mit Gedenktafeln aus dem ehemaligen Exekutionsbereich

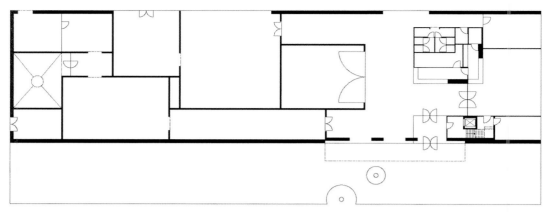

Floor plan, ground floor of the entrance building    Eingangsgebäude, Grundriss Erdgeschoss

On the second floor, invisible from the outside, the entrance pavilion contains office space surrounding an inner courtyard. On the first floor, a lobby, a café, an auditorium, and exhibition rooms link to create a path leading to the outside—to the reconstructed part of the camp.

Inside the building, there is a permanent exhibition dedicated to the camp's history, while temporary exhibitions interpret subjects such as good and evil, discrimination and prejudice from a contemporary perspective. This thematic generalization is typical of this national monument which does not explicitly articulate a Jewish identity—either in its expositions or in its architecture or landscaping. Nor was this a motive that informed the architectural design.

If the Kamp Vught National Monument is not explicitly or exclusively Jewish, its sheer presence cannot be interpreted but as a pointed request for attention to the history of this site which, to a large degree, is a Jewish history. Of the approximate 140,000 Jews who lived in the Netherlands at the beginning of the war, only twenty-one percent survived. After the war, this history was for the most part obscured by a pragmatic form of reuse: in the barracks, the SS was replaced by the Dutch army; a part of the camp was turned into a penitentiary—today one of the most heavily guarded prisons in the Netherlands; and from 1951 until 1992 the housing barracks served as accommodation—intended to be temporary—for Moluccans who, in the Indonesian struggle for independence, took the side of the Dutch and consequently had to flee.

Hans Ibelings

Werk vermittelt immer den Eindruck, als wäre es schon seit langem an seinem jeweiligen Ort.

Im Eingangsgebäude sind in dem von außen unsichtbaren ersten Stockwerk um einen Innenhof angeordnete Büroräume untergebracht. Im Erdgeschoss bilden ein Foyer, ein Café, ein Auditorium und Ausstellungsräume eine Flucht, die nach außen, in den rekonstruierten Teil des Lagers, führt.

Im Gebäude ist eine Dauerausstellung der Geschichte des Lagers gewidmet, während Wechselausstellungen Themen wie ›Gut und Böse‹, ›Diskriminierung‹ und ›Vorurteile‹ aus heutiger Sicht beleuchten. Diese thematische Verallgemeinerung ist kennzeichnend für die Nationale Gedenkstätte Kamp Vught, die weder in den Ausstellungen noch in der Architektur oder Landschaftsgestaltung ausdrücklich eine jüdische Identität bekundet. Diese hat auch beim Bauentwurf als Motiv keine Rolle gespielt.

Mag die Nationale Gedenkstätte Kamp Vught auch nicht ausdrücklich oder ausschließlich jüdisch sein, so kann ihr bloßes Vorhandensein doch nicht anders aufgefasst werden als als ein prägnanter Appell, der Geschichte dieses Ortes, die in bedeutendem Maß eine jüdische Geschichte ist, Aufmerksamkeit zu schenken – von den ca. 140.000 zu Kriegsbeginn in den Niederlanden lebenden Juden überlebten nur 21 Prozent. Nach dem Krieg wurde diese Geschichte durch eine pragmatische Form der Wiederverwendung der Infrastruktur des Lagers weitgehend verdrängt: In den Kasernen machte die SS der niederländischen Armee Platz, ein Teil des Lagers wurde in eine Strafvollzugsanstalt – inzwischen eines der schwerstbewachten Gefängnisse in den Niederlanden – umfunktioniert, und in der Zeit von 1951 bis 1992 dienten die Wohnbaracken als vorübergehend gedachte Unterkunft für Molukker, die sich im indonesischen Unabhängigkeitskampf auf die Seite der Niederlande geschlagen hatten und deshalb hatten fliehen müssen.

Hans Ibelings

Page    Seite 67
Entrance building of the memorial
Eingangsgebäude der Gedenkstätte

Pages    Seiten 68/69
Entrance building with model of the former concentration camp
Eingangsgebäude mit dem Modell des ehemaligen Konzentrationslagers

Memorial room with 750 plaques containing the names, dates of birth, and dates of death of those murdered in the camp
Gedenkraum mit 750 Tafeln mit den Namen sowie den Geburts- und Sterbedaten der im Lager ermordeten Menschen

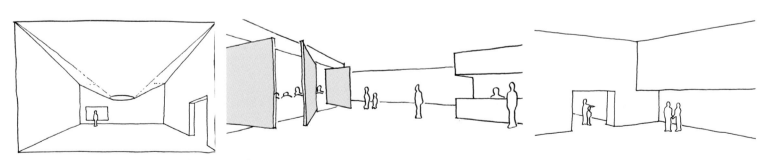

Perspective sketches of interior    Perspektivische Innenraum-Skizzen

Page    Seite 70
Facade with narrow terracotta and recessed plaster stripes
Fassade mit schmalen Terrakotta- und zurückgesetzten Putzstreifen

Frank O. Gehry

# The Jerusalem Museum of Tolerance – A Project of the Simon Wiesenthal Center

**Museum der Toleranz Jerusalem – Ein Projekt des Simon Wiesenthal Center**

Jerusalem | Israel
2000 – 2006 / 2007

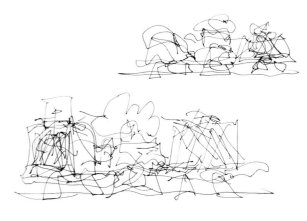

Design sketches by Frank O. Gehry    Entwurfsskizzen von Frank O. Gehry

By placing this iconic building in a city which nowadays so badly needs tolerance, the Simon Wiesenthal Center expects to facilitate reconciliation and foster peace between Palestinians and Israelis. The municipality of Jerusalem hopes to achieve a kind of "Bilbao-effect" where Frank O. Gehry's famous Guggenheim Museum (1991–1997) generated new life into the city, putting it on the map and onto every tourist's "must see" agenda.

Frank O. Gehry (born 1928 as Frank Goldberg in Canada) belongs among the most talented and original architects of late twentieth-century architecture. His career started with anti-refinement ad-hocism, collage, and "cheap tech" emphasizing the unfinished as in the Gehry House in Santa Monica (1977–78). Gradually, he moved on to more and more sophisticated structures and materials, trying out almost all formal languages of the period with great inventiveness and success. In the late 1980s and 1990s, his opus was ascribed to Deconstructivism. This ascription, probably by mistake, raised the issue of "Jewishness" in his architecture which, in an explicit sense, would have to be denied.

Commissioned by the Simon Wiesenthal Center in Los Angeles, on a built area of 21,600 square meters, the Jerusalem Museum of Tolerance is his first building designed for a Jewish institution. It is an ensemble of functionally and formally diverse, sculpturally shaped elements. The project provides exhibition and conference facilities to support programs that promote the ideals of tolerance and civility among diverse cultures. Its prominent site in West Jerusalem, close to the Old City and near Independence Park, includes two parcels which are connected by a bridge.

The ensemble includes the Museum of Tolerance, an international conference center, a multi-purpose Grand Hall, an auditorium, and support facilities. The museum, clad in Jerusalem stone, contains individual clustered galleries visible from the central atrium and from the adjacent conference facilities as well as the Grand Hall. A cafeteria and restaurant, enclosed by panes of glass, are

Mit der Errichtung dieses ikonenhaften Gebäudes in einer Stadt, in der Toleranz gegenwärtig eine dringende Notwendigkeit darstellt, hofft das Simon Wiesenthal Center die Versöhnung und den Frieden zwischen Israelis und Palästinensern zu fördern. Gleichzeitig erhoffen sich der Auftraggeber und die Stadt Jerusalem eine Art ›Bilbao-Effekt‹, denn in Bilbao brachte Frank O. Gehrys berühmtes Guggenheim Museum (1991–97) neues Leben in die Stadt und setzte diese auf die Landkarte der Orte, die jeder Reisende unbedingt gesehen haben sollte.

Frank O. Gehry (1928 als Frank Goldberg in Kanada geboren) gehört zu den originellsten Architekten des späten 20. Jahrhunderts. Am Anfang seiner Karriere vertrat er eine Art ›Spontanarchitektur‹ und realisierte mit preiswerter Bautechnik Gebäude-Collagen, bei denen er wie beim Haus Gehry in Santa Monica (1977/78) den unfertigen Charakter des Baus betonte. Im Lauf der Zeit wurde seine Architektur anspruchsvoller, er verwendete hochwertigere Materialien und erprobte mit viel Fantasie und Erfolg die verschiedenen Formensprachen seiner Zeit. Gehrys Bauten der späten 1980er und der 1990er Jahre wurden dem Dekonstruktivismus zugeschrieben. Wahrscheinlich ist dies eine unkorrekte Zuordnung, die aber die Frage nach dem ›jüdischen Charakter‹ seiner Architektur ins Spiel bringt, der in expliziter Form allerdings wohl verneint werden muss.

Das Jerusalemer Museum der Toleranz wird im Auftrag des in Los Angeles ansässigen Simon Wiesenthal Center auf einer Grundfläche von 21.600 m² errichtet und ist Gehrys erster Bau für eine jüdische Institution. Es handelt sich dabei um ein Ensemble funktional und formal unterschiedlicher, plastisch geformter Baukörper. Das Programm umfasst verschiedene Bereiche für Veranstaltungen und Lernmöglichkeiten zur Förderung wechselseitiger Toleranz und des Respekts zwischen Juden und den Angehörigen anderer Glaubensrichtungen. Der prominente Bauplatz in West-Jerusalem in der Nähe der Altstadt und in der Nachbarschaft des Independence Park umfasst zwei Grundstücke, die über eine Brücke miteinander verbunden werden.

Site plan    Lageplan

Interior of the Grand Hall. Model    Innenraum der Mehrzweckhalle. Modell

located adjacent to the museum which is clad in titanium panels. The conference center consists of two distinct buildings, the Conference Theater and the Educational Center. The Conference Theater, clad in blue titanium panels, houses a 250-seat primary conference facility with a research center located above. The Educational Center provides space for nine smaller conference rooms with a library above and is articulated as a cluster of boxes clad in Jerusalem stone. The turbine-like, titanium clad Grand Hall houses a 350-seat auditorium for film presentations and serves as an icon for the whole ensemble.

The $120 million project has provoked its share controversy in Israel because of its procedural and architectural/urban facets. Jerusalemites do not want to sacrifice their lively public square for any new building. More importantly, the collage character and undulating shapes of the project are perceived as disregarding the local architecture—historic and modern alike—something perhaps admissible in Bilbao but not in Jerusalem. The otherwise stimulating "industrial-waste aesthetic" is at odds with the three-thousand-year-old architectural heritage of Jerusalem—Jewish, Christian, and Muslim—in a city where it supposed to foster mutual understanding and tolerance.

Rudolf Klein

Das Ensemble wird ein Museum der Toleranz, ein internationales Konferenzzentrum, eine große Mehrzweckhalle und einen Vortragssaal mit Dienst- und Nebenräumen enthalten. Das mit einer Fassade aus Jerusalemer Stein verkleidete Museum beherbergt einzelne, in Gruppen zusammengefasste Galerien, die vom zentralen Atrium, vom angrenzenden Konferenzzentrum und von der Mehrzweckhalle aus einsehbar sind. Ein voll verglaster Cafeteria- und Restaurantbereich befindet sich neben dem Museum, ebenso ein mit Titanplatten verkleideter Museumsshop. Das Konferenzzentrum besteht aus zwei Gebäuden, dem Theatersaal und dem Bildungszentrum. Ersteres umfasst einen Hauptsaal mit 250 Sitzplätzen; darüber befindet sich ein mit blauen Titanplatten verkleidetes Forschungszentrum. Das Bildungszentrum ist mit neun kleineren Konferenzräumen und einer darüber liegenden Bibliothek ausgestattet und als Ansammlung von Boxen ausgebildet, die mit Jerusalemer Stein verkleidet sind. Die turbinenförmige, titanverkleidete Mehrzweckhalle beherbergt ein Auditorium mit 350 Sitzen für Filmvorführungen und funktioniert als das ikonische Element der Gesamtanlage.

Das auf 120 Millionen US-Dollar veranschlagte Projekt war wegen seiner verfahrenstechnischen und architektonisch-städtebaulichen Aspekte in Israel umstritten. Die Jerusalemer tun sich schwer damit, den belebten öffentlichen Platz in der Nähe der Altstadt für einen Neubau zur Verfügung zu stellen. Aufgrund des collagenhaften Charakters und der mehrfach geschwungenen Baukörper des Ensembles befürchten sie, dass es sich nicht in die Architektur des Ortes einfügt – sowohl die historische als auch die moderne –, was in Bilbao vielleicht zulässig erscheint, offensichtlich aber nicht in Jerusalem. Gehrys andernorts stimulierende ›Industriebrachenästhetik‹ passt nach Ansicht vieler nicht zu dem 3000 Jahre alten architektonischen Erbe der Stadt Jerusalem – ob jüdisch, christlich oder muslimisch –, in der es doch gegenseitiges Verständnis und Toleranz fördern soll.

Rudolf Klein

Total view from the west with theater, museum, and café. Model    Gesamtansicht von Westen mit Theater, Museum und Café. Modell

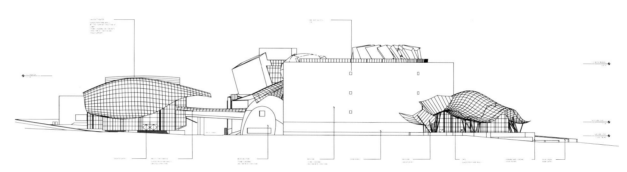

**West elevation**    Ansicht von Westen

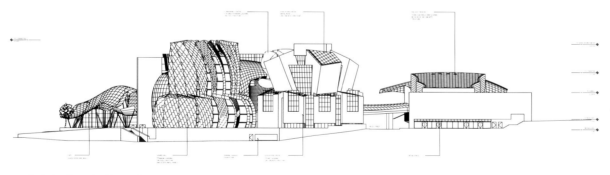

**East elevation**    Ansicht von Osten

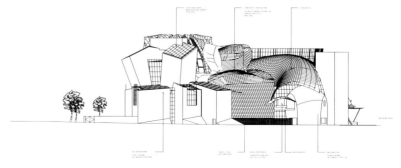

**North elevation**    Ansicht von Norden

**Pages**    Seiten 76/77
Model studies of the Grand Hall
Modellstudien der Mehrzweckhalle

Frank O. Gehry    **Jerusalem Museum of Tolerance**    **Museum der Toleranz Jerusalem**

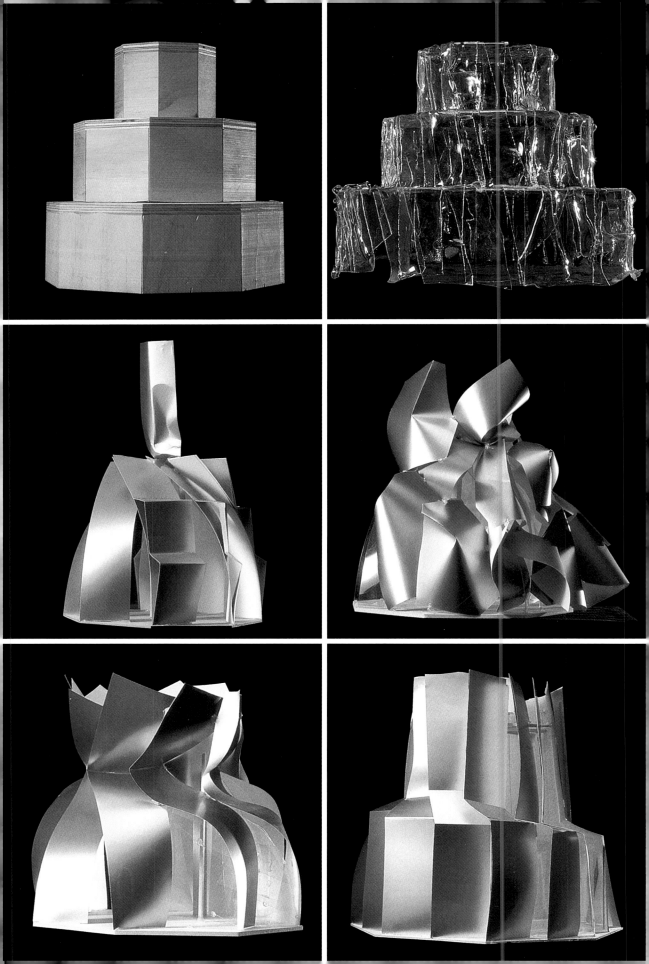

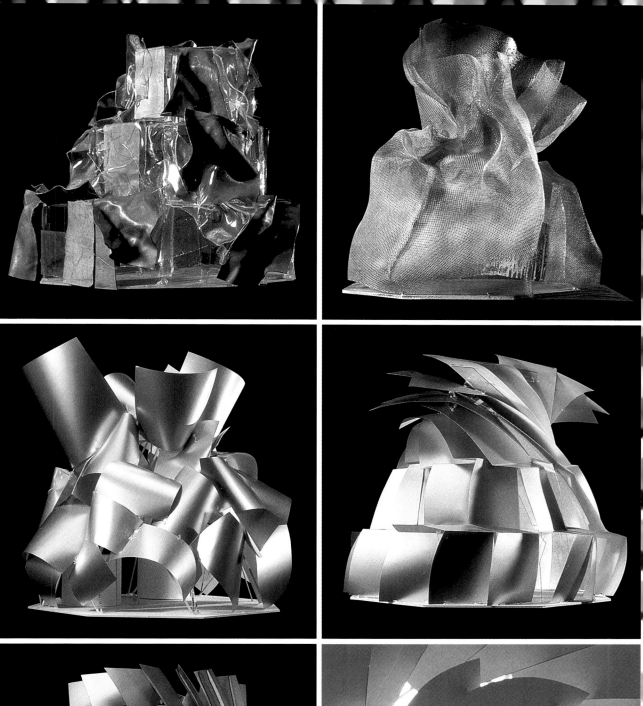

Daniel Libeskind

**Jewish Museum Berlin**
**Jüdisches Museum Berlin**

Berlin, Germany | Deutschland
1989–1999

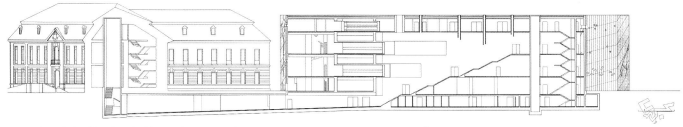

Section through the old and new buildings with transition in basement    Schnitt durch Alt- und Neubau mit dem Übergang im Untergeschoss

Daniel Libeskind's architectural conception for the Jewish Museum in Berlin builds on a highly complex matrix of meanings that link it with the city's Jewish tradition. The project, awarded first place in the 1989 competition and subsequently revised, was originally intended as an integrative structure that would connect the Jewish Museum with the existing Berlin Museum, in the adjacent baroque Collegienhaus. In 1998, the Jewish Museum became an independent institution. The Berlin Museum moved to a new site, and its former building is now used as a reception area and for temporary exhibitions.

Symbolically embodying memories of Jewish history in Berlin and Germany, the new building was already opened for tours in 1999, to an overwhelming public response. Its actual inauguration came with the installation of the permanent exhibition in 2001. In the meantime, the museum has not only become one of the country's most popular museums and a Berlin landmark, its unusual form has become a worldwide icon of Jewish identity and the Holocaust, which the architecture intrinsically embodies.

Libeskind described his conception, in which both visible and invisible aspects of Jewish culture come into play as, "Between the Lines." The museum's ground plan, reminiscent of a lightning bolt, derived from a dialogue between two double-lines, repeatedly angled, that defined the sculptural building volume. The intersections between these lines form a total of five empty spaces, known as "voids," spaced at irregular intervals within the structure. These symbolize the absence of German Jewish citizens who were forced to emigrate or were murdered by the Nazis, as well as the obliteration of their world, which played such an important role in Berlin's history. At the same time, Libeskind embedded his project in the urban context and the history of ideas in Berlin.

The new, four-story building volume approaches the existing historical building at three points, forming two courtyards, one of which is dedicated to the Jewish poet Paul Celan. The facade is sheathed in zinc panels into which seemingly arbitrarily criss-crossing window bands

Das architektonische Konzept des Jüdischen Museums von Daniel Libeskind ist auf einer höchst komplexen Matrix der Bedeutungen aufgebaut, die den Bau mit der jüdischen Tradition Berlins verbindet. Das im Wettbewerb von 1989 erstplatzierte und in der Folge überarbeitete Projekt war ursprünglich als integratives Modell gedacht, als Einbindung des Jüdischen Museums in das bereits bestehende Berlin Museum im benachbarten Barockbau des Kollegienhauses. Seit 1998 ist das Jüdische Museum eine autonome Institution. Das Berlin Museum wurde an einen anderen Ort verlegt, der Altbau dient nun für Wechselausstellungen und als Empfangsbereich.

Als symbolische Verkörperung der Erinnerungen an die jüdische Geschichte Berlins und Deutschlands wurde das neue Gebäude bereits ab 1999 unter großer Beteiligung der Öffentlichkeit für Architekturführungen zugänglich, bevor es mit der Einrichtung der Dauerausstellung 2001 als eigentliches Museum eröffnet wurde. Inzwischen ist es nicht nur eines der erfolgreichsten Museen und gleichzeitig eines der Wahrzeichen Berlins, sondern seine ungewöhnliche Form hat sich auch weltweit als ikonische Architektur für jüdische Identität und den Holocaust eingeprägt, die in dem Bau untrennbar verbunden sind.

Libeskind nannte sein Konzept, in das sowohl das Sichtbare der jüdischen Kultur als auch das Unsichtbare integriert ist, »Between the Lines«. Der der Form eines Blitzes vergleichbare Grundriss des Museums beruht auf dem Dialog zweier Doppellinien, aus denen sich der mehrfach abgewinkelte, skulptural wirkende Baukörper konstituiert. An den Schnittstellen der beiden Linien entstanden insgesamt fünf Leerräume, so genannte ›voids‹, die den Museumsbau als unregelmäßige Sequenz durchziehen. In ihnen manifestiert sich die Abwesenheit der emigrierten und ermordeten jüdischen Mitbürger und die Auslöschung ihrer für Berlin so bedeutsamen Welt während des Nationalsozialismus. Gleichzeitig verknüpfte Libeskind sein Projekt mit dem städtischen Kontext und der Geistesgeschichte Berlins.

Der viergeschossige Baukörper nähert sich dem Altbau an drei Stellen an, wodurch zwei Höfe gebildet werden, von denen einer dem jüdischen Dichter Paul Celan

Page    Seite 78
Facade detail
with cut in windows
Fassadenausschnitt mit
eingeschnittenen Fenstern

are incised. Independent of the interior structure, these have the effect of autonomous graphic design elements in their own right. Access to the museum is by way of the old building's main entrance. To the right of the vestibule, in an empty space echoing the configuration of one of the voids, stairs lead down to the basement floor. Here, the path divides into two corridors, illuminated by lighting bands, and intersected after a short distance by a further corridor. The right-hand corridor, known as the Axis of Exile, leads to the Garden of Exile outside the building. The intersecting corridor, the Axis of the Holocaust, also leads outside, to the Holocaust Tower—two special memorial sites in this building dedicated to remembrance. The corridor leading straight ahead, the Axis of Continuity, rises gradually to meet the main stairway, which provides access to the uppermost of the new museum's three exhibition floors. Above this is a fourth floor reserved for offices and workshops.

Due to the museum's unusual plan, the interior spaces form a continually surprising and impressive sequence, penetrating all of the floors and extending around the voids, which are sparingly illuminated by daylight from above. Only the last of these five internal voids is accessible, and it conveys an overwhelming sense of the vacancy left by the extermination of the Jews and their culture in the Third Reich.

Angeli Sachs

gewidmet ist. Die Fassade besteht aus einer Zinkverkleidung, in die verschiedene Öffnungen und sich scheinbar willkürlich kreuzende Fensterbänder eingeschnitten sind, so dass sie unabhängig von der inneren Struktur zum autonomen, zeichenhaften Gestaltungselement wird. Das Museum wird über den Haupteingang des Altbaus erschlossen. Rechts vom Eingang wurde ein den ›voids‹ nachgebildeter Leerraum eingestellt, in dem eine Treppe in das Untergeschoss führt. Dort gabelt sich der Weg in zwei durch Lichtbänder betonte Gänge, die kurz darauf von einem weiteren Gang gekreuzt werden. Der rechte Gang, als Achse des Exils bezeichnet, führt zum außerhalb des Gebäudes liegenden Garten des Exils, die Querachse, Achse des Holocaust genannt, führt zum ebenfalls externen Holocaust-Turm – zwei besondere Orte des Gedenkens in diesem Bau der Erinnerung. Geradeaus erreicht der leicht ansteigende Gang als Achse der Kontinuität die Haupttreppe, die bis in das oberste der drei Ausstellungsgeschosse des Neubaus führt. Darüber befindet sich ein weiteres Geschoss für Büros und Werkstätten.

Der ungewöhnliche Grundriss des Museums schafft eindrucksvolle und ungewöhnliche Raumfolgen, die sich um die alle Stockwerke des Museums durchstoßenden und von oben belichteten ›voids‹ erstrecken. Nur das letzte dieser fünf internen ›voids‹ ist betretbar, und hier kann man noch einmal die Leere erfahren, die durch die Vernichtung der Juden und ihrer Kultur während des Nationalsozialismus entstanden ist.

Angeli Sachs

**Pages**  Seiten 82/83
**Garden of Exile with 49 concrete columns**
Der Garten des Exils mit 49 Betonpfeilern

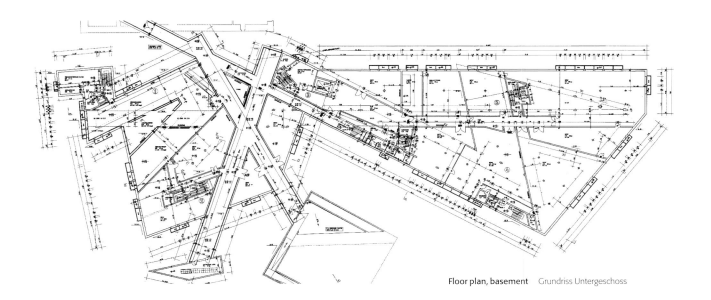

Floor plan, basement    Grundriss Untergeschoss

View from the northwest of the new and old buildings. Left: Garden of Exile with Holocaust tower in background
Blick von Nordwesten auf den Neu- und Altbau. Links der Garten des Exils, dahinter der Holocaust-Turm

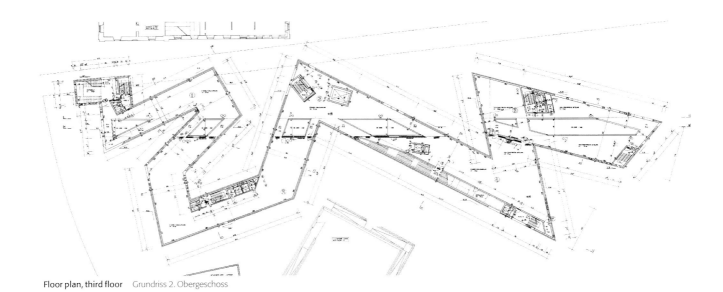

Floor plan, third floor   Grundriss 2. Obergeschoss

Main staircase    Haupttreppe

Two of the exhibition rooms, empty and with objects
Zwei der Ausstellungsräume, leer und mit Exponaten

Page    Seite 85
Final void with installation *Fallen Leaves* by Menashe Kadishman
Das letzte ›void‹ mit der Installation *Gefallenes Laub* von Menashe Kadishman

Daniel Libeskind

**Jewish Museum
San Francisco**
**Jüdisches Museum
San Francisco**

San Francisco,
California | Kalifornien | USA
Since | seit 1998

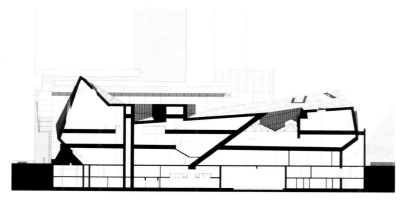

Longitudinal section    Längsschnitt

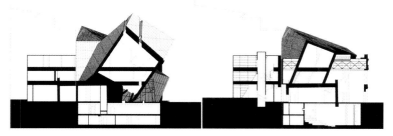

Cross sections    Querschnitte

One of the first buildings erected in San Francisco after the Great Earthquake of 1906 was a power plant. The turbines in the brick building designed by Willis Polk supplied the electricity needed for the city's reconstruction. They provided the devastated metropolis with fresh energy, or, poetically speaking, infused it with new life. "To life," in Hebrew *L'Chai'm*, was also the concept adopted by architect Daniel Libeskind for his conversion of the former power plant, a protected monument, into the Jewish Museum San Francisco. The project's title, program, and metaphor in one, can be interpreted on various levels: it describes the intent to revitalize the defunct power plant by giving it a new function; it reflects the curators' hope that the planned museum would invigorate the debate on the significance of Jewish tradition for the present and future; and it was part of the project to revive the power plant's surroundings, the rundown area South of Market, by establishing cultural institutions such as Mario Botta's San Francisco Museum of Modern Art. Not least of all, L'Chai'm represented a further example of Libeskind's art of providing his buildings with a super-structure of ideas.

The architect suggested that the term L'Chai'm be taken quite literally as the basis of the conversion. His plans envisage the development of three-dimensional volumes out of the contours of the two Hebrew letters of the word Chai, which would penetrate the existing structure like sharp-edged implants. This calculated collision represents what Libeskind sees as an architectural variant on the Jewish tradition of expanding upon the texts of the Hebrew Bible, the Talmud, and other reli-

Eines der ersten Gebäude, das in San Francisco nach dem großen Erdbeben von 1906 errichtet wurde, war ein Kraftwerk. Die Turbinen in dem Ziegelbau des Architekten Willis Polk lieferten den Strom, der für den Wiederaufbau der Stadt nötig war. Sie verhalfen der zerstörten Metropole zu frischer Energie, hauchten ihr, poetisch gesprochen, neues Leben ein. »To Life«, hebräisch »L'Chai'm«, zu Deutsch »Zum Leben«, heißt auch das Konzept des Architekten Daniel Libeskind für den Umbau der denkmalgeschützten Backsteinhalle zum Sitz des Jewish Museum San Francisco. Der Titel, Programm und Metapher zugleich, lässt sich auf mehreren Ebenen deuten: Er beschreibt das Vorhaben, das stillgelegte Kraftwerk mittels einer neuen Funktion zu revitalisieren; er spiegelt die Hoffnung der Kuratoren, ihr künftiges Haus könne die Debatte über die Bedeutung der jüdischen Überlieferung für Gegenwart und Zukunft beleben; er fügt sich ein in das Projekt, die Umgebung des Kraftwerks, den heruntergekommenen Bezirk South of Market, durch die Ansiedlung von Kulturinstitutionen wie Mario Bottas San Francisco Museum of Modern Art aufzuwerten. Und nicht zuletzt beweist »L'Chai'm« neuerlich Libeskinds Kunst, seinen Bauten stets auch einen schillernden geistigen Überbau zu verpassen.

Der Architekt hat vorgeschlagen, den Begriff »L'Chai'm« ganz wörtlich zur Basis des Umbaus zu machen. Seine Pläne sehen vor, aus den Umrissen der beiden hebräischen Buchstaben des Wortes Chai dreidimensionale Körper zu entwickeln, die den Altbau wie scharfkantige Implantate durchstoßen sollen — eine kalkulierte Kollision, die Libeskind als architektonische Variante der jüdischen Tradition interpretiert, Texte der hebräischen Bibel, des Talmud

gious writings by means of ever-new commentaries and exegeses. In fact, little would remain of the historical building except its long, plain brick facade. Behind it would open a foyer, extending the full height of the building, with a café and shops. All of the exhibition areas and rooms for the museum's educational department and administration would be located in the diagonally-placed new buildings, whose metal cladding, graphically zigzagging window apertures, and complicated, inter-folding spaces recall other Libeskind designs, such as the Jewish Museum Berlin or the Felix-Nussbaum-Haus in Osnabrück. The two lower floors would house an auditorium and a library.

When the project was presented in February 2000, its cost was estimated at sixty million dollars, to be raised principally through donations. After the dot.com bubble burst and the American economy plunged in the wake of the terrorist attacks of 11 September 2001, these plans proved unrealistic. An abortive attempt to merge the Jewish Museum San Francisco with the Judah L. Magnes Museum in nearby Berkeley delayed the project still further. The inauguration, foreseen for autumn 2003, has been postponed indefinitely, and Libeskind's designs, according to the museum management, have been shelved. The construction costs are to be lowered and the museum floor area reduced by forty percent. One can only speculate what effect these cuts will have on the architecture. The clients emphasize that Libeskind is still their architect of choice, but before asking him to submit new, less elaborate plans, the financing must be secured. When, and in what form, the Jewish Museum San Francisco will materialize remains very much an open question.

Heinrich Wefing

und anderer religiöser Schriften durch immer neue Kommentare und Glossen fortzuschreiben. Tatsächlich aber bliebe von dem historischen Bau kaum mehr als die lang gestreckte, schlichte Ziegelfassade. Dahinter soll sich ein haushohes Foyer mit Café und Museumsshop öffnen. Alle Ausstellungsbereiche sowie die Flächen für die Museumsdidaktik und die Verwaltung befinden sich in den schräg gestellten Neubauten, die mit ihrer Metallverkleidung, der zuckenden Grafik der Fensteröffnungen und den komplizierten Raumfaltungen an andere Entwürfe Libeskinds wie das Jüdische Museum Berlin oder das Felix-Nussbaum-Haus in Osnabrück anknüpfen. In den beiden Untergeschossen sollen ein Vortragssaal und eine Bibliothek untergebracht werden.

Als das Projekt im Februar 2000 vorgestellt wurde, sollte es sechzig Millionen Dollar kosten und überwiegend durch Spenden finanziert werden. Nach dem Platzen der dot.com-Blase und dem Einbruch der amerikanischen Wirtschaft im Gefolge der Terroranschläge vom 11. September 2001 haben sich diese Pläne jedoch als unrealistisch erwiesen. Der missglückte Versuch, das Jewish Museum San Francisco mit dem Judah L. Magnes Museum im benachbarten Berkeley zu verschmelzen, hat das Bauvorhaben noch weiter zurückgeworfen. Die für Herbst 2003 vorgesehene Eröffnung ist auf unbestimmte Zeit verschoben worden, Libeskinds Entwürfe sind nach Auskunft der Museumsleitung Makulatur. Erwogen wird eine Senkung der Baukosten und eine Reduzierung des Raumprogramms um vierzig Prozent. Welche Auswirkungen diese Einschnitte auf die Architektur haben werden, lässt sich nur ahnen. Die Verantwortlichen betonen zwar, Daniel Libeskind sei weiterhin der Architekt ihres Vertrauens. Ehe er aber um neue, weniger üppige Pläne gebeten werden soll, will das Museum die Finanzierung sicherstellen. Wann und in welcher Gestalt das Jewish Museum San Francisco entstehen wird, ist daher ungewiss.

Heinrich Wefing

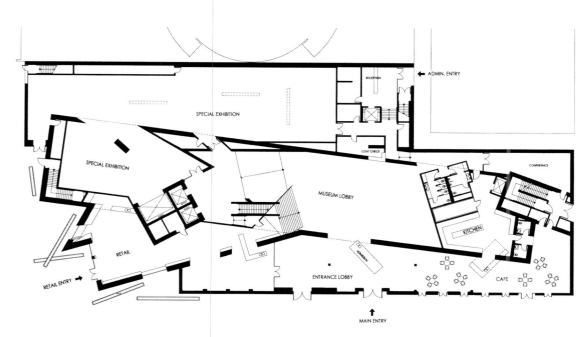

Floor plan, ground floor
Grundriss Erdgeschoss

Brick facade of the original power plant with main entrance of the museum. Computer simulation
Die Ziegelfassade des ehemaligen Kraftwerks mit dem Haupteingang des Museums. Computersimulation

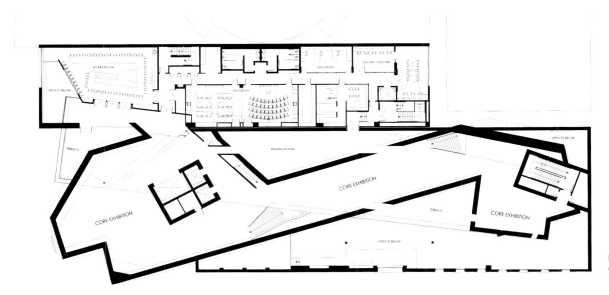

Floor plan, third floor
Grundriss 2. Obergeschoss

View from northwest. Computer simulation    Ansicht von Nordwesten. Computersimulation

Page    Seite 91
**Entrance lobby. Computer simulation**
Eingangshalle. Computersimulation

Moshe Safdie

**Yad Vashem Holocaust Museum**
Yad Vashem Holocaust Museum

Jerusalem | Israel
1997–2004

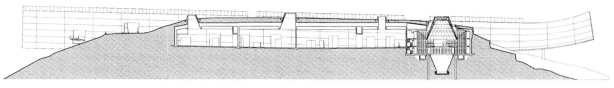

Longitudinal section  Längsschnitt

Passing through the reinforced concrete triangle-axis that penetrates the hillside of Jerusalem's mountains to become the new Historic Museum of Yad Vashem, one is overwhelmed by its exalting and original space. (Its size extends over an area of about 3,500 square meters, with a length of 175 meters and a height of 16 meters.) Looking up to the top of the triangle, which contains a continuous stream of skylights, a flow of daylight reveals a blue Jerusalem sky whose spatial shrinkage and plenitude suggests the Kabbalistic concept of divine withdrawal. This stripe of light recalls Barnett Newman's sign—the "zip"—which was placed in his wide canvas as a channel of spiritual tension; in the same stream of thinking, the prismatic, linear structure reminds one of the hovering feelings between the oppressive and the exuberant, experienced while observing Barnett Newman's *Broken Obelisk* (1963–67).

Moshe Safdie, who maintains offices in Boston, Toronto, and Jerusalem and who is the architect of buildings such as the Hebrew Union College in Jerusalem and the Skirball Museum and Cultural Center in Los Angeles, chose the triangular form as one structurally stable enough to support the pressure of the earth upon the prism, as well as one that would dramatically bring light from above onto the floor below. Moreover, the triangular cross-section varies throughout the prism: Both ends dramatically cantilever out of the mountain to form the entrance and exit. As one begins the journey and the ascent towards the light and exit point, the roof descends across the mountain while the floor slopes at a grade of five percent. This dynamic sequence of spaces forces the visitor to move through in a zigzag, to and from one chapter to the other, while maintaining a view from beginning to end, appropriate to the linear character of the museum with its pre-determined sequences of experiences divided into sub-sections.

Unlike an art museum, in which even light is required as a way of viewing objects, this museum contrasts blasts of daylight with areas of considerable darkness, particularly when required for audio-visual presentations. The changing play of sunlight that penetrates the clear to diffused glass skylight of the prism is used for dramatic impact; at any given moment it reflects differently as the surface warps on either side of the visitor. The result is an

Wenn man die lange Achse des dreieckigen Prismas aus Stahlbeton abschreitet, das einen Hang im Bergland von Jerusalem durchdringt, um in Zukunft das neue Historische Museum der Gedenkstätte von Yad Vashem zu beherbergen, ist man überwältigt von diesem erhebenden und originellen Bauwerk (mit einer Grundfläche von rund 3500 m², einer Länge von 175 m und einer Höhe von 16 m). In den First des Dreieckprismas ist eine fortlaufende Reihe von Oberlichtern integriert. Das einströmende Tageslicht enthüllt den blauen Himmel über Jerusalem, dessen durch den schmalen Dachausschnitt gebündeltes Licht das kabbalistische Konzept des göttlichen Rückzugs zu verkörpern scheint. Der Lichtstreifen erinnert aber auch an Barnett Newmans Bildmotiv des ›Zipps‹ (Reißverschlusses), den er wie einen Kanal für spirituelle Spannung auf seine großen Leinwände malte. Wenn man diesen Gedanken weiterspinnt, erinnert die lineare Konstruktion an das Hin- und Hergerissensein zwischen Niedergedrücktheit und Überschwang, das man bei der Betrachtung von Barnett Newmans *Broken Obelisk* (1963–67) empfindet.

Der Architekt Moshe Safdie, der Büros in Boston, Toronto und Jerusalem unterhält und unter anderem das Hebrew Union College in Jerusalem sowie das Skirball Museum and Cultural Center von Los Angeles gebaut hat, entschied sich für die Dreieckskonstruktion, weil sie strukturell stabil genug ist, um dem Erddruck standzuhalten, und weil sie es erlaubt, den Lichteinfall von oben mit dramatischer Wirkung zu inszenieren. Die Querschnitte durch das dreieckige Prisma variieren: Die beiden Enden kragen eindrucksvoll aus dem Berghang vor und bilden jeweils Eingang und Ausgang. Wenn man vom Eingang zum Licht am anderen Ende und damit zum Ausgang geht, neigt sich die Decke durch den Berg nach unten, während der Fußboden mit einem Gefälle von fünf Prozent nach oben aufsteigt. Die dynamische Raumsequenz zwingt den Besucher zu einem Zickzack-Kurs — hin und her von einem Themenkomplex zum anderen —, während er den gesamten zentralen Achsenraum beim Durchqueren stets von einem Ende zum anderen überblicken kann. Das entspricht dem linearen Charakter des Ausstellungsdesigns mit seinen festgelegten historischen Abschnitten, die ihrerseits weiter unterteilt sind.

Anders als bei einem Kunstmuseum, in dem eine gleichmäßige Ausleuchtung für die Betrachtung der Expo-

Page    Seite 92
The new Holocaust History Museum penetrates the hillside.
Das neue Museum für die Geschichte des Holocaust durchstößt den Hügel.

Model of the entire structure    Modell der Gesamtanlage

*anti*-archaeological or geological character, similar to top-lit underground chambers in stone quarries. Within the chapter room galleries, the skylights are localized and the exhibit design adapted to take advantage of them. At night, the skylights form powerful abstract sculptural objects in the landscape.

The Historic Museum is part of the Har Hazikaron (the Mount of Remembrance) complex, which includes a new Hall of Names, galleries for changing exhibitions and Holocaust art, an information center, and a synagogue. If this extensive program had been set atop Har Hazikaron in conventional buildings, it would have permanently altered the pastoral character of this national preserve, which the Yad Vashem management was eager to maintain, along with the prominence of Ohel Yizkor (the Hall of Remembrance), an architectural landmark of the original 1953 structure. The relatively low elevation of the entrance requires considerable ascent for visitors to the ridge of the hill. Thus, an underground scheme maintains a continuity of levels by cutting under the ridge and providing for a visitor's path with only one level change from entry to exit.

In response to these considerations, and out of conviction that traditional buildings with traditional galleries are an inappropriate setting for telling the story of the Holocaust, the alternative scheme of a prismatic, underground structure evolved, expertly and innovatively conceived by architect Moshe Safdie.

Mordechai Omer

nate erforderlich ist, kontrastiert Safdie hier lichtdurchflutete mit weitgehend abgedunkelten Räumen – letztere hauptsächlich für audiovisuelle Präsentationen. Das durch die Oberlichter aus transparentem und diffusem Glas einfallende Sonnenlicht erzeugt wechselnde Reflexe, da die Wandflächen zu beiden Seiten unregelmäßig geformt sind. Das Ergebnis ist ein ›anti-archäologischer‹ beziehungsweise geologischer Raumcharakter, der an einen von oben beleuchteten unterirdischen Steinbruch denken lässt. Die Galerieabteilungen haben eigene Dachlaternen, und die Exponate sind darin so installiert, dass sie von der natürlichen Beleuchtung durch diese Oberlichter profitieren. Nachts bilden die Dachlaternen eindrucksvolle abstrakte Objekte in der Hügellandschaft.

Das Historische Museum gehört zum Baukomplex auf dem Har Hasikaron (Berg des Gedenkens), der auch eine neue Hall of Names (Halle der Namen), Galerien für Wechselausstellungen und Holocaust-Kunst, ein Informationszentrum und eine Synagoge umfasst. Wenn dieses umfangreiche Raumprogramm in konventionellen Bauten auf der Hügelkuppe des Har Hasikaron untergebracht worden wäre, hätte es den ländlichen Charakter dieses Geländes für immer verändert – und diesen wollte die Leitung von Yad Vashem auf jeden Fall erhalten, ebenso den ungehinderten Blick auf das beherrschende Gebäude der Gedenkstätte, die Ohel Yiskor (Gedenkhalle), ein Baudenkmal und Wahrzeichen der ursprünglichen Anlage von 1953. Die relativ niedrige Eingangsfassade verlangt Besuchern die Mühe ab, bis zur Hügelkuppe hinaufzusteigen. Im Innern, also unterhalb der Kuppe, wird dann die Anzahl der Geschossebenen auf zwei beschränkt, so dass die Besucher nur einmal einen Höhenunterschied zu überwinden haben.

In Erfüllung dieser Auflagen und in der Überzeugung, dass konventionelle Museumsbauten mit herkömmlichen Ausstellungsräumen ungeeignete Orte zur Darstellung der Geschichte des Holocaust sind, hat Moshe Safdie sein alternatives Konzept einer prismatischen Untergrundstruktur überzeugend und innovativ entwickelt.

Mordechai Omer

Hall of Names and exit of the Holocaust History Museum   Die Halle der Namen und der Ausgang des Museums für die Geschichte des Holocaust

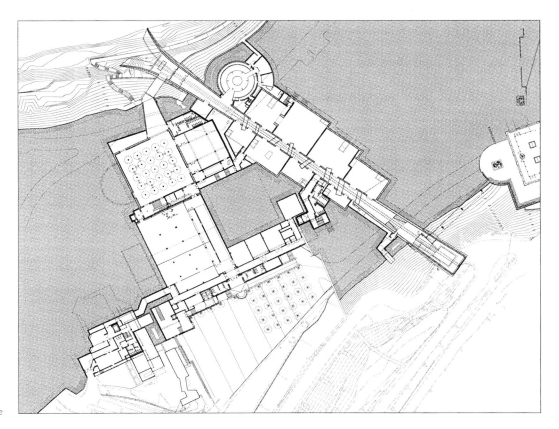

Museum floor plan
Grundriss Museumsebene

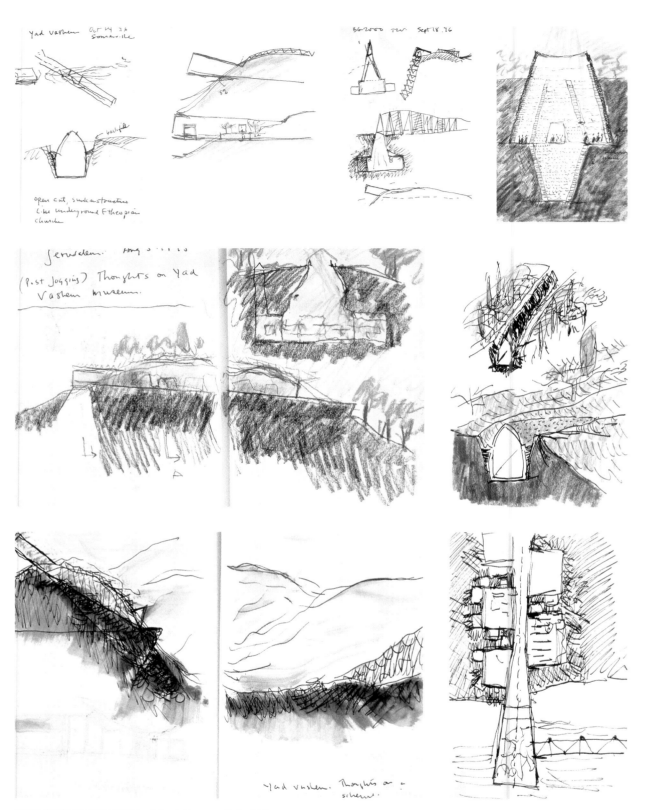

Design sketches by Moshe Safdie   Entwurfsskizzen von Moshe Safdie

Page   Seite 97
The building opens like an over-sized
funnel to the surrounding landscape.
Wie ein überdimensionaler Trichter
öffnet sich das Gebäude zur Landschaft.

Mario Botta

**Cymbalista Synagogue
and Jewish Heritage Center**
Cymbalista-Synagoge
und Jüdisches Kulturzentrum

Tel Aviv | Israel
1996–1998

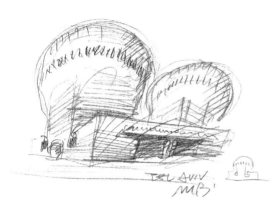

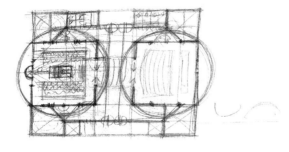

Design sketches by Mario Botta    Entwurfsskizzen von Mario Botta

Mario Botta, born in 1943 in Ticino, established his reputation with small villas. His true stature as an architect, however, was revealed much later in sacred buildings such as the Cymbalista Synagogue, inaugurated in May 1998. With this fortress-like house of God rising up on the campus of Tel Aviv University, Botta surpassed himself—and this despite the fact that he had never entered a synagogue until Norbert Cymbalista, the Swiss benefactor, requested a design from him in late 1995. Intuition and a feeling for the transcendental guided Botta to a solution that can be named in a single breath with Frank Lloyd Wright's Beth Sholom Synagogue in Elkins Park (1953–59), one of the most spectacular synagogue buildings of the twentieth century.

Yet unlike Wright, whose Reform synagogue hardly differs from a church, Botta invented a new type of building—a double synagogue consisting of two nearly identical rooms. Above a rectangular socle measuring 22 by 29 meters, two cubic structures each 10.5 meters per side, rise in strict symmetry, expanding skywards into cylinders measuring 15 meters in diameter. This freestanding gem, clad in red Verona dolomite, is the first architecturally significant campus synagogue since 1957–58, when Heinz Rau and David Reznik built their legendary synagogue at the Givat Ram campus of Hebrew University in Jerusalem. Thereafter, with the exception of Zvi Hecker's bunker-like Negev Synagogue of 1969, no sacred building has emerged that could compare to Botta's masterpiece. It is impressive alone for its multifarious historical references, extending from the cubic synagogue spaces of Rhenish Romanesque through the Prague Altneuschul down to Judith Stolzer's tower-like Wehrsynagoge in Hadera.

The north entrance is accentuated by two coupled round pillars, recalling the portal of Solomon's Temple flanked by the bronze columns Jachin and Boaz. This leads into a vestibule that opens on the left to the Judaica Museum and synagogue proper, and on the right to the *beth midrash* (the room reserved for Torah studies) and the auditorium in the "West Tower." While this is used for cultural activities as well as for Reform and Conservative services, the interior of the "East Tower", whose small apse and torah shrine are oriented toward Jerusalem, is conceived as an Orthodox synagogue. In the interest of maintaining spatial unity, a gallery was omitted and a women's section was placed on the level of the entrance, symbolically separated by a balustrade as in some ancient

Pages    Seiten 98/99
Facade detail
Fassadenausschnitt

Page    Seite 100
Building detail
Gebäudeausschnitt

Es waren kleine Villen, die Mario Bottas Ruhm begründeten; doch seine wahre Größe erlangte der 1943 geborene Tessiner Architekt erst viel später mit Sakralbauten wie der im Mai 1998 eingeweihten Cymbalista-Synagoge. Mit diesem festungsartig sich auf dem Campus der Tel Aviv University erhebenden Gotteshaus übertraf Botta sich selbst – und dies, obwohl er noch nie eine Synagoge betreten hatte, als Norbert Cymbalista, der Schweizer Stifter, ihn Ende 1995 um einen Entwurf bat. Doch Intuition und ein Gespür für das Transzendentale ließen ihn eine Lösung finden, die in einem Atemzug mit Frank Lloyd Wrights Beth-Sholom-Synagoge in Elkins Park (1953–59), dem spektakulärsten Synagogenbau des 20. Jahrhunderts, genannt werden darf.

Doch anders als Wright, dessen Reformsynagoge sich kaum von einer Kirche unterscheidet, erfand Botta einen neuen Bautyp: eine aus zwei nahezu identischen Räumen bestehende Doppelsynagoge, bei der aus einem rechteckigen Sockelbau von 22 × 29 m Grundfläche in strenger Symmetrie zwei würfelförmige Volumen von je 10,5 m Kantenlänge wachsen und sich himmelwärts zu Zylindern von 15 m Durchmesser weiten. Bei diesem mit rotem

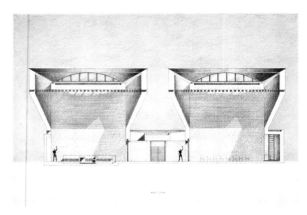

Longitudinal section   Längsschnitt

synagogues. A step leads down to the men's section around the *bimah*, or lectern, where, as in the psalm, the men raise "their voice out of the depths" in prayer.

Light filters into the towers through segments—four at a time—which are left open between the ceiling (which itself resembles a *huppah*, or wedding canopy) and the rounded end of the roof. The towers, clad in Tuscan pie-tra dorata, are transformed into a cosmic metaphor by the movement of the sun. Like a contemporary inter-pretation of a gate to the heavenly Jerusalem, this architecture fulfils the promise of Louis I. Kahn's project-ed, but never built, Hurva Synagogue in Jerusalem. In secular Tel Aviv, Botta's twin-towered bastion of faith also takes on a sociopolitical significance as a meeting place for two diverging religious and lay population groups whose concord is so crucial to Israel's future.

Roman Hollenstein

For a detailed analysis, see: Roman Hollenstein, "Mario Botta's Cymbalista Synagogue in Tel Aviv" in *Mario Botta, The Cymbalista Synagogue and Jewish Heritage Center, Tel Aviv University*, Milan 2001, pp. 25–36.

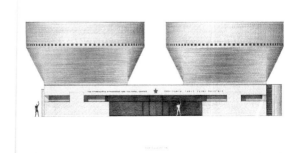

North elevation   Ansicht von Norden

Veroneser Dolomiten-Stein verkleideten Solitär handelt es sich um die erste architektonisch bedeutende Campus-Synagoge seit 1957/58, als Heinz Rau und David Reznik in Jerusalem auf dem Givat-Ram-Campus der Hebrew University ihr legendäres Gotteshaus bauten. Danach ist in Israel – Zvi Heckers bunkerartige Negev-Synagoge von 1969 ausgenommen – kein Sakralbau mehr entstanden, der sich mit Bottas Meisterwerk messen könnte – be-eindrucken doch allein schon die vielfältigen historischen Bezüge, die von den kubischen Synagogenräumen der rheinischen Romanik über die Prager Altneuschul bis hin zu Judith Stolzers turmförmiger Wehrsynagoge in Hadera reichen.

Der durch zwei gekuppelte Rundpfeiler akzentuierte Nordeingang, der an das von den Bronzesäulen Jachin und Boas flankierte Portal von Salomons Tempel erinnert, führt in eine Vorhalle, von der aus man nach links in das Judaica-Museum und die eigentliche Synagoge, nach rechts aber in den Beth Midrasch genannten Raum für das Thorastudium und in den Versammlungssaal im West-›Turm‹ gelangt. Während dieser für kulturelle Aktivitäten, aber auch für Reform- und Konservative Gottesdienste genutzt wird, ist der mit seiner kleinen Apsis und dem Thoraschrein nach Jerusalem orientierte Ost-›Turm‹ im Inneren als orthodoxe Synagoge konzipiert. Allerdings wurde, um die räumliche Einheit nicht zu stören, auf eine Empore verzichtet und das wie in einigen antiken Synagogen nur symbolisch durch ein Geländer abgetrennte Frauenabteil auf dem Niveau des Eingangs eingerichtet. Eine Stufe führt hinab zu dem um die Bima, das Lesepult, angeordneten Bereich der Männer, die von hier – dem Psalm folgend – »ihre Stimme aus der Tiefe« zum Gebet erheben.

Durch je vier Segmente, die im Übergang von der quadratischen, an eine Chuppa, einen Hochzeitsbaldachin, erinnernden Decke zu dem runden Dachabschluss ausge-spart sind, flutet Licht in die beiden mit toskanischer Pietra dorata ausgekleideten ›Türme‹, die durch den Gang der Sonne gleichsam in kosmische Metaphern verwandelt werden. Damit löst das wie die zeitgenössische Interpreta-tion eines Tors zum himmlischen Jerusalem anmutende Gotteshaus das Versprechen von Louis I. Kahns nie reali-sierter Hurva-Synagoge in Jerusalem ein. Bottas doppel-türmiger Burg des Glaubens kommt im säkularen Tel Aviv aber auch gesellschaftspolitische Bedeutung zu als Ort der für die Zukunft Israels wichtigen Begegnung zwischen den sich auseinander lebenden religiösen und laizistischen Bevölkerungsgruppen.

Roman Hollenstein

Für eine ausführliche Analyse siehe: Roman Hollenstein, »Mario Botta's Cymbalista Synagogue in Tel Aviv«, in: *Mario Botta: The Cymbalista Synagogue and Jewish Heritage Center. Tel Aviv Uni-versity*, Mailand 2001, S. 25–36.

Pages   Seiten 104/105
The synagogue ceiling resembles a huppah
Die an eine Chuppa erinnernde Synagogendecke

**North facade with main entrance**  Nordfassade mit dem Haupteingang

**Floor plan, ground floor**  Grundriss Erdgeschoss

Floor plan, upper level  Grundriss Dachebene

Entry hall. Left: auditorium entrance.
Right: synagogue entrance
Eingangshalle. Links der Eingang zum Auditorium,
rechts der zur Synagoge

Synagogue ceiling
Decke der Synagoge

View into the auditorium
Blick ins Auditorium

Page    Seite 107
Synagogue interior
Innenraum der Synagoge

Will Bruder

**Temple Kol Ami**
**Kol-Ami-Synagoge**

Scottsdale, Arizona | USA
1992–1994, 2002/2003

Perspective drawings by Will Bruder    Perspektivzeichnungen von Will Bruder

How does a semi-mystical, non-Jewish architect design a synagogue in the middle of the sprawl of one of the United States' fastest growing cities? When Will Bruder received the commission to design the Temple Kol Ami sanctuary and school in Scottsdale, Arizona, in 1992, he felt far enough removed from any Jewish tradition that he took his whole (small) office to Jerusalem. There, he and his associates found themselves impressed by an unexpected sense of similarity between the center of Jewish life and its furthest suburban periphery. The desert climate and the inward turned, rough-hewn rock response to that climate in the Old City reminded them of what they held dear about Arizona. Back in Scottsdale, Bruder chose to carve a sense of sensual spirituality out of and with that geologic and climatic condition. Instead of either referring directly to Israel or trying to make a contextual work in the sprawl of Phoenix, he decided to carve a sense of community out of—what is in both an abstract and a physical sense—an alien, harsh landscape.

The project that resulted is a closed compound, presenting its stepped concrete block walls with naked force to its suburban neighbors. The offset blocks catch the light and help alleviate the massiveness of the form, while one gesture, a split glass plane propped up in front of the sanctuary's sloping face, marks the project's spiritual core. This is a "desert community," says Bruder, meant to remind us "of Masada and Jerusalem." But it is also a secure haven for Jews far away from their spiritual home—residents of a placeless metropolis who can park their cars off the street and enter through one small slot into a place that is defined, sheltered, cool, and safe.

Wie kann ein nur halbwegs mystisch veranlagter nichtjüdischer Architekt eine Synagoge mitten in einem ausufernden Stadtrandgebiet einer der am schnellsten wachsenden Städte der Vereinigten Staaten bauen? Als Will Bruder 1992 den Auftrag zum Entwurf der Kol-Ami-Synagoge mit Schule in Scottsdale, Arizona, erhielt, fühlte er sich so weit von jeder jüdischen Tradition entfernt, dass er zunächst einmal mit sämtlichen Mitarbeitern (er hat nur wenige) nach Jerusalem reiste. Dort waren sie alle überrascht und beeindruckt, wie sehr das jüdische Leben in seinem Zentrum dem in seiner äußersten Peripherie ähnelt. Das Wüstenklima und die diesem Klima entsprechende nach innen gekehrte Anlage der Jerusalemer Altstadt mit ihren Häusern und Gebäuden aus grob behauenen Steinen erinnerte sie an vertraute Anblicke in Arizona. Nach Scottsdale zurückgekehrt, beschloss Bruder, aus und mit diesen geologischen und klimatischen Gegebenheiten ein Gefühl sinnlicher Spiritualität herauszuarbeiten. Statt an der Peripherie der Stadt Phoenix direkte Bezüge zu Israel herzustellen oder den Versuch zu machen, kontextuell zu arbeiten, entschied er sich dafür, in dieser im übertragenen wie im konkreten Sinne unwirtlichen, harten Landschaft durch den Synagogenkomplex ein Gefühl der Gemeinschaft zu vermitteln.

Das Ergebnis ist ein ummauertes Ensemble, das den vorstädtischen Nachbarn seine abgestuften Betonsteinmauern mit unverhüllter Kraft zukehrt. Die gegeneinander versetzten Steine fangen das Sonnenlicht ein und tragen dazu bei, die Massivität der Bauform zu mildern, während ein anderes Element – eine an die geneigte Vorderfassade des Tempels angelehnte gespaltene Glasscheibe – auf die spirituelle Nutzung des Gebäudes hinweist. Es ist eine »Wüstensiedlung«, so Bruder, die uns an Massada und

Within the compound, a long axis of shade trees stretches through the block, stringing together the classrooms, communal spaces, offices, and the sanctuary. Everywhere, the alchemy of architecture transforms the simplest forms and materials into a refined element that both shelters and abstracts. An undulating canopy of corrugated Plexiglas held up by steel beams, the stage front-like walls of the school, and the blocks themselves, which are of a standard size and finish, are all bits and pieces taken from the outside world of residential developments, industrial parks and roadside stands. Here, these familiar fragments are composed in such a manner that one actually notices them, and can find beauty even in these humble components of desert living.

The sanctuary itself is like a suburban home, abstracted and increased in scale. One enters into a low lobby through a rough-hewn wood door, set in a glass plane, and then turns into the main space. There, everything falls away. The curving, sloping walls that led one from the parking lot to the community center serve to both enclose the community at its moment of concentration and to guide one's eye to the carefully buffered light that enters past the Temple's signature, a knife's blade of glass, on the outside. A low window balances this flood of sunlight and looks out onto a garden offering a refined piece of desert landscape.

A butterfly roof plays with one's sense of weight and enclosure, while the ark with its cherry wood doors contains the torah scrolls with a luxurious, but primitive certainty. With a push and a pull, a curve and a sense of enclosure, with rough-hewn majesty and an abstraction of the outside world, Bruder has turned this small, suburban outpost of Jewish civilization into a place where a tradition of cherishing knowledge and community can both be safely housed and find an understanding of the place it came from and now resides.

Aaron Betsky

Jerusalem erinnern soll. Es ist aber auch ein sicherer Hafen für Juden, die fern ihrer spirituellen Heimat leben, Bewohner einer gesichtslosen Großstadt. Sie können ihre Autos auf der Straße parken, um dann durch einen schmalen Spalt einen klar umrissenen, geschützten, kühlen und sicheren Ort zu betreten.

Hier im Inneren verläuft eine lange Reihe Schatten spendender Bäume durch die gesamte Hofanlage und verbindet die Klassenzimmer, Gemeinschaftsräume, Büros und die Synagoge miteinander. Überall verwandelt die architektonische Alchemie die einfachsten Formen und Materialien in raffinierte Komponenten, die zugleich schützen und abstrahieren. Ein Baldachin aus gewelltem Plexiglas auf Stahlträgern, die proszeniumartigen Mauern der Schule und die handelsüblichen genormten Betonsteine – all das sind Bestandteile, die der ›Außenwelt‹ der Wohnsiedlungen, Gewerbeparks und Straßenverkaufsstände entnommen wurden. Hier werden diese vertrauten Elemente so zusammengefügt, dass man sie bewusst wahrnimmt und sogar in diesen bescheidenen Alltagsdingen des Wüstendaseins Schönheit entdecken kann.

Die Synagoge selbst wirkt wie ein aus einer Vorortsiedlung hierher versetztes und maßstäblich vergrößertes Haus. Durch eine mit Glas eingefasste rustikale Holztür betritt man einen niedrigen Vorraum und wendet sich zum großen Synagogenraum. Hier lässt man alles hinter sich. Die geschwungenen und geneigten Mauern, die einen vom Parkplatz zum Gemeindehaus geleitet haben, dienen hier dazu, die Gläubigen in ihrer Konzentration auf die religiöse Handlung zu umfassen und den Blick auf das sorgfältig gedämpfte Licht zu lenken, das durch den schmalen Glasschlitz einfällt, der von außen gesehen das Erkennungsmerkmal der Synagoge bildet. Ein niedriges Fenster ergänzt diesen Lichteinfall und gibt Blick auf einen Garten, ein veredeltes Stück Wüstenlandschaft.

Das Schmetterlingsdach der Synagoge spielt mit der Wahrnehmung des Betrachters von Schwere und Geschlossenheit, während die Kirschbaumtüren des Thoraschreins die Thorarollen mit luxuriöser und doch ursprünglicher Gewissheit verbergen. Mit Präsenz und Rückzug, Schwung und dem Sinn für Geborgenheit, mit grob behauener Würde und Abgeschiedenheit von der Außenwelt hat Bruder diesen kleinen vorstädtischen Außenposten der jüdischen Zivilisation in einen Ort verwandelt, der die Tradition, das Wissen und die Gemeinschaft wertzuschätzen, in seinen Mauern bewahrt und zum tieferen Verständnis des Ursprungsortes und der gegenwärtigen Heimat der Juden beiträgt.

Aaron Betsky

View of entire area   Blick auf die Gesamtanlage

Main entrance of the building   Haupteingang des Gebäudes

Synagogue interior   Innenraum der Synagoge

**Pages**   Seiten 112/113
**Courtyard of school area**
Innenhof des Schulbereichs

Interior of a classroom    Innenraum eines Klassenzimmers

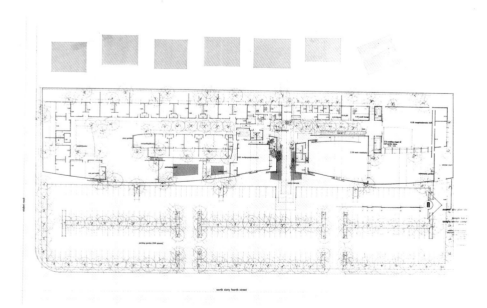

Floor plan    Grundriss

Page    Seite 115
**Facade detail**
Fassadenausschnitt

Will Bruder    **Temple Kol Ami**    Kol-Ami-Synagoge

Zvi Hecker

**Jewish Cultural Center Duisburg**
**Jüdisches Gemeindezentrum**
**Duisburg Mülheim Oberhausen**

Duisburg, Germany | Deutschland
1996 – 1999

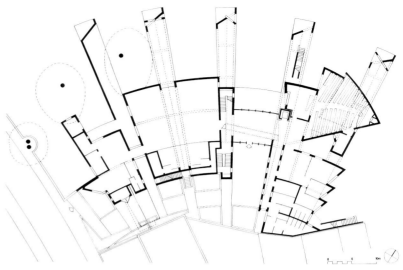

Floor plan, ground floor   Grundriss Erdgeschoss

The Jewish community in Duisburg, a harbor and manufacturing city in the West German mining region, shares its fate with many others in Germany. A Jewish community has existed there since the twelfth century, when the city was under direct imperial rule. After the pogrom of 1938, after the Holocaust, war, and emigration, its membership in Duisburg and Mülheim had shrunk to sixty. Since then, thanks to the immigration of Russian Jews of German descent, the community has increased to over two thousand members.

Zvi Hecker received the commission to build the community center after a competition whose contributors included Daniel Libeskind. Like Libeskind, Hecker has an unconstrained approach to symbolically charged and, at the same time, geometrically controlled configurations. He associates the five folds of the fan-like structure with epochs of German-Jewish coexistence, from the arrival of the Jewish community alluded to in the first wing to the new, postwar beginning symbolized by the fifth wing and its swing to the east. The image of an open book also plays into the configuration, which at the same time stands for the first five letters of the Hebrew alphabet and possibly for the five Books of Moses. But the radial double disks of the facades with their perforated surfaces also recall loading cranes, remnants of Duisburg's past as a lumber port—or the fingers of an open hand—or the points of a star.

The structure exudes self-confidence, neither closing itself off from the outside world nor making itself inconspicuous; yet it avoids every pretentious gesture. Its entrance appears of secondary importance, suitable in Hecker's view for a Diaspora community. The visitor passes under a section of the building which projects daringly (containing the caretaker's apartment) and

Die jüdische Gemeinde in Duisburg, der Hafen- und Fabrikstadt im westdeutschen Montanrevier, teilt ihr Schicksal mit vielen Gemeinden in Deutschland. Eine jüdische Gemeinschaft gab es in der reichsunmittelbaren Stadt seit dem 12. Jahrhundert. Nach dem Pogrom von 1938, nach Holocaust, Krieg und Emigration war die Zahl ihrer Mitglieder in Duisburg und Mülheim auf sechzig Personen zusammengeschmolzen. Einwanderungen jüdischer Russland-Deutscher haben die Gemeinde wieder auf mehr als 2000 Mitglieder anwachsen lassen.

Den Auftrag für ein Gemeindezentrum erhielt Zvi Hecker nach einem Wettbewerb, bei dem er sich unter anderem gegen Daniel Libeskind durchsetzte. Auch Hecker hat einen unverstellten Zugang zu symbolisch aufgeladenen und zugleich geometrisch kontrollierten Figuren. Die fünf Faltungen des Gebäudefächers bezieht er auf Epochen des deutsch-jüdischen Zusammenlebens: von der Ankunft der jüdischen Gemeinde, auf die der erste Flügel verweist, bis zum fünften, der, nach Osten geschwenkt, den Neubeginn symbolisiert. Das Bild des Buches mit aufgeschlagenen Seiten spielt hinein, die zugleich für die ersten fünf Buchstaben des hebräischen Alphabets stehen sollen und womöglich auch für die fünf Bücher Mose. Aber die radialen, an ihren Kopfstücken perforierten Doppelscheiben erinnern auch an Portalkräne, die aus der Vergangenheit des Duisburger Holzhafens überdauert haben könnten. Oder an die Finger einer geöffneten Hand. Oder an die Zacken eines Sterns.

Der Bau zeigt Selbstbewusstsein, schließt sich nicht ab, macht sich nicht klein, vermeidet aber jede auftrumpfende Geste. Sein Eingang wirkt wie nebensächlich, einer Diaspora-Gemeinde angemessen, wie Hecker findet. Der Besucher unterquert einen waghalsig auskragenden Gebäuderiegel (mit der Hausmeisterwohnung) und gerät in

enters a small courtyard. Somewhere between the third and fourth radials the foyer opens, over-spanned by a bridge clad in corrugated metal, and the planned uses nest between the radii. On the eastern side, a triangular prism projects out of the last radial—the synagogue itself. Hecker had intended to sheath it in slate but, due to the expense, had to make do with black paint.

With one exception, all the materials are ordinary: exposed concrete, white stucco, wood, steel, zinc. Imported Jerusalem stone, in this case in gradations of red rather than yellow, is limited to the interior floors and balustrades. The simplicity of the other building materials was dictated by the limited budget. But polished elegance was not Hecker's aim to begin with. If worship and religious services are ancient human activities, shouldn't the place in which they are practiced have archaic, even primitive qualities?

The community center was erected under the auspices of the International Building Exhibition Emscher Park. The multipartite structure projects into the newly laid-out park, conceived as a "Garden of Memories" by the Israeli sculptor Dani Karavan. Set off by the construction relics integrated by Karavan, Hecker's architecture exudes contemporary presence. The fact that the Garden of Memories invokes not only the industrial past of the terrain but, thanks to the new Community Center, a chapter of religious and political history with its highs and lows, lends the locale an additional metaphysical dimension.

Wolfgang Pehnt

einen kleinen Innenhof. Irgendwo öffnet sich das Foyer zwischen dritter und vierter Radiale, überspannt von einer wellblechverkleideten Gebäudebrücke. Zwischen den Halbmessern haben sich die notwendigen Nutzungen eingenistet. An der Ostseite drängt ein Dreiecksprisma durch die letzte Radiale, die Synagoge. Hecker wollte sie außen verschiefern, musste sich aber aus Kostengründen mit einem schwarzen Anstrich begnügen.

Mit einer Ausnahme sind alle Materialien gewöhnlich: Sichtbeton, weißer Putz, Holz, Stahl, Zink. Importierter Jerusalem-Stein, hier in rötlichem und nicht gelbem Farbspiel, ist auf Böden und Brüstungen des Inneren beschränkt. Die Armut der übrigen Baustoffe ergab sich aus dem niedrigen Budget. Doch polierte Eleganz ist ohnehin nicht Heckers Fall. Wenn Anbetung und Gottesdienst uralte Handlungen des Menschen sind: Darf oder muss dann nicht auch der Ort, an dem sie ausgeübt werden, archaische, ja primitive Qualitäten haben?

Der Bau wurde unter dem Protektorat der Internationalen Bauausstellung Emscherpark realisiert. Das vielgliedrige Gebäude greift in den neu angelegten Park aus, den der israelische Bildhauer Dani Karavan als ›Garten der Erinnerungen‹ konzipiert hat. Neben den Baurelikten, die Karavan integrierte, entfaltet Heckers Bauwerk zeitgenössische Präsenz. Dass der ›Garten der Erinnerungen‹ nicht nur die industrielle Vergangenheit des Terrains beschwört, sondern dank dem neuen Gemeindezentrum auch ein Stück religiöser und politischer Geschichte mit ihren Tiefen und Untiefen, gibt dem Ort eine zusätzliche, metaphysische Dimension.

Wolfgang Pehnt

Pages    Seiten 120/121
Total view from the north
Gesamtansicht von Norden

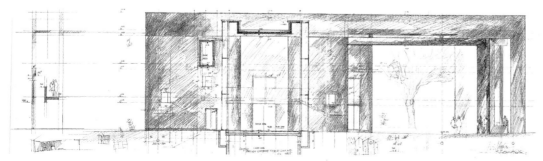
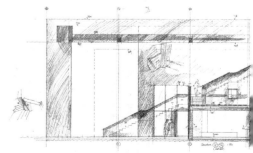

Design drawings by Zvi Hecker
Section through entrance foyer looking west. 7/19/1997 (left)
Section G—G. 8/9/1997 (middle)
Section synagogue. 9/15/1997 (right)

Entwurfszeichnungen von Zvi Hecker
Schnitt durch das Eingangsfoyer, Blick nach Westen. 19.7.1997 (links)
Schnitt G—G. 9.8.1997 (Mitte)
Schnitt Synagoge. 15.9.1997 (rechts)

**Floor plan** Grundriss

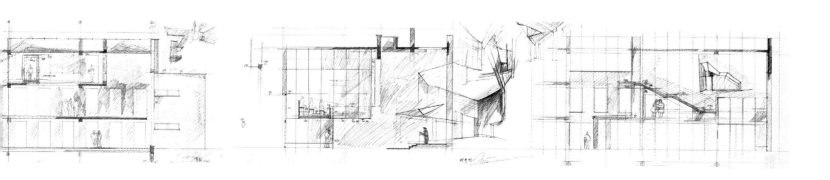

Staircase    Treppenhaus

Synagogue interior
Innenraum der Synagoge

Wandel Hoefer Lorch + Hirsch

**New Synagogue Dresden**
**Neue Synagoge Dresden**

Dresden, Germany | Deutschland
1997–2001

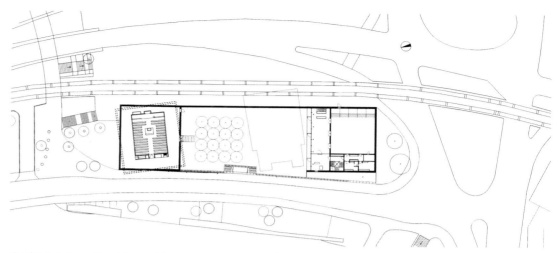

Site plan, including outline of destroyed Semper synagogue   Gesamtplan mit den Umrissen der zerstörten Semper-Synagoge

Wandel Hoefer Lorch, in occasional collaboration with Nikolaus Hirsch, is one of the German architecture firms that have dealt most intensively with the memory of the Shoah. The absence of the Jews murdered in the Third Reich and the destruction of their culture is a leitmotif of their work, which can be seen in their monuments on Börneplatz in Frankfurt (1995), and *Track 17* at the former deportation station of Berlin-Grunewald (1998). Likewise, their new synagogue and Jewish community center in Dresden stands under the paradigm of disappearance and destruction—of both the old synagogue and Dresden's city center. The old synagogue, an oriental, neo-Byzantine domed building with Romanesque elements, was built according to Gottfried Semper's design in 1838–1840. It contained an interior in a Moorish-Byzantine style and was torched in the Night of Broken Glass, 9–10 November 1938, and was subsequently razed. Dresden's city center was destroyed during Allied air raids in February 1945, as World War II neared its end.

In Dresden, this caesura is being addressed by an extensive reconstruction program. Its claim to continuity is, at best, difficult to ascribe to German history and has nothing at all to do with Jewish history there. This may explain why the Jewish community in Dresden chose the synagogue design of Wandel Hoefer Lorch + Hirsch, even though it placed only third in a Europe-wide competition. Located on the historical lot, now reduced to a narrow strip at the east edge of the Brühl'sche Terrasse and city center, the design consists of two solitary structures on an elongated socle which define a courtyard. On the far side, a busy traffic artery leads to the bridge that crosses to the newer part of town, Dresden Neustadt.

In addition to considering the urban context, the architects looked into the special characteristics of

Wandel Hoefer Lorch, teilweise in Zusammenarbeit mit Nikolaus Hirsch, ist eines der Architekturbüros in Deutschland, die sich am intensivsten mit der Erinnerung an die Shoah auseinander gesetzt haben. Folglich ist eines der Leitmotive ihrer Arbeit das Verschwinden der im Nationalsozialismus ermordeten Juden und ihrer Kultur, dem sie sich über ihre Mahnmale für den Frankfurter Börneplatz (1995) und das *Gleis 17* am ehemaligen Deportationsbahnhof Berlin-Grunewald (1998) angenähert haben. Auch der Neubau der Synagoge und des jüdischen Gemeindezentrums in Dresden steht unter dem Paradigma des Verschwindens und der Zerstörung: sowohl der nach einem Entwurf von Gottfried Semper 1838–40 als orientalisch-byzantinischer Kuppelbau mit romanischen Stilelementen und einer maurisch-byzantinischen Innendekoration errichteten Synagoge, die in der ›Reichskristallnacht‹ vom 9./10. November 1938 in Brand gesteckt und anschließend abgetragen wurde, als auch der Zerstörung der Dresdner Altstadt durch die alliierten Bombenangriffe am Ende des Zweiten Weltkriegs im Februar 1945.

Dieser Zäsur begegnet man in Dresden mit einem groß angelegten Rekonstruktionsprogramm, dessen Anspruch auf eine scheinbare Kontinuität sich schon auf deutsche Geschichte schwer, aber auf jüdische Geschichte in Deutschland ganz sicher nicht übertragen lässt. Deswegen entschied sich die jüdische Gemeinde zu Dresden 1997 in einem europaweit ausgeschriebenen Realisierungswettbewerb für den Entwurf der drittplatzierten Architekten Wandel Hoefer Lorch + Hirsch, die das inzwischen auf einen schmalen Streifen reduzierte historische Grundstück am Ostrand der Brühl'schen Terrasse und der Altstadt mit zwei Solitären auf einem lang gestreckten Sockel besetzten, welche zwischen sich einen Hof definieren. Auf der anderen Seite führt eine viel befahrene Verkehrsachse vorbei, die auf die Brücke zur Dresdner Neustadt führt.

Page   Seite 124
Synagogue interior
with brass curtain
Innenraum der Synagoge
mit dem Messingvorhang

Wandel Hoefer Lorch + Hirsch   **New Synagogue Dresden**   Neue Synagoge Dresden

125

Jewish synagogue architecture, and asked themselves how historical and contemporary aspects of Jewish identity and migration could be translated into architectural terms. The results of these reflections led them to base their design both on the Temple, symbol of homeland and permanence, and on the tabernacle, symbol of the wanderings of the Jewish people, which the architects describe as the "fundamental architectural experience of Judaism." They also approached this theme by way of a second strategy, that of materials.

The synagogue is a monolith twenty-four meters in height, whose complex, tensioned form results from a step-by-step rotation of orthogonal levels that serve to orient the wall of the torah shrine in the direction of Jerusalem. The facade, a closed surface interrupted only by the courtyard entrance and four small windows on the back wall, consists of cast stones whose color and texture echo the Elbe sandstone widely used in Dresden's buildings—including the original synagogue. The exterior configuration and facade structure of the new building, referring to the motif of the Temple, are also clearly evident in the interior, since the walls are unclad and all utilities are integrated in them. In this impressive interior a weave of brass, suspended like a canopy, defines the actual ritual space of the synagogue. This semi-transparent curtain conveys an analogy to the tabernacle and is adorned with a series of Stars of David that evoke a highly festive atmosphere. Below this curtain is an expansive wooden structure that contains the visitors' gallery, pews, back wall with *aron hakodesh* (Torah shrine, whose doors are adorned with inlay work), and *bimah* (lectern).

In Reform synagogues of the nineteenth century, the lectern tended to be moved to the front wall with the torah shrine, in an increasing adoption of the spatial organization of Christian churches. Wandel Hoefer Lorch + Hirsch's conception reverses this assimilation tendency. Here, the lectern is centrally located, creating a non-hierarchical space in which the rituals take on a more participatory character. The space is illuminated by daylight from above and by suspended lamps.

Across from the synagogue stands the community center, whose glazed facade with wooden framing (open to the courtyard) sets a contrast to the introverted block of the synagogue with its focus on worship and concentration. The multi-purpose building with café, festival hall, kitchen, administration offices, library and archive, classrooms, and a roof terrace, serves not only the Dresden Jewish community's internal concerns but also an exchange with the public. The site as a whole is thus not only a demarcated space for the Jewish center but an urban plaza. The Jewish community which, thanks to immigration, has grown to nearly 500 members since 1989, now performs a dual integrational function of new members into the community and of the community into the city.

Zusätzlich zu der Auseinandersetzung mit dem städtebaulichen Kontext beschäftigten sich die Architekten mit den speziellen Charakteristika jüdischer Sakralarchitektur und fragten sich, wie sich die historischen und aktuellen Phänomene der jüdischen Identität und Migration in Architektur übertragen ließen. Als Resultat dieser Überlegungen führten sie ihren Entwurf einerseits auf den Tempel, den man als Symbol für Heimat und Dauerhaftigkeit bezeichnen könnte, und andererseits auf das Stiftszelt, Symbol für die Wanderschaft des jüdischen Volkes, zurück, die sie als die »architektonischen Grunderfahrungen des Judentums« bezeichnen. Diesem Thema näherten sie sich über ihre zweite Strategie, das Material, an.

Die Synagoge ist ein Monolith von 24 m Höhe, dessen komplexe und gespannte Form aus einer schrittweisen Drehung orthogonaler Ebenen entsteht, deren Funktion es ist, die Wand mit dem Thoraschrein Richtung Jerusalem auszurichten. Die bis auf den hofseitigen Eingang und vier kleine Fenster an der Rückwand geschlossene Fassade besteht aus Formsteinen, die in ihrer Farbe und Materialität den städtebaulichen Bezug zu dem in Dresden meist verwendeten Elbsandstein herstellen, aus dem auch der Vorgängerbau errichtet war. Gleichzeitig ist die äußere Erscheinung und Fassadenstruktur der Synagoge, die auf das zuvor schon erwähnte Motiv des Tempels verweist, auch im Inneren deutlich wahrnehmbar, da die Wände nicht verkleidet und sämtliche Installationen in sie integriert sind. In diesen eindrucksvollen Innenraum ist ein Messinggeflecht, das den eigentlichen rituellen Raum der Synagoge definiert, wie ein Baldachin eingehängt. Hier zeigt sich die Analogie zum Stiftszelt; gleichzeitig hat der mit einer Reihe von Davidsternen verzierte, halb transparente Vorhang einen ausgesprochen festlichen Charakter. Unter diesen Vorhang ist ein hölzernes Großmöbel eingestellt, das die hier für Besucher verwendete Empore, die Bänke, die Stirnwand mit dem Aron ha-Kodesch (Thoraschrein), dessen Türen mit Intarsienarbeiten verziert sind, und die in der Mitte platzierte Bima (Lesepult) enthält. Hatten die Reformsynagogen im 19. Jahrhundert dazu tendiert, die Bima an die Rückwand der Synagoge mit dem Thoraschrein heranzurücken und damit zunehmend die Raumorganisation christlicher Kirchen übernommen, so geht das Raumkonzept von Wandel Hoefer Lorch + Hirsch hinter diese Assimilationsbestrebungen zurück und sieht eine mittige Disposition vor, die einen unhierarchischen Raum schafft, in dem die rituelle Handlung eher partizipatorischen Charakter hat. Belichtet wird der Raum durch Tageslicht von oben und abgehängte Lampen.

Gegenüber der Synagoge liegt das Gemeindezentrum, dessen zum Hof offene, mit Holz versetzte Glasfassade einen Gegensatz zu dem introvertierten, ganz auf Andacht und Konzentration gerichteten Kubus der Synagoge darstellt. Das multifunktionale Gebäude mit Café, Festsaal, Küche, Verwaltung, Bibliothek und Archiv, Unterrichtsräumen und einer Dachterrasse dient nicht nur den internen Belangen der Dresdner jüdischen Gemeinde, sondern

Total view. Left: synagogue. Right: community center    Gesamtansicht. Links die Synagoge, rechts das Gemeindezentrum

This openness is also proclaimed by the Hebrew inscription over the synagogue entrance, "May My house be a house of worship for all peoples" (Isaiah 56:7). The new synagogue and community center, inaugurated on 9 November 2001, marked a self-confident and encouraging new beginning. At the same time, the Semper synagogue and with it the history of the former Jewish community in Dresden, live on in the rescued golden Star of David at the entrance, several original sandstone blocks integrated in the masonry, and the ground plan of its destroyed predecessor inscribed in the courtyard of the new building.

Angeli Sachs

auch dem Austausch mit der Öffentlichkeit. Damit wird die Gesamtanlage gleichzeitig definierter Raum des jüdischen Zentrums und städtischer Platz, und die durch Immigranten seit 1989 auf fast 500 Mitglieder gewachsene Gemeinde erbringt nun eine doppelte Integrationsleistung der neuen Mitglieder in die Gemeinde und der Gemeinde in die Stadt.

Auch der in hebräischen Buchstaben über der Eingangstür der Synagoge eingravierte Spruch »Mein Haus sei ein Haus der Andacht allen Völkern« (Jesaja 56,7) kündet von dieser Offenheit. Die am 9. November 2001 eröffnete neue Synagoge und das Gemeindezentrum sind ein selbstbewusster und ermutigender Neubeginn. Gleichzeitig bleiben die Semper-Synagoge und damit die Geschichte der früheren jüdischen Gemeinde Dresdens in dem geretteten goldenen Davidstern im Eingang der Synagoge, einigen eingemauerten originalen Sandsteinquadern und dem in den Hof eingeschriebenen Grundriss des vernichteten Vorgängerbaus spürbar.

Angeli Sachs

**Community center**  Gemeindezentrum

**Page**  Seite 128
**Synagogue**  Synagoge

**Page** Seite 131
Synagogue vestibule, interior
Eingangsbereich der Synagoge von innen

Synagogue interior with bima and Torah shrine. Above: canopy-like brass curtain
Innenraum der Synagoge mit der Bima und dem Thoraschrein, darüber der baldachinartige Messingvorhang

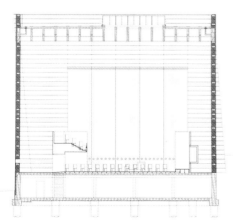

Longitudinal section through the synagogue
Längsschnitt durch die Synagoge

Wandel Hoefer Lorch

**Jewish Center Jakobsplatz**
**Jüdisches Zentrum Jakobsplatz**

Munich | München,
Germany | Deutschland
Since | seit 2001

Urban design competition model with synagogue, museum, and community center
Städtebauliches Wettbewerbsmodell mit Synagoge, Museum und Gemeindezentrum

On 9 November 2003, sixty-five years after the night of the pogrom, the cornerstone of the new Jewish Center in Munich was laid. This new center on Jakobsplatz consists of a synagogue, a community center, and Jewish Museum. This was a historic moment not only for the Jewish community but for the city as a whole. More than most other German cities, Munich is burdened by the legacy of Nazism, having been the "Capital of the Movement," the starting point of the Night of Broken Glass on 9–10 November 1938, and the site of the first concentration camp in nearby Dachau. As in Dresden, the synagogues in Munich were destroyed in 1938. The main synagogue on Herzog-Max-Strasse (consecrated in 1887) was leveled on Hitler's personal orders as early as June of that year. The return to the heart of the city from the postwar, backyard site of the sole surviving synagogue on Reichenbachstrasse, was a clear sign on the part of the city and the Jewish community that Jewish life was again to become a visible and integral part of life in Munich. Not even plans by neo-Nazis—discovered in advance of the event—to violently disrupt the cornerstone laying ceremony could alter this commitment.

The two-phase competition was won by the firm Wandel Hoefer Lorch. Three differently configured building volumes were integrated in the demanding and contextually difficult site on St. Jakobsplatz. The community center abuts existing historical structures, while the synagogue and Jewish Museum are conceived as free-standing, smaller blocks that redefine the urban space in a convincing way. A formal link among the three building volumes is established by the facade material, a warm-toned travertine, enlivened by various surface textures from polished to rough-split slabs.

The community center, housing a range of facilities for school, education, and events as well as a restaurant, a welfare center, and administration offices, is a complex structure not only in terms of its diverse functions. The

Als am 9. November 2003, 65 Jahre nach der Pogromnacht, der Grundstein für das aus Synagoge, Gemeindezentrum und Jüdischem Museum bestehende Jüdische Zentrum am Jakobsplatz in München gelegt wurde, war dies nicht nur für die Jüdische Gemeinde, sondern für die ganze Stadt ein bedeutsamer historischer Moment. Durch seine Geschichte als ehemalige ›Hauptstadt der Bewegung‹, als Ausgangsort der ›Kristallnacht‹ vom 9. auf den 10. November 1938 und als Standort des ersten Konzentrationslagers in Dachau ist München stärker als viele andere Städte durch die Geschichte des Nationalsozialismus belastet. Ähnlich wie in Dresden wurden 1938 auch in München die Synagogen zerstört, die 1887 eingeweihte Hauptsynagoge an der Herzog-Max-Straße auf persönlichen Befehl Hitlers sogar schon im Juni 1938. Die Rückkehr aus der Hinterhofsituation der Nachkriegszeit in der einzigen erhaltenen Synagoge an der Reichenbachstraße in das Herz der historischen Altstadt ist denn auch als ein deutliches Zeichen der Stadt und der Gemeinde zu verstehen, jüdisches Leben wieder zu einem sicht- und erfahrbaren Teil des städtischen Lebens werden zu lassen. Daran konnten auch Attentatspläne von Neonazis auf die Grundsteinlegung, die im Vorfeld der Veranstaltung aufgedeckt wurden, nichts ändern.

Der zweistufige Wettbewerb wurde von dem Architekturbüro Wandel Hoefer Lorch gewonnen. In die städtebaulich anspruchsvolle und kontextuell schwierige Situation am St.-Jakobs-Platz integrieren die Architekten drei unterschiedlich geformte Baukörper. Das Gemeindezentrum schließt dabei an die bestehende historische Bebauung an, die Synagoge und das Jüdische Museum sind als frei stehende, kleinere Kuben konzipiert, die den Stadtraum auf überzeugende Weise neu definieren. Ein formaler Zusammenhang der drei Baukörper wird durch das Fassadenmaterial des warm getönten Travertins erreicht, der durch unterschiedliche Oberflächentexturen von geschliffen bis gebrochen differenziert eingesetzt wird.

Page Seite 132
Material study for facades
Materialstudien für die Fassaden

mono-functional synagogue and museum buildings have correspondingly straightforward configurations. Like that in Dresden, the Munich synagogue combines features of both Temple and tabernacle. Yet here, the translucent tent of meeting, based on the geometry of the Star of David, rises above the monolithic socle to become a symbol visible from afar, especially by night. And as in Dresden, the interior is centrally organized, with galleries extending along the longitudinal walls.

In the Jewish Museum, the effect is reversed. A closed block containing exhibition rooms rises above a glazed ground floor which doubles as display window and public space where activities are accessible to view. The 750-square-meter exhibition area of this municipal institution will be devoted principally to the life and culture of Judaism, with an emphasis on Munich and temporary exhibitions on related topics.

For Jews in Munich, the beginning of construction of the Jewish Center—currently the largest project of its type in Europe—marked a homecoming. As the chairwoman of the Jewish community in Munich, Charlotte Knobloch, said at the cornerstone laying, "Today, after exactly sixty-five years, I too have truly and entirely come back home."

Angeli Sachs

Das Gemeindezentrum, das eine ganze Bandbreite von Einrichtungen für Schule, Bildung und Veranstaltungen sowie ein Restaurant, eine Sozialstation und Büros für die Verwaltung enthalten soll, ist nicht nur von seinen Funktionen her ein komplexes Gebäude. Die monofunktionalen Gebäude der Synagoge und des Museums erscheinen in ihrer Gestalt klarer ausgeprägt. Die Synagoge vereint wie die in Dresden die Charakteristika des Tempels und des Zelts. Diesmal erhebt sich das transluzente, auf der Geometrie des Davidsterns basierende Zelt von außen sichtbar über dem monolithischen Sockel und wird so, vor allem bei Dunkelheit, zu einem weithin sichtbaren Symbol werden. Der Innenraum ist auch hier zentral organisiert, die Emporen befinden sich an den Längswänden.

Bei dem Jüdischen Museum ist der Effekt umgekehrt — dort erhebt sich der geschlossene Block der Ausstellungsräume über einem verglasten Erdgeschoss, das als Schaufenster und zugleich öffentlicher Raum die Aktivitäten sichtbar machen soll. Die städtische Institution wird auf ihren 750 m² Ausstellungsfläche vor allem Leben und Kultur des Judentums, mit einem Schwerpunkt auf München, darstellen sowie darüber hinausreichende Wechselausstellungen zeigen.

Für die Juden in München bedeutet der Baubeginn für das Jüdische Zentrum, übrigens das zur Zeit größte jüdische Projekt in Europa, Heimkehr und Heimat. Ihre Vorsitzende Charlotte Knobloch sagte bei der Grundsteinlegung: »Denn heute, nach genau 65 Jahren, bin auch ich wieder ganz in meiner Heimat angekommen.«

Angeli Sachs

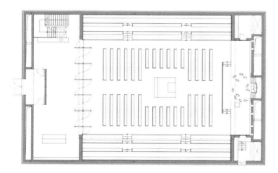

**Floor plan, synagogue**   Grundriss der Synagoge

**Longitudinal and cross section of the synagogue**
Längs- und Querschnitt der Synagoge

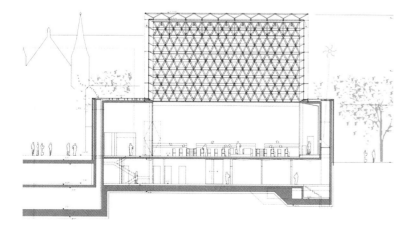

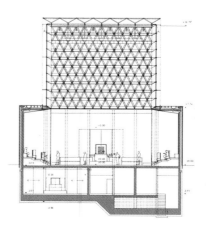

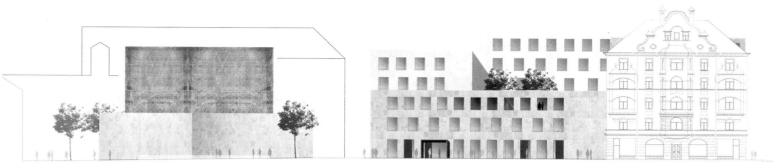

Total view. Left: the synagogue with the Jewish Museum in the background. Right: the community center
Gesamtansicht. Links die Synagoge, dahinter das Jüdische Museum, rechts das Gemeindezentrum

North elevation of the Jewish Museum
Nordansicht des Jüdischen Museums

West elevation of the synagogue with entrance
Westansicht der Synagoge mit dem Eingang

Schools
Schulen

Zvi Hecker

**Jewish Primary School Berlin**
Heinz-Galinski-Schule

Berlin, Germany | Deutschland
1990–1995

Axonometric view
Axonometrie

Despite a restless life resulting from his Jewish descent, the widely travelled Zvi Hecker is no global player. The fluctuations on the stock exchange of aesthetic opinion have left him unaffected. In the 1960s and '70s he persistently explored the potentials of closely layered, polyhedral crystalline structures that permitted condensed construction in limited areas. For Hecker, geometry is no self-referential mathematical game—it provides formulae for the expression of organic life. His buildings in Israel frequently employed the form of the spiral, in particular the geometry of the sunflower, whose blossoms are defined by the intersection points of radius and concentric arc segments.

In the floor plan for the Heinz Galinski School in Berlin, this configuration is superimposed on that of a book with open pages. The Hebrew the word for "book" (*sefer*) forms the basis for the word "school" (*beth sefer*, "house of the book"). For a culture that for the greater part of its history was unable to define itself in terms of a certain territory and was dependent in exile on the read and interpreted word, the book represented a unifying factor. This wandering people may not have been able to carry their temple along with them, but they could carry the book. Hecker has now opened it in Berlin as well.

His pre and elementary school is located in the Grunewald district. It continues the tradition of the Jewish school in Berlin, especially the Jewish Free School of the late eighteenth century, which was attended by Jewish and Christian children alike. Hecker had to defend his unusual configuration in face of many obstacles—from budget stipulations to building and zoning laws and, not least, his own working conditions. Part of the project was finished in the air-raid shelter of his neighborhood in Tel Aviv as Saddam Hussein's missiles were raining down. The plans truly have the look of battlefields, with their continually shifting intermediate states, corrections and explanations. That they were finally put

Trotz seines bewegten Lebenslaufs, den ihm sein jüdisches Schicksal auferlegt hat, ist der weit gereiste Zvi Hecker kein ›global player‹. Die jeweiligen Kursschwankungen an der ästhetischen Meinungsbörse berühren ihn nicht. Ausführlich und hartnäckig hat er sich in den 1960er und 1970er Jahren mit polyedrischen Kristallstrukturen in dichten Packlagen auseinander gesetzt, die konzentriertes Bauen auf knapper Fläche ermöglichen sollten. Geometrie ist für Hecker kein selbstgenügsames mathematisches Spiel, sie bietet ihm eine Formel organischen Lebens. Bei seinen Bauten in Israel hat ihn mehrfach die Spirale beschäftigt, vor allem die Geometrie der Sonnenblume, deren Blütenstände sich aus den Schnittpunkten von Radien und konzentrischen Kreisbögen ergeben.

Im Grundriss der Berliner Heinz-Galinski-Schule überlagert sich diese Figur mit dem Bild des Buches und seiner aufgeschlagenen Seiten. Das Wort Buch (sefer) bildet im Hebräischen die Grundlage für das Wort Schule (beth sefer, Haus des Buches). Für eine Kultur, die sich in den längsten Epochen ihrer Geschichte nicht durch ein Territorium definieren konnte und im Exil auf das gelesene und gedeutete Wort angewiesen war, bedeutete das Buch ein einheitsstiftendes Moment. Den Tempel konnte das Volk der Wanderer nicht mit sich tragen, wohl aber das Buch. Hecker schlug es auch in Berlin auf.

Die Vor- und Grundschule liegt im Berliner Grunewald. Sie setzt die Tradition des jüdischen Berliner Schulwesens fort, vor allem der ›jüdischen Freyschule‹ vom Ende des 18. Jahrhunderts, die jüdische und christliche Kinder gemeinsam unterrichtet hatte. Hecker musste seine ungewöhnliche Baufigur im Clinch mit den wirtschaftlichen Vorgaben, dem Bau- und Nachbarschaftsrecht und nicht zuletzt mit seinen eigenen Arbeitsbedingungen durchsetzen. Ein Teil der Projekte entstand im Luftschutzkeller seines Wohnviertels in Tel Aviv, als es Saddam Husseins Raketen ausgesetzt war. Die Pläne sind wahrhafte Schlachtfelder mit immer neuen Zwischenzuständen, Korrekturen,

into practice can be credited largely to Hecker's contact architect in Berlin, Inken Baller.

Schoolchildren, teachers, and guests are received by a seven-cornered plaza, an empty space like the storm center of the building. From there, the building's wings seem virtually to fly outward—the auditorium wing, which can be used as a synagogue or concert hall, and the curving wedges housing the classrooms and playrooms of the all-day school. The connections between the separate sections are highly unusual in character. Gently rising and falling bridges and corridors clad with sheet metal snake their way through the various levels of the building complex.

In terms of color, Hecker has exerted restraint: white stucco surfaces, gray painted concrete, anthracite—gray sheathing, silver—gray metal elements, rust-brown window frames. Conflicts, breaks, and collisions remain limited to the floor plans and building volumes. This school building is neither beholden to one-dimensional logic nor to an over-protectiveness of children. It contains dark zones and unexpected challenges—just like the real world, about which the children are already beginning to learn as they attend their school.

Wolfgang Pehnt

Erklärungsversuchen. Um ihre Umsetzung hat sich Heckers Berliner Kontaktarchitektin Inken Baller verdient gemacht.

Empfangen werden Kinder, Lehrer und Gäste auf einem siebeneckigen Platz, der leeren Mitte, dem Sturmzentrum des Bauwerks. Von hier aus scheinen die Gebäudeflügel förmlich davonzufliegen: der Teil, den eine als Synagoge oder Konzertsaal nutzbare Aula einnimmt, und die gekrümmten Keile, in denen Klassen- und Spielräume für den Ganztagsbetrieb liegen. Höchst ungewöhnlich ist die Verbindung der einzelnen Bauteile. Wie Schlangengewürm winden sich auf den verschiedenen Ebenen leicht ansteigende und abfallende, außen blechverkleidete Brücken und Gänge durch den Baukomplex.

In der Farbigkeit übte Hecker Zurückhaltung: weiße Putzflächen, grau gestrichener Beton, anthrazitfarbene Verkleidungen, silbergraues Metall, rostbraune Fensterrahmen. Konflikte, Brüche und Zusammenstöße bleiben den Grundrissen und Bauvolumen überlassen. Dieser Schulort folgt nicht eindimensionaler Logik, auch nicht protektionistischer Kinderfreundlichkeit. Er birgt Dunkelzonen und unüberschaubare Herausforderungen – gleich der großen Welt. Die Kinder lernen es schon beim Gebrauch ihres Schulhauses.

Wolfgang Pehnt

Design sketch by Zvi Hecker from the initial design stage
Entwurfsskizze von Zvi Hecker aus der ersten Entwurfsphase

**Page** Seite 141
Design sketches by Zvi Hecker.
*Rainwater Collection,*
1/9–1/10/1993, mixed media on paper (above);
Facade details,
3/29–4/15/1993, mixed media on paper (bottom)
Entwurfsskizzen von Zvi Hecker.
*Rainwater Collection,*
9.–10.1.1993, Mischtechnik auf Papier (oben);
Fassadendetails,
29.3.–15.4.1993, Mischtechnik auf Papier (unten)

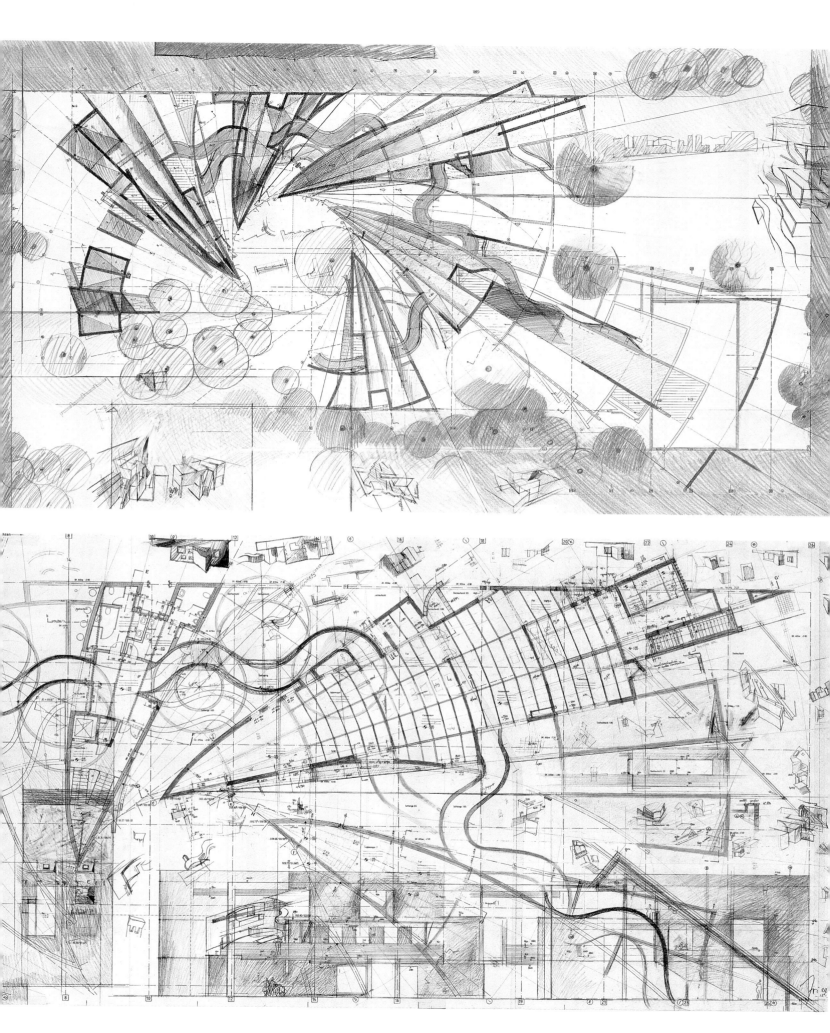

Zvi Hecker **Jewish Primary School Berlin** Heinz-Galinski-Schule

The structure contains a multifarious formal language.    Das Gebäude verfügt über eine vielfältige Formensprache.

**Page**    Seite 142
The individual building volumes are connected by a serpentine hall.
Die einzelnen Baukörper werden durch einen schlangenförmigen Gang verbunden.

**Pages**    Seiten 144/145
**Aerial view**    Gesamtaufnahme aus der Luft

Adolf Krischanitz

**New World School**
**Neue Welt Schule**

Vienna | Wien, Austria | Österreich
1992 – 1994

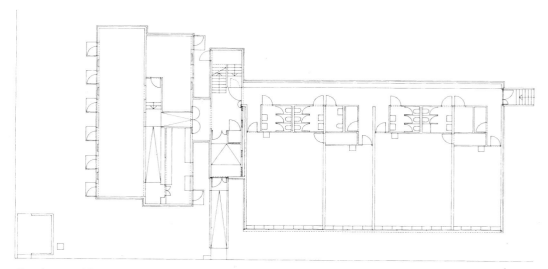

Floor plan, ground floor   Grundriss Erdgeschoss

Vienna, District II — Leopoldstadt — Mazzesinsel: In the symbolic topography of the city, the municipal district on the opposite side of the Danube Canal has been closely associated with its Jewish inhabitants ever since the establishment of the ghetto (1624–1670). The Jewish kindergarten and school designed by the subtle minimalist Adolf Krischanitz are also located here, though not in the area of the former ghetto, rather on prominent sites in the erstwhile royal parks of the Prater and Augarten. Contrary to the usual practice, the architect himself was able to choose the construction sites together with the client. Both buildings were commissioned by a foundation established by Ronald S. Lauder, who served as American ambassador in Vienna from 1986–87. Since 1987, the Ronald S. Lauder Foundation has been furthering the religious training and general education of Jewish children in central Eastern Europe, a task made ever more pressing by the increasing immigration of Russian Jews to the region.

In the case of the Neue Welt Schule (New World School), it was an existing municipal kindergarten that suggested the choice of a construction site in the Prater, near the Lusthaus. The idea underlying the design was to establish various links with the surrounding landscape: first, by positioning the structural elements to take into account an existing population of old trees; second, through the large window areas; and finally, through the building's unusual color scheme. The blackish–gray of the pigmented concrete facade was the result of a collaboration with the Swiss artist Helmut Federle, who also selected the colors and materials for the interior. What at

Wien II. Bezirk — Leopoldstadt — Mazzesinsel: In der symbolischen Topografie der Stadt ist der Gemeindebezirk jenseits des Donaukanals seit der Gründung des neuzeitlichen Ghettos (1624–70) eng mit seinen jüdischen Bewohnern verbunden. Hier befinden sich auch der jüdische Kindergarten und der Schulbau des subtilen Minimalisten Adolf Krischanitz, allerdings nicht im Bereich des einstigen Ghettos, sondern an prominenten Stellen in den ehemals kaiserlichen Grünanlagen des Praters und des Augartens. Ungewöhnlicherweise durfte der Architekt die Bauplätze in Absprache mit dem Auftraggeber bestimmen. Beide Bauten wurden von der Stiftung von Ronald S. Lauder, der 1986/87 amerikanischer Botschafter in Wien war, in Auftrag gegeben. Die Ronald S. Lauder Foundation fördert seit 1987 die durch die vermehrte Immigration der russischen Juden noch dringlicher gewordene religiöse Erziehung und die Schulbildung jüdischer Kinder in Mittelosteuropa.

Im Fall der Neue Welt Schule war es ein städtischer Kindergarten, der den Anknüpfungspunkt für die Wahl des Bauplatzes im Prater in der Nähe des Lusthauses bot. Die Leitidee des Entwurfs war die Verbindung zur Landschaft auf möglichst vielfältige Weise: zunächst durch die Positionierung der Baukörper, die auf den alten Baumbestand Rücksicht nahm, dann durch die großen Fensterflächen und die ungewöhnliche Farbigkeit. Das Schwarzgrau der durchgefärbten Betonfassade ist das Ergebnis der Zusammenarbeit mit dem Schweizer Künstler Helmut Federle, der auch das Farb- und Materialkonzept im Inneren entwickelte: Was auf den ersten Blick befremdlich wirkt, fügt sich auf den zweiten selbstverständlich in die Palette der Aulandschaft ein; dunkel sind die oft nasse Erde und die

View from northwest of the staggered building volumes    Blick von Nordwesten auf die gestaffelt angeordneten Baukörper

first sight may appear strange soon turns out to be naturally integrated in the palette of the river meadows outside. Their damp earth and the nearby tree trunks often take on a dark hue which is set off, like the building's interior walls, by the greenish-yellow of foliage and grass.

As if carefully stacked and then shifted by an inadvertent movement, the building volumes are staggered in terms of height and position. The projections and recessions correspond to clearly defined functions. The two-story tract houses a cafeteria, utilities, and administration, while the one-story tract is divided into common rooms for the children, with a narrow stairwell sandwiched in between.

Viewed from outside, nothing points to the building's purpose as a kindergarten, let alone a kindergarten for Jewish children. No "child-friendly" playground equipment or symbolic explanations provide orientation for the observer. Yet, the building is more than the often-quoted "neutral shell" waiting to be filled with content and life. Rather, it is an extremely expressive shell that employs architectural means of the most fundamental kind—a truly self-confident architecture.

Ruth Hanisch

Baumstämme der näheren Umgebung, grünlich-gelb — wie die Wände im Inneren — sind Blätter und Gras.

Wie sorgfältig aneinander gereiht und dann durch eine unbedachte Bewegung verrutscht, sind die Baukörper in Höhe und Lage gestaffelt. Den Vor- und Rücksprüngen entsprechen klar unterschiedene Funktionen: Der zweigeschossige Trakt nimmt Speisesaal, Technik und Verwaltung auf, der eingeschossige die Gruppenräume der Kinder, dazwischen liegt das schmale Treppenhaus.

Von außen besehen lässt nichts auf die Bestimmung des Baus als Kindergarten, als einen für jüdische Kinder zumal, schließen. Keine ›kindgerechten‹ Spielereien, keine symbolischen Erklärungen orientieren den Betrachter. Und dennoch handelt es sich hier nicht nur um die oft zitierte ›neutrale‹ Hülle, die erst mit Inhalten und Leben zu füllen wäre. Es handelt sich vielmehr um eine höchst ausdrucksstarke Hülle, die sich auf die ihr ureigensten Mittel des Architektonischen konzentriert — eine ›selbstbewusste‹ Architektur.

Ruth Hanisch

Pages    Seiten 150/151
The windows reflect the surroundings, thereby including them in the building. Die Fenster spiegeln die Umgebung wider und beziehen sie so in das Gebäude mit ein.

View into the park from a group room    Blick aus einem Gruppenraum in den Park

Adolf Krischanitz

**Lauder Chabad School**
**Lauder Chabad Schule**

Vienna | Wien, Austria | Österreich
1996 – 1999

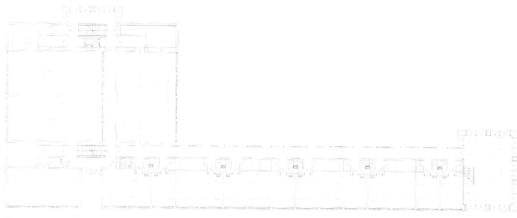

Floor plan, ground floor   Grundriss Erdgeschoss

The Lauder Chabad School has stood since 1999 on the grounds of a provisional Jewish children's home behind the old brick wall of the Augarten, in the immediate proximity of one of Vienna's anti-aircraft towers. In a strange shift of meaning, these World War II defense structures, scattered around the city, are now generally understood as admonitory anti-war monuments. Here, the dark silhouette of the tower dominates the site, both physically and symbolically.

The building volume absorbs the dominant elements in the surroundings—the tower and wall. The three-story tract with classrooms extends between a nearly square stairwell tower and a tract containing administration offices, cafeterias, and synagogue. The tower-like impression of the two flanking structures results not from a difference in height but from a very conscious use of deep window reveals and their relationship to the wall surface. Krischanitz himself increased the challenge of the task by employing a single type of window for the entire school. Depending on whether the windows were set flush with the interior wall, as in the flanking structures, or flush with the exterior wall, as in the classroom tract, an immensely different architectural impression resulted. The sole exception to this scheme was the complete glazing of the classroom tract facing the park wall.

Functionally, the spatial arrangement is much more diversified than in the New World School. The Campus is attended by children from preschool to final examination. The rooms are used by a kindergarten, elementary, and middle school, with corresponding rooms for administration, library, and the necessary sanitary facilities. Beyond this, religious criteria had to be taken into account. Both cafeterias include separate areas for the preparation of dairy and meat dishes, and the gymnasiums and workrooms are designed for separate use by boys and girls. The three-aisle prayer room on the top floor of the administration tract, for which Krischanitz also designed the textile furnishings, has a women's gallery and

Auf dem Gelände eines provisorischen jüdischen Kinderheims hinter der alten Ziegelmauer des Augartens und in unmittelbarer Nähe zu einem der Wiener Flaktürme steht seit 1999 die Lauder Chabad Schule. Die über das Stadtgebiet verstreuten Türme der Flugabwehr werden heute in einer seltsamen Bedeutungsverschiebung generell als Mahnmal gegen den Krieg empfunden. Die dunkle Silhouette dominiert den Bauplatz sowohl physisch wie inhaltlich.

Die Volumetrie des Baus nimmt die dominierenden Elemente der Umgebung – Turm und Mauer – auf. Zwischen einem annähernd quadratischen Treppenhausturm und einem Trakt für Verwaltung, Speisesäle und Synagoge wird ein dreigeschossiger Trakt mit den Klassenräumen eingespannt. Der turmartige Eindruck der beiden Kopfbauten wird nicht durch eine Höhendifferenz erreicht, sondern durch den kalkulierten Einsatz von tiefen Fensterlaibungen und ihrem Verhältnis zur Wandfläche. Krischanitz hat die Herausforderung der Aufgabe für sich selbst noch erhöht, indem er nur einen einzigen Fenstertypus für die gesamte Schule verwendete. Je nachdem, ob dieser nun innenbündig wie in den Kopfbauten oder außenbündig wie im Klassentrakt eingebaut wurde, verändert sich der Ausdruck der Architektur immens. Als einzige Ausnahme wurde die Vollverglasung des Klassentraktes zur Parkmauer zugelassen.

Funktional ist das Raumprogramm wesentlich diversifizierter als in Krischanitz' Neue Welt Schule; der Campus kann Kinder von der Krabbelstube bis zur Reifeprüfung aufnehmen. Das Raumprogramm umfasst Kindergarten, Volksschule und Mittelschule mit den entsprechenden Räumen für Verwaltung und Bibliothek sowie den notwendigen Sanitäreinrichtungen. Darüber hinaus waren die religiösen Vorgaben zu berücksichtigen: In beiden Speisesälen wurden zwei Küchennischen für die getrennte Zubereitung von Milch- und Fleischspeisen eingerichtet; Turnsäle und Werkräume sind für Mädchen und Knaben getrennt benutzbar. Der dreischiffige Andachtsraum im obersten Geschoss des Verwaltungstraktes, für den Krischanitz auch die textile Ausstattung entwarf, verfügt über Frauenempore

North elevation   Ansicht von Norden

Torah shrine. The room serves as a synagogue for both the school and the congregation.

Except for the prayer room of the Lauder Chabad Campus, the architect employed no religious or secular symbolism in either building. Yet their design, nevertheless, reflects the Jewish tradition in Vienna. Krischanitz established clear links with Viennese architecture of the interwar period, in which Jewish architects and clients played a key role. Their conception of culture was nourished by profound tolerance and openness. One of their most brilliant representatives was Josef Frank, an outspoken critic of dogma of whatever origin, who was forced to flee Vienna on the advent of Austrian fascism.

Both buildings stand quietly and impressively on their site. They are anchored in a way that is not obtrusive, but by no means arbitrary, either. The classical lines of their design and the durability of their materials (concrete, Untersberg marble, bronze, and oak) combine with an almost visionary aspect which reflects the client's intentions: to ensure that the experiences of Jewish children in a future Austrian society will be as well-founded and natural as the architecture of their schools.

Ruth Hanisch

und Thoraschrein. Er steht als Synagoge für die Schule sowie für die Gemeinde zur Verfügung.

Außerhalb des eigentlichen Kultraums des Lauder Chabad Campus hat der Architekt keine religiöse oder profane Symbolik bei den beiden Bauten verwendet. Und dennoch bezieht sich ihre Erscheinung auf die jüdische Tradition Wiens. Krischanitz knüpft deutlich an die Wiener Architektur der Zwischenkriegszeit an, die stark von jüdischen Architekten und Auftraggebern geprägt war. Deren Kulturbegriff war von einer großen Toleranz und Offenheit getragen. Einer ihrer geistreichsten Vertreter war Josef Frank, bitterer Kritiker sämtlicher Dogmen, der vor dem Austrofaschismus aus Wien flüchten musste.

Beide Bauten stehen ruhig und nachdrücklich an ihren jeweiligen Orten. Sie sind dort in einer Weise verankert, die nicht aggressiv ist, aber auch keinesfalls beliebig. Die Klassizität ihrer Gestaltung und die Dauerhaftigkeit ihrer Materialien (Beton, Untersberger Marmor, Bronze und Eiche) verbindet sich mit einem geradezu visionären Zug, der den Intentionen des Auftraggebers entgegenkommt: Die Erfahrungen jüdischer Kinder in einer österreichischen Gesellschaft der Zukunft sollen der Solidität und Selbstverständlichkeit des hier Gebauten entsprechen.

Ruth Hanisch

**Pages**   Seiten 156/157
**View from the east with neighboring watchtower**
Ansicht von Osten mit dem benachbarten Flakturm

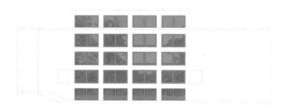

West elevation   Ansicht von Westen

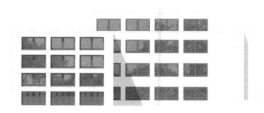

East elevation   Ansicht von Osten

South elevation   Ansicht von Süden

Synagogue/auditorium   Synagoge/Auditorium

Entrance hall   Eingangshalle

Library interior   Innenraum der Bibliothek

Adolf Krischanitz   **Lauder Chabad School**   Lauder Chabad Schule

Al Mansfeld,
Haim Kehat, Michael Mansfeld,
Judith Mansfeld

**Yavne Religious High School**
**Yavne-Schule,**
**religiöse Oberschule**

Ramat Alon, Haifa | Israel
1995–1998, 2000/2001

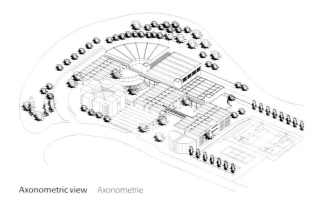

Axonometric view   Axonometrie

The Orthodox Yavne School is a late work of Al Mansfeld, who was born in St. Petersburg in 1912. After escaping the turmoil of the October Revolution, Mansfeld honed his drawing talent in Berlin during the 1920s, and from 1931 to 1935 studied architecture in Berlin and Paris. After unsuccessful attempts to find employment in France, he emigrated to Palestine, then still a British mandated territory. In 1937, he opened an architecture firm in Haifa with Munio Weinraub, a former Bauhaus member, and one-time collaborator of Mies van der Rohe. By the time the state of Israel was established in 1948, their firm had become one of the country's most renowned. In 1950 they won a project competition for a new government district in Jerusalem, the building of which, however, was not further pursued.

In 1960 Al Mansfeld and Dora Gad were awarded first prize for their competition design for the Israel Museum, submitted under the title "Growth, Change and Incertainty." After permission to build was granted, this project occupied them for three decades, until 1993. Today, the museum complex dominates the crest of Neve Sha'anan hill west of Jerusalem's Old City. It has the appearance of having grown organically from a modular order and is now considered a classic, one of the finest buildings of Israeli modernism.

The Yavne Upper School for fourteen- to eighteen-year-old boys was based on the same elementary structuralist vocabulary as the artfully interlocked pavilions of the Israel Museum. The school lies embedded in a gently sloping valley below Ramat Alon, a habitat intended primarily for immigrants from the Soviet Union. Ramat Alon was designed along the lines of Mediterranean coastal towns by Mansfeld and his junior partners Haim Kehat and Michael and Judith Mansfeld. The school might be viewed as the spiritual nexus of the area, were it not for the fact that only about ten percent of the population are observant Jews and only a few families send their sons to this school, whose curriculum, divided equally between religious and secular subjects, is not exactly popular there.

The majority of the approximately 700 students come from the Greater Haifa area and some from even farther away. Accommodation is provided by a dormitory integrated in the harmoniously balanced complex. After

Die orthodoxe Yavne-Schule in Haifa ist ein Spätwerk des 1912 in St. Petersburg geborenen Architekten Al Mansfeld, der, den Wirren der Oktoberrevolution entkommen, im Berlin der ›Goldenen Zwanziger‹ sein Zeichentalent trainierte und von 1931 bis 1935 in Berlin und Paris Architektur studierte. Nach vergeblicher Arbeitssuche in Frankreich wanderte er in das damalige britische Mandatsgebiet Palästina ein, wo er zusammen mit Munio Weinraub, dem ehemaligen Bauhaus-Angehörigen und zeitweiligen Mitarbeiter Mies van der Rohes, im Jahr 1937 in Haifa ein Architekturbüro eröffnete, das zur Zeit der Staatsgründung 1948 zu den renommiertesten im Land gehörte. 1950 gewann es den Ideenwettbewerb für den Bau des neuen Regierungsviertels in Jerusalem, der jedoch nicht weiterverfolgt wurde. 1960 erhielten Al Mansfeld und Dora Gad den ersten Preis für ihren unter dem Leitsatz »Growth, Change and Incertainty« eingereichten Wettbewerbsentwurf für das Israel-Museum, das sie nach Erhalt des Bauauftrags drei Jahrzehnte lang bis 1993 beschäftigte. Heute ist der nach einer modularen Ordnung in dominanter Lage scheinbar organisch gewachsene Museumskomplex auf dem Kamm des Neve-Sha'anan-Hügels westlich der Jerusalemer Altstadt ein Klassiker und einer der besten Bauten der israelischen Moderne.

Die Yavne-Oberschule für Jungen im Alter von 14 bis 18 Jahren entstammt dem gleichen strukturalistisch-elementaristischen Vokabular wie die kunstvoll verschränkten Pavillons des Israel-Museums. Die Schule liegt unterhalb des von Mansfeld und seinen Juniorpartnern Haim Kehat, Michael und Judith Mansfeld speziell für Einwanderer aus der Sowjetunion nach dem Vorbild mediterraner Küstenstädte geplanten Habitats Ramat Alon in eine abflachende Talsenke eingebettet. Man könnte sie als dessen spirituellen Bezugspunkt ansehen, wüsste man nicht, dass nur etwa zehn Prozent seiner Bewohner gläubige Juden sind und nur wenige Familien ihre Söhne in diese Schule schicken, deren paritätisch in religiöse und weltliche Fächer unterteiltes Unterrichtsprogramm nicht gerade populär ist.

Die Mehrheit der ca. 700 Schüler kommt aus dem Großraum Haifa, einige von noch weiter her. Sie können in dem innerhalb des harmonisch ausgewogenen Ensembles gelegenen Dormitorium wohnen. Die Schüler werden auf der Plaza empfangen und zur Linken sogleich in die von acht quadratischen Bastionen umstandene,

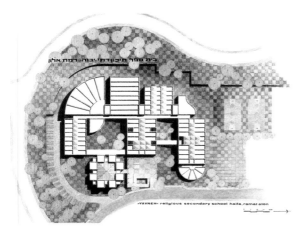

Site plan    Lageplan

entering the plaza, students proceed straight to the two-story synagogue surrounded by eight square bastions, whose basement contains a spacious hall that serves as a central instruction facility and is also used for informal meetings and social services. Its pyramidal roof has a glazed peak through which light falls on the central *bima*, and which seems to hover weightlessly above a circumambient window band. This feature reflects a masterful control of illumination and conveys a sublime recollection of the tabernacle, the symbol of the exodus. The impression is augmented by the transparency of the diagonally set glass bricks. Incidental decor is waived, with the exception of the vegetation evoking the Tree of Life located around the torah niche. As in every synagogue in the world, the niche is oriented towards the Temple Mount in Jerusalem.

Apart from the synagogue, this compositionally and functionally balanced complex evinces no further religious references. The administration tract and faculty conference rooms overlook the entrances and exits, and link the instruction area with the rounded tract which houses the common rooms: cafeteria, college hall, library, and club house. The rectangular classrooms and shop rooms receive natural light from the north and south. The lower courtyard, located between the faculty house and classrooms, contains a garden with proliferating flowerbeds, shade trees and small bench niches. In the publicly accessible upper courtyard, green lawns and a broad, sweeping stairway invite rendezvous and recreation, and provide a site for cultural events. Next to the gymnasium there are open grounds, which are also available for use by children and adolescents from the settlement. The "fifth facade," the roof, is accentuated by an accumulation of small transparent pyramids, echoing the synagogue roof, which rises above the faculty, instruction, and dormitory tract. For the neighbors, this roof offers a sign, visible day and night, that the congruence of faith and knowledge is still vital.

Anna Teut

zweigeschossige Synagoge geleitet, die im Souterrain eine geräumige Halle für informelle Begegnungen und soziale Dienste beherbergt, im Übrigen als zentrales Lehrhaus dient. Überdacht wird sie von einer Pyramide, durch deren gläserne Spitze das Licht auf die zentrale Bima herabflutet, während sie selbst, durch das umlaufende Fensterband ihrer lastenden Schwere enthoben, zu schweben scheint. Ohne Frage zeigt sich hier eine meisterhafte Lichtführung und sublime Erinnerung an das Stiftszelt, das Symbol der Wanderung – eine Impression, die durch die Transparenz der Glasbausteine über Eck noch verstärkt wird. Auf beiläufiges Dekor wird konsequent verzichtet; ausgenommen ist die den Lebensbaum assoziierende vegetabile Umrandung der Thoranische, die hier, wie in allen Synagogen der Welt, auf den Tempelberg in Jerusalem ausgerichtet ist.

Abgesehen von der Synagoge zeigt die kompositorisch und funktional ausgewogene Gesamtanlage keine weiteren religiösen Merkmale. Verwaltungstrakt und Lehrerarbeitsräume kontrollieren die Ein- und Ausgänge und verbinden den Lernbereich mit den nach außen gerundeten Gemeinschaftsräumen: Mensa, Kollegsaal, Bibliothek und Clubhaus. Die rechteckigen Klassen- und Werkräume werden von Norden und Süden belichtet. Der zwischen dem Lehrerhaus und den Klassenräumen gelegene untere Hof ist ein Garten mit üppigen Rabatten, schattigen Bäumen und kleinen Bankplätzen. Im öffentlich zugänglichen oberen Hof laden der grüne Rasen und die breite, schön geschwungene Treppenanlage zu Entspannung, Treffs und kulturellen Veranstaltungen ein. Neben der Sporthalle gibt es freie Plätze, die auch von Kindern und Jugendlichen der Siedlung genutzt werden. Die ›Fünfte Fassade‹, das Dach, wird lesbar gemacht durch die Kumulation kleiner, der Synagogenspitze nachgebildeter, transparenter Pyramiden über dem Lehr-, Lern- und Schlaftrakt – für die Nachbarn bei Tag und in der Nacht ein Zeichen, dass die Übereinstimmung von Glauben und Wissen lebendig ist.

Anna Teut

Floor plan, ground floor    Grundriss Eingangsebene

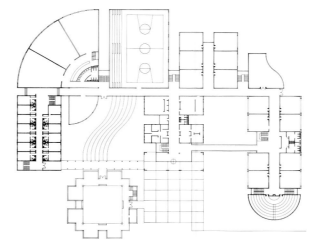

View from the northeast of students' residence, the teachers' offices, and synagogue
Blick von Nordosten auf das Schülerwohnheim, das Lehrerhaus und die Synagoge

**Connecting bridge to the classrooms**    Verbindungssteg zu den Klassenräumen

**Synagogue interior**    Innenraum der Synagoge

Mehrdad Yazdani | Cannon Design

**Sinai Temple Akiba Academy**
**Sinai Temple Akiba Academy**

Los Angeles, California | Kalifornien
USA
1998 / 1999

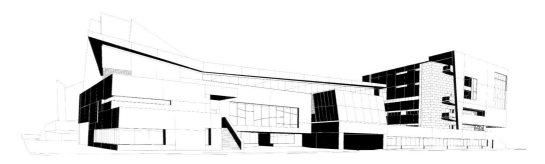

Perspective view from the south    Perspektive von Süden

Many describe Los Angeles as a city devoid of an architectural identity, an opinion derived, in large part, from the city's characteristic sprawl and lack of a definable center. It is precisely because Los Angeles is a connection of semi-autonomous cities that it provides the ideal crucible for mixing cultures and style. There is no predominant tradition in this city, the Santa Monica School direction in art and architecture coming as close to a signature style as post–World War II modernism. Perhaps Los Angeles' relatively young age explains its unique position among world cities—it is culturally open-minded without deeply-rooted prejudices that often accompany long history and tradition.

The Sinai Temple Akiba Academy Expansion provides a perfect example of how adroitly Los Angeles merges the past, present, and future. The original Sinai Temple, a 1960s modern building designed by Sidney Eisenshtat, a disciple of Frank Lloyd Wright, is not significantly different than other religious structures of various faiths along Wilshire Boulevard. The academy (for students from pre-school through eighth grade) achieves the sophistication of its upscale, conservative West Los Angeles neighborhood and the stately temple which it adjoins, without gratuitously acknowledging either context or purpose.

Like Yazdani's other work, including the Yeshiva Boys' School and future Kabbalah Center in Los Angeles, the 80,000 square foot Akiba Academy is both sophisticated and exuberant. The building program—60,000 square foot of classrooms, basketball court, rooftop playground, exterior courtyard; 150,000 square foot of parking, drop-off and pick-up area, meeting rooms, and multi-purpose hall—is prodigious. The buildings that formerly accommodated these functions had consumed the portion of the site where higher density was possible. Yazdani's approach was to access more of the site by massing the building into distinct, differently-sized components of varied form—some angled, some bowed, some linear. This massing offered several advantages. The smaller components, which accommodate special func-

Viele beschreiben Los Angeles als eine Stadt ohne architektonische Identität. Diese Einschätzung beruht zum großen Teil auf der charakteristischen Flächenausbreitung der Stadt und dem Fehlen eines klar erkennbaren Zentrums. Gerade weil Los Angeles eigentlich aus einer Verbindung halb autonomer Städte besteht, verkörpert es den idealen Schmelztiegel für verschiedene Kulturen und Stile. In dieser Stadt gibt es keine vorherrschende Kunst- und Architekturtradition, und die Santa-Monica-Schule ist hier ein ebenso typischer Stil wie die Moderne nach dem Zweiten Weltkrieg. Vielleicht erklärt das verhältnismäßig junge Alter von Los Angeles seine einzigartige Stellung unter den Weltstädten: Es ist kulturell aufgeschlossen und frei von den eingefleischten Vorurteilen, die so häufig mit einer langen Geschichte und Tradition einhergehen.

Der Erweiterungsbau der zur Sinai-Synagoge gehörenden Akiba Academy liefert das beste Beispiel dafür, wie geschickt Los Angeles Vergangenheit, Gegenwart und Zukunft zu verschmelzen weiß. Die Sinai-Synagoge – ein von dem Frank-Lloyd-Wright-Schüler Sidney Eisenshtat entworfener moderner Bau der 1960er Jahre – unterscheidet sich nicht wesentlich von den Sakralbauten anderer Konfessionen am Wilshire Boulevard. Die Academy (Vorschule und Schule bis zur 8. Klasse) erreicht die Kultiviertheit der konservativen, gehobenen Nachbarschaft in West Los Angeles und der angrenzenden imposanten Synagoge, ohne dabei ihren Kontext oder Zweck zu übernehmen.

Wie Yazdanis andere Bauten – darunter die Yeshiva Boys' School und das künftige Kabbalah Center in Los Angeles – ist auch die Akiba Academy mit ihren etwa 7400 m² Fläche zugleich elegant und lebendig. Das umfangreiche Bauprogramm umfasste 5600 m² für Klassenzimmer, Basketballfeld, Spielplatz auf dem Dach, Außenhof sowie 14.000 m² für Parkplätze, Kurzzeitparkstreifen, Aufenthaltsräume und Mehrzweckhalle. Die Bauten und Anlagen, in denen diese Funktionen zuvor untergebracht gewesen waren, nahmen den Geländeabschnitt ein, der eine dichtere Bebauung erlaubte. Yazdani wollte mehr offenen Raum schaffen und gestaltete das Academy-Gebäude deshalb als Ansammlung deutlich unterscheidbarer,

View from the south    Ansicht von Süden

tion and meeting rooms, were placed on the southwest portion of the site to relate to the lower scale of the immediately-adjacent residential area. A larger component was placed along the site's east edge, creating a wall that shields the outdoor courtyards and terraces formed by the lower-scaled elements from the noise and activity of the boulevard. This organization also allowed internalization of drop-off and pick-up lanes mitigating long lines of traffic along major streets.

The academy's east elevation along Beverly Glen Boulevard is more restrained than the smaller volumes. Classrooms are stacked on three floors at this end of the building, with a basketball court and rooftop garden above. The luminous precast concrete and glass facade is carefully articulated, and by contrasting the heavier form, dark concrete, and multi-colored stained glass of the temple, it emphasizes the sacred role of the older structure rather than overpowering it.

One has to believe that Yazdani's design for the Akiba Academy was an adventurous direction for the temple. The expansion may be respectful, but it makes its presence known with no attempt to blend in unobtrusively.

Danette Riddle

verschieden großer und geformter Baukörper – einige spitzwinklig, andere gebogen, andere linear. Diese Gestaltung bot mehrere Vorteile. Die kleineren Bauvolumen, in denen Sonderfunktionen und Aufenthaltsräume untergebracht sind, platzierte Yazdani im Südwestabschnitt des Geländes, um zu dem kleineren Maßstab des angrenzenden Wohngebiets überzuleiten. Einen größeren Baukörper platzierte er am Ostrand des Areals, so dass dieser die kleineren Außenhöfe und Terrassen wie eine Mauer vom Lärm und hektischen Treiben des Boulevards abschirmt. Diese Anordnung erlaubte es außerdem, die Vor- und Zufahrten ins Innere der Anlage zu verlegen und so lange Schlangen haltender Wagen in den öffentlichen Straßen zu vermeiden.

Die Ostfassade der Academy zum Beverly Glen Boulevard wirkt zurückhaltender als die kleineren Baukörper. Die Klassenzimmer sind an diesem Ende des Gebäudes auf drei Etagen übereinander angeordnet; auf dem Dach befinden sich ein Basketballfeld und ein Dachgarten. Die glänzende Fassade aus hellen Betonfertigteilen und Glas ist sorgfältig gegliedert. Sie bildet ein Gegengewicht zur Synagoge mit ihrer massiveren Form aus dunklem Beton und Buntglasfenstern und unterstreicht die sakrale Funktion des älteren Gebäudes eher, als dass sie dieses übertrumpft.

Es ist anzunehmen, dass Yazdanis Akiba Academy für die Synagogengemeinde ein Abenteuer darstellte. Der Erweiterungsbau mag zwar dem Bestand gegenüber respektvoll sein, behauptet sich aber dennoch selbstbewusst, ohne den Versuch zu machen, sich unauffällig einzufügen.

Danette Riddle

Pages    Seiten 166/167, 173
**Facade detail of the Jewish Museum Berlin by Daniel Libeskind**
Fassadenausschnitt des Jüdischen Museums Berlin von Daniel Libeskind

Exterior of the assembly hall    Versammlungsraum von außen

View from the southeast. A winding wall of Jerusalem stone guides from the visitor's entrance to the assembly room.
Ansicht von Südosten. Eine gebogene Wand aus Jerusalemer Stein führt vom Besuchereingang zum Versammlungsraum.

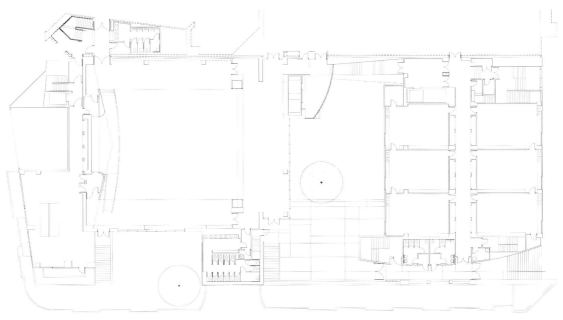

Floor plan, second floor    Grundriss 1. Obergeschoss

# Appendix
## Anhang

## Architects | Architekten

### Ralph Appelbaum

Ralph Appelbaum Associates
New York, USA
London, United Kingdom | Großbritannien
www.raany.com

Ralph Appelbaum (b. 1942 in New York), who founded RAA in 1978, has had extensive involvement in every facet of museum planning and exhibition design. His renowned and award-winning work includes the United States Holocaust Memorial Museum in Washington, DC, the American Museum of Natural History in New York, and the news technology museum—the Newseum—in Arlington, Virginia. He is a frequent lecturer at national and international conferences on a wide variety of issues related to museum design.

Ralph Appelbaum (geb. 1942 in New York), der RAA 1978 gründete, ist vor allem im Bereich der Museumsplanung und des Ausstellungsdesigns engagiert. Seine anerkannten und mit zahlreichen Preisen ausgezeichneten Arbeiten schließen das United States Holocaust Memorial Museum in Washington, D.C., das American Museum of Natural History in New York und das news technology museum – the Newseum – in Arlington, Virginia, ein. Auf nationalen und internationalen Konferenzen hält er regelmäßig Vorträge zu einer großen Bandbreite von Themen im Bereich des Museumsdesigns.

### Mario Botta

Lugano, Switzerland | Schweiz
www.botta.ch

Mario Botta (b. 1943 in Mendrisio) opened his own architecture firm in Lugano in 1969. Subsequent to numerous guest professorships, he has taught at the Academy of Architecture in Mendrisio, Ticino—which he founded—since 1969. His work encompasses the entire spectrum of both public and private construction, and has been awarded numerous prizes and honors. He is considered one of the most important contemporary architects for religious architecture. Among his most important buildings in this area are, alongside the Cymbalista Synagogue, the cathedral of Evry near Paris (1988–95) and the chapel on the peak of Mount Tamaro in Ticino (1990–95).

1969 gründete Mario Botta (geb. 1943 in Mendrisio) sein eigenes Büro in Lugano. Nach zahlreichen Gastprofessuren lehrt er seit 1996 an der von ihm gegründeten Architekturakademie in Mendrisio, Tessin. Botta, der mit zahlreichen Preisen und Ehrungen ausgezeichnet wurde und dessen Werk die ganze Bandbreite privater und öffentlicher Bauaufgaben umfasst, gilt als einer der wichtigsten zeitgenössischen Architekten für religiöse Architektur. Zu seinen wichtigsten Bauten in diesem Bereich zählen neben der Cymbalista-Synagoge die Kathedrale von Evry bei Paris (1988–95) und die Kapelle auf dem Gipfel des Monte Tamaro im Tessin (1990–95).

### Will Bruder

Phoenix, Arizona, USA
www.willbruder.com

Will Bruder (b. 1946 in Milwaukee, Wisconsin), an autodidact in the field of architecture, is in fact a trained sculptor. Following training with Gunnar Birkerts and Poalo Soleri, he opened his own office in 1974. In numerous already completed projects, he attempts to align form and function with the desires of his clients. Through the creative implementation of programs and situations, he has garnered the reputation of one who makes something extraordinary out of the ordinary. His most well-known buildings include the Phoenix Central Library (1998) and the Scottsdale Museum of Contemporary Art (1999).

Will Bruder (geb. 1946 in Milwaukee, Wisconsin), als Architekt Autodidakt, ist ausgebildeter Bildhauer. Nach einer Ausbildungszeit bei Gunnar Birkerts und Poalo Soleri gründete er 1974 sein eigenes Büro. In seinen zahlreichen inzwischen ausgeführten Projekten bemüht er sich, die Form der Funktion und den Wünschen seiner Klienten anzupassen. Seine kreative Umsetzung des Programms und der Situation hat ihm dabei den Ruf eingebracht, aus dem Gewöhnlichen das Außergewöhnliche zu machen. Zu seinen bekanntesten Bauten zählen die Phoenix Central Library (1998) und das Scottsdale Museum of Contemporary Art (1999).

### Claus en Kaan

Claus en Kaan Architecten
Amsterdam and | und Rotterdam, The Netherlands | Niederlande
www.clausenkaan.com

Felix Claus (b. 1956 in Arnhem) and Kees Kaan (b. 1961 in Breda) have, since 1988, run one of the most innovative young architecture firms in the Netherlands. Their clearly structured buildings derive their tension and extraordinary aspects from the implementation of diverse building materials, both natural and industrial. One of their most important projects is the reception pavilion of Zorgvlied cemetery in Amsterdam (1995–98). Felix Claus is guest professor at RWTH Aachen, Germany and head of the atelier at the Academy of Architecture, Amsterdam. Kees Kaan has various teaching positions at technical colleges and the University of Kyoto.

Felix Claus (geb. 1956 in Arnhem) und Kees Kaan (geb. 1961 in Breda) betreiben seit 1988 zusammen eines der innovativsten der jüngeren Architekturbüros der Niederlande. Ihre klar strukturierten Bauten beziehen ihre Spannung und überraschenden Aspekte aus dem Einsatz und Kontrast unterschiedlichster Materialien natürlicher oder industrieller Herkunft. Ein wichtiges ihrer zahlreichen Projekte ist der Empfangspavillon des Friedhofs Zorgvlied in Amsterdam (1995–98). Felix Claus ist Gastprofessor an der RWTH Aachen und leitet das Atelier an der Academy of Architecture in Amsterdam, Kees Kaan hat verschiedene Lehraufträge an europäischen Hochschulen und der Universität von Kyoto.

## Frank O. Gehry

Frank O. Gehry & Associates, Inc.
Santa Monica, California | Kalifornien, USA
www.foga.com

Frank O. Gehry (b. 1929 in Toronto) opened his firm in Los Angeles in 1962. Following his design for the Guggenheim Museum in Bilbao (1991–97), he has become one of the most important and well-known architects working today. The designs of his formally very unusual structures, result from an extensive modeling process, in multiple scales, in which the functional and formal aspects of the project are explored in detail. Other significant buildings include the Walt Disney Concert Hall in Los Angeles (2003) and the Vitra Design Museum in Weil am Rhein (1987–89). Among his other international honors, Gehry was awarded the Pritzker Prize in 1989.

Frank O. Gehry (geb. 1929 in Toronto), der sein Büro 1962 in Los Angeles eröffnete, gehört spätestens seit seinem spektakulären Entwurf für das Guggenheim Museum in Bilbao (1991–97) zu den heute wichtigsten und bekanntesten Architekten. Der Designprozess seiner formal ungewöhnlichen Bauten beruht auf einer extensiven Modellierung in verschiedenen Maßstäben, bei denen die funktionalen und formalen Aspekte des Projekts detailliert untersucht werden. Weitere bedeutende Bauten sind die Walt Disney Concert Hall in Los Angeles (2003) und das Vitra Design Museum in Weil am Rhein (1987–89). Neben zahlreichen anderen internationalen Ehrungen erhielt Gehry 1989 den Pritzker-Preis.

## Zvi Hecker

Tel Aviv, Israel
Berlin, Germany | Deutschland
www.zvihecker.com

Following studies in architecture and painting, Zvi Hecker (b. 1931 in Krakow) opened an office in Israel in 1959. He has also been a guest professor at numerous architecture schools in Europe and the USA. Many of his projects, including the Ramot Housing in Jerusalem or the Palmach Museum of History in Tel Aviv, were built in Israel. He has, however, realized a number of projects in Europe, like those mentioned in this book. Alongside numerous honors, Hecker's work has been exhibited worldwide, and he has represented Israel at different times at the Architecture Biennale of Venice.

Nach einem Studium der Architektur und Malerei eröffnete Zvi Hecker (geb. 1931 in Krakau) sein Büro 1959 in Israel. Daneben war er Gastprofessor an zahlreichen Architekturschulen in Europa und den USA. Viele seiner Projekte wie das Ramot Housing in Jerusalem oder das Palmach Museum of History in Tel Aviv sind in Israel entstanden. Inzwischen realisiert er aber, wie die Beispiele dieses Buchs zeigen, auch bedeutende Projekte in Europa. Neben zahlreichen Ehrungen wurden Heckers Arbeiten weltweit ausgestellt, und er repräsentierte Israel verschiedene Male auf der Architekturbiennale von Venedig.

## Adolf Krischanitz

Vienna | Wien, Austria | Österreich
www.krischanitz.at

In 1970 Adolf Krischanitz (b. 1946 in Schwarzach, Pongau), together with Angela Hareiter and Otto Kapfinger, formed the consortium "Missing Link." In 1979 he went on to open his own architecture firm in Vienna. Since 1992 he has been professor for design and urban renewal at the University of Arts in Berlin. One of his most important early works, together with Herzog & de Meuron and Otto Steidle is the Settlement Pilotengasse in Vienna (1987–92). Next to his work in residential and city planning, he has increasingly created public buildings and exhibition pavilions. One of the most important projects of this minimalist-leaning architect is the conversion of the Museum Rietberg in Zurich (2002–04).

1970 gründete Adolf Krischanitz (geb. 1946 in Schwarzach, Pongau) mit Angela Hareiter und Otto Kapfinger die Arbeitsgemeinschaft Missing Link, bevor er 1979 sein eigenes Architekturbüro in Wien eröffnete. Seit 1992 hat er eine Professur für Entwerfen und Stadterneuerung an der Universität der Künste in Berlin. Eines seiner bedeutendsten Frühwerke ist zusammen mit Herzog & de Meuron und Otto Steidle die Siedlung Pilotengasse in Wien (1987–92). Neben seinen Domänen Wohn- und Städtebau entstehen zunehmend auch öffentliche Bauten und Ausstellungspavillons. Das wichtigste aktuelle Projekt des dem Minimalismus nahe stehenden Architekten ist der Umbau des Museums Rietberg in Zürich (2002–04).

## Daniel Libeskind

Studio Daniel Libeskind
New York, USA
www.daniel-libeskind.com

Daniel Libeskind (b. 1946 in Lodz) is an international figure in architectural practice and urban design. He is well-known for introducing a new critical discourse into architecture and for his multi-disciplinary approach. His work ranges from building major cultural institutions including: museums and concert halls, landscape, and urban projects; to stage design, installations, and exhibitions. His most acclaimed buildings are the Felix Nussbaum Haus in Osnabrück, Germany (1998), the Jewish Museum Berlin (1999), and the Imperial War Museum North in Manchester (2002). In 2003 he won the competition to rebuild the World Trade Center in New York.

Daniel Libeskind (geb. 1946 in Lodz) ist ein internationaler Protagonist der Architektur und Stadtplanung. Er ist bekannt für seine Einführung eines neuen kritischen Diskurses in die Architektur und für seinen interdisziplinären Ansatz. Seine Projekte reichen von bedeutenden Kulturinstitutionen wie Museen und Konzerthallen, Landschafts- und städtebaulichen Projekten bis zu Bühnenbild, Installationen und Ausstellungen. Er lehrte an zahlreichen Universitäten als Gastprofessor und wurde vielfach ausgezeichnet. Seine bekanntesten Gebäude sind das Felix Nussbaum Haus in Osnabrück (1998), das Jüdische Museum Berlin (1999) und das

Imperial War Museum North in Manchester (2002). 2003 gewann er den Wettbewerb für den Wiederaufbau des World Trade Center in New York.

## Al Mansfeld

Tirat ha Carmel, Israel
architects@mansfeld-kehat.co.il

Al Mansfeld (b. 1912 in St. Petersburg) is one of the pioneers and most important protagonists of modern architecture and urban planning in Israel. From 1937, first in partnership with Munio Weinraub and then with his own firm, he designed and built numerous kibbutz and trade union buildings, residential housing, as well as public and urban development projects. His most famous building is the Israel Museum in Jerusalem (1959–93, with Dora Gad). As a professor at the Technion in Haifa, he influenced the concepts and styles of generations of young architects.

Al Mansfeld (geb. 1912 in St. Petersburg) ist einer der Pioniere und wichtigsten Vertreter der modernen Architektur und des Städtebaus in Israel, wo er ab 1937 zunächst mit Munio Weinraub und dann mit seinem eigenen Büro zahlreiche Kibbuz- und Gewerkschaftsbauten, Wohnanlagen, öffentliche Gebäude und städtebauliche Projekte realisierte. Sein bedeutendster Bau ist das Israel-Museum in Jerusalem (1959–93, mit Dora Gad). Als Professor am Technion in Haifa prägte er konzeptionell und stilistisch Generationen von jungen Architekten.

## Moshe Safdie

Moshe Safdie and Associates Inc.
Somerville, MA, USA
Jerusalem, Israel
Toronto, Ontario, Canada | Kanada
www.msafdie.com

In 1964, Moshe Safdie (b. 1938 in Haifa) opened his own architecture office in Montreal for the construction of Habitat for *Expo '67*. Safdie has built numerous Jewish institutions. Some of his foremost works in both Israel and the USA are the Hebrew Union College in Jerusalem (1976–88), various memorials such as the Yad Vashem Children's Holocaust Memorial in Jerusalem (1976–87), and the Skirball Museum and Cultural Center in Los Angeles (1986–95). He has been a professor at different universities in Canada, Israel, and the USA, most recently at the Harvard University Graduate School of Design. He has published numerous articles and books and has been recognized with many awards.

Moshe Safdie (geb. 1938 in Haifa) gründete 1964 in Montreal sein eigenes Architekturbüro für den Bau von Habitat für die *Expo 1967*. Safdie hat viel für jüdische Institutionen gebaut; einige seiner Hauptwerke in Israel und den USA sind das Hebrew Union College in Jerusalem (1976–88), verschiedene Mahnmale wie das Yad Vashem Children's Holocaust Memorial in Jerusalem (1976–87) und das Skirball Museum and Cultural Center in Los Angeles (1986–95). Er war Professor an verschiedenen

Universitäten in Kanada, Israel und den USA, zuletzt an der Harvard University Graduate School of Design. Er publizierte zahlreiche Artikel und Bücher und wurde mehrfach ausgezeichnet.

## Wandel Hoefer Lorch + Hirsch

Saarbrücken, Germany | Deutschland
www.wandel-hoefer-lorch.de

Wandel Hoefer Lorch (Andrea Wandel, b. 1963 in Saarbrücken; Hubertus Wandel, b. 1926 in Meseritz; Rena Wandel Hoefer, b. 1959 in Saarbrücken; Andreas Hoefer, b. 1955 in Hamburg; Wolfgang Lorch, b. 1960 in Nürtingen), in occasional cooperation with the Frankfurt-based Nikolaus Hirsch (b. 1964 in Karlsruhe) is one of the German architecture firms who have explored most intensively the memory of the Holocaust. Important works on this subject are their memorial for Frankfurt's Börneplatz (1995) and *Gleis 17* at the former deportation station Berlin-Grunewald (1998). Their synagogue with community center in Dresden and their design for the Jewish Center on Jakobsplatz in Munich have garnered accolades and have received numerous awards. Wolfgang Lorch is professor at the Technical University of Darmstadt; Nikolaus Hirsch has a teaching position at the Architectural Association in London.

Wandel Hoefer Lorch (Andrea Wandel, geb. 1963 in Saarbrücken, Hubertus Wandel, geb. 1926 in Meseritz, Rena Wandel Hoefer, geb. 1959 in Saarbrücken, Andreas Hoefer, geb. 1955 in Hamburg, Wolfgang Lorch, geb. 1960 in Nürtingen), teilweise in Zusammenarbeit mit dem in Frankfurt lebenden Nikolaus Hirsch (geb. 1964 in Karlsruhe), ist eines der Architekturbüros in Deutschland, die sich am intensivsten mit der Erinnerung an den Holocaust auseinander gesetzt haben. Wichtige Arbeiten in diesem Zusammenhang sind ihre Mahnmale für den Frankfurter Börneplatz (1995) und das *Gleis 17* am ehemaligen Deportationsbahnhof Berlin-Grunewald (1998). Ihre Synagoge mit Gemeindezentrum in Dresden und ihr Entwurf für das Jüdische Zentrum am Jakobsplatz in München fanden große Beachtung und wurden mehrfach ausgezeichnet. Wolfgang Lorch hat eine Professur an der TU Darmstadt, Nikolaus Hirsch einen Lehrauftrag an der Architectural Association in London.

## Mehrdad Yazdani

Yazdani Studio of Cannon Design
Los Angeles, California | Kalifornien, USA
www.cannondesign.com

Since he began practicing as an architect in 1987, Mehrdad Yazdani (b. 1959 in Kerman, Iran) is credited as being a catalyst in the Los Angeles design revolution. He has received significant attention for producing a new generation of public buildings that combine stimulating design and function. He began his professional career at the Los Angeles office of Ellerbe Becket in 1987; in 1994 he joined Dworsky Associates, which was acquired by Cannon Design in 2000. Besides the Sinai Temple Akiba Academy, he also designed the Yeshiva University

Boys' High School Los Angeles. His work has been exhibited in major museums and galleries. He regularly lectures at various American universities and architecture-related institutions.

Seit Mehrdad Yazdani (geb. 1959 in Kerman, Iran) 1987 als Architekt zu arbeiten begann, wird er als einer der Katalysatoren der Design-Revolution in Los Angeles betrachtet. Seine Entwürfe einer neuen Generation von öffentlichen Gebäuden, die stimulierendes Design mit Funktionalität verbinden, erhielten viel Anerkennung. Er begann seine professionelle Laufbahn 1987 im Büro von Ellerbe Becket, 1994 wechselte er zu Dworsky Associates, die 2000 von Cannon Design übernommen wurden. Neben der Sinai Temple Akiba Academy entwarf er auch die Yeshiva University Boys' High School Los Angeles. Seine Arbeiten wurden in wichtigen Museen und Galerien ausgestellt. Er hält regelmäßig Vorträge an amerikanischen Universitäten und Architekturinstitutionen.

## Curators and Editors | Kuratoren und Herausgeber

### Angeli Sachs

Is an art historian and editor-in-chief for architecture and design, based in Munich. She has worked at the Frankfurter Kunstverein, the German Architectural Museum, and the Institute for the History and Theory of Architecture at the ETH Swiss Federal Institute of Technology in Zurich. Her work includes several exhibitions and publications on art and architecture of the twentieth and twenty-first century.

Kunsthistorikerin und Cheflektorin für Architektur und Design in München. Zuvor Mitarbeiterin des Frankfurter Kunstvereins, des Deutschen Architektur Museums und des Instituts für Geschichte und Theorie der Architektur an der Eidgenössischen Technischen Hochschule Zürich. Verschiedene Ausstellungen und Publikationen zur Kunst und Architektur des 20. und 21. Jahrhunderts.

### Edward van Voolen

Is an art historian and rabbi. He is curator of the Jewish Historical Museum in Amsterdam and lectures at the Abraham Geiger College in Berlin. He has taught at several universities in Amsterdam, Potsdam, and Chicago. His work includes numerous exhibitions and publications on Jewish art, culture, and religion.

Kunsthistoriker und Rabbiner. Kustos und Kurator des Jüdischen Historischen Museums in Amsterdam und Gastdozent am Abraham Geiger Kolleg in Berlin. Lehrtätigkeit an verschiedenen Hochschulen in Amsterdam, Potsdam und Chicago. Zahlreiche Ausstellungen und Publikationen zu jüdischer Kunst, Kultur und Religion.

## Authors | Autoren

### Aaron Betsky

Is an art historian and architect, and since 2001 director of the Netherlands Architecture Institute in Rotterdam. Prior to that, he was curator of architecture, design, and digital projects at the San Francisco Museum of Modern Art, and was an instructor and coordinator of special projects at the Southern California Institute of Architecture (SCI–Arc). His work includes numerous exhibitions, publications, and lectures on architecture and design.

Kunsthistoriker und Architekt, seit 2001 Direktor des Niederländischen Architekturinstituts in Rotterdam. Zuvor Kurator für Architektur, Design und digitale Projekte am San Francisco Museum of Modern Art sowie Dozent und Projektkoordinator am Southern California Institute of Architecture (SCI-Arc). Zahlreiche Ausstellungen, Publikationen und Vorträge zu Architektur und Design.

### Stephen Fox

Is an architectural historian in Houston and a fellow of the Anchorage Foundation of Texas.

Architekturhistoriker in Houston und Stipendiat der Anchorage Foundation of Texas.

### Samuel D. Gruber

Is director of the Jewish Heritage Research Center (Syracuse, NY), research director of the U.S. Commission for the Preservation of America's Heritage Abroad (USCPAHA), and consultant for the World Monuments Fund (WMF) and the Hanadiv Charitable Foundation. He has taught at several universities and is the author of numerous books and articles about medieval architecture, Jewish art and architecture, and historic preservation.

Direktor des Jewish Heritage Research Center (Syracuse, NY), Forschungsdirektor der U. S. Commission for the Preservation of America's Heritage Abroad (USCPAHA) und Consultant für den World Monuments Fund (WMF) und die Hanadiv Charitable Foundation. Lehrtätigkeit an verschiedenen Universitäten und Autor zahlreicher Bücher und Artikel über mittelalterliche Architektur, jüdische Kunst und Architektur sowie Denkmalschutz.

### Ruth Hanisch

Is an art historian and has worked on many exhibitions of architecture and art history in Vienna. She was also an assistant at the Institute for History and Theory of Architecture at the ETH in Zurich. She has teaching positions at the University of Vienna and the Strathclyde University Glasgow.

Kunsthistorikerin. Mitarbeit bei zahlreichen Ausstellungen zu architektur- und kulturhistorischen Themen in Wien. Danach Assistentin am Institut für Geschichte und Theorie der Architektur an der ETH Zürich. Lehraufträge an der Universität Wien und der Strathclyde University Glasgow.

## Roman Hollenstein

Is a historian of art and architecture, and features editor at the *Neue Zürcher Zeitung* for architecture, monument preservation, design, and Jewish and Islamic art. His work includes various teaching positions as well as publications on contemporary Swiss architecture, museums, and synagogue architecture.

Kunst- und Architekturhistoriker, Feuilleton-Redakteur bei der *Neuen Zürcher Zeitung* mit den Schwerpunkten Architektur, Denkmalpflege, Design, jüdische und islamische Kunst. Verschiedene Lehraufträge und Publikationen zur zeitgenössischen Schweizer Architektur, Museums- und Synagogenarchitektur.

## Hans Ibelings

Is an art historian and architecture critic, based in Amsterdam. His work includes several publications on Dutch architecture, architecture and globalization, landscape architecture, and monographs on Dutch architects.

Kunsthistoriker, lebt als Architekturkritiker in Amsterdam. Zahlreiche Publikationen zur niederländischen Architektur, Architektur und Globalisierung, Landschaftsarchitektur und Monografien über niederländische Architekten.

## Rudolf Klein

Professor of modern architectural history and theory at Tel Aviv University, has published monographs on Zvi Hecker, Peter Eisenman, Tadao Ando, Joze Plecnik, and twentieth century architectural theory. He currently researches nineteenth century synagogues and architecture designed by Jewish architects.

Professor für Architekturgeschichte und -theorie der Moderne an der Universität von Tel Aviv. Publikationen über Zvi Hecker, Peter Eisenman, Tadao Ando, Joze Plecnik und Architekturtheorie des 20. Jahrhunderts. Gegenwärtig forscht er über Synagogen des 19. Jahrhunderts und Architektur jüdischer Architekten.

## Michael Levin

Is an art and architectural historian, based in Jerusalem. He has taught at several Israeli universities and colleges, and served as chief curator and later director of the Tel Aviv Museum of Art. His work includes numerous publications on modern architecture and art.

Kunst- und Architekturhistoriker in Jerusalem. Lehrtätigkeit an verschiedenen israelischen Hochschulen. Früherer Chefkurator und Direktor des Tel Aviv Museum of Art. Zahlreiche Publikationen zur modernen Architektur und Kunst.

## Mordechai Omer

Director and chief curator of the Tel Aviv Museum of Art, is a professor of modern art at the Tel Aviv University. He was curator of numerous exhibitions in Israel and abroad, including the Israeli contribution to the 2003 Biennale in Venice. His work includes numerous publications on Israeli and international artists.

Direktor und Chefkurator des Tel Aviv Museum of Art und Professor für moderne Kunst an der Universität von Tel Aviv. Er hat zahlreiche Ausstellungen in Israel und im Ausland kuratiert, darunter 2003 die Beteiligung von Israel an der Biennale in Venedig. Zahlreiche Publikationen über israelische und internationale Künstler.

## Wolfgang Pehnt

Is a historian of architecture and critic, and lives in Cologne. He is professor at Ruhr-University Bochum and member of the Academy of Arts in Berlin and the Bavarian Academy of Fine Arts in Munich. His work includes numerous publications on nineteenth and twentieth century architecture.

Architekturhistoriker und -kritiker, lebt in Köln. Professor an der Ruhr-Universität Bochum und Mitglied der Akademie der Künste, Berlin, und der Bayerischen Akademie der Schönen Künste, München. Zahlreiche Veröffentlichungen zur Architektur des 19. und 20. Jahrhunderts.

## Danette Riddle

Director of corporate communications for the global architecture/engineering firm DMJM, based in Los Angeles. She was editor of *L.A. Architect Magazine* and has edited and contributed to several books and magazines.

Kommunikationsdirektorin der globalen Architektur- und Ingenieurfirma DMJM, lebt in Los Angeles. Zuvor Redakteurin des *L.A. Architect Magazine*, Beiträge in verschiedenen Büchern und Zeitschriften.

## Anna Teut

Is an architecture, literature, and art historian, residing in Berlin. She is editor of the *Sonntagsblatt* and *Die Welt* and co-publisher of *Daidalos*. Her work includes publications primarily on the architecture of the Third Reich, and about Al Mansfeld and Max Liebermann.

Architektur-, Literatur- und Kunsthistorikerin in Berlin. Redakteurin des *Sonntagsblatts* und der *Welt*, Mitherausgeberin von *Daidalos*. Publikatio-

nen vor allem zur Architektur des Dritten Reichs, über Al Mansfeld und Max Liebermann.

## Heinrich Wefing

Is a jurist and correspondent for the *Frankfurter Allgemeine Zeitung* for the West Coast of the USA, and is based in San Francisco. Prior to this, he was an *FAZ* reporter in Berlin. His work includes numerous publications, most recently on the Chancellor's Office in Berlin.

Jurist, Korrespondent der *Frankfurter Allgemeinen Zeitung* für die amerikanische Westküste mit Sitz in San Francisco. Zuvor berichtete er sechs Jahre lang für die *FAZ* aus Berlin. Zahlreiche Veröffentlichungen, zuletzt über das Berliner Kanzleramt.

## James E. Young

Professor of English and Judaic Studies at the University of Massachusetts, Amherst, and Chair of the Department of Judaic and Near Eastern Studies. He previously held teaching positions at other American universities. He is the author of numerous books and articles, and is guest curator of the Jewish Museum of New York on the subject of memory and the Holocaust. He is a member of various committees such as the central Holocaust memorial in Berlin and the memorial at the World Trade Center in New York.

Professor für English and Judaic Studies an der University of Massachusetts, Amherst, und Dekan des Department of Judaic and Near Eastern Studies. Davor Lehrtätigkeit an verschiedenen anderen amerikanischen Universitäten. Autor zahlreicher Bücher und Artikel sowie Gastkurator des Jewish Museum, New York, über Erinnerung und den Holocaust. Mitglied verschiedener Kommissionen wie für das zentrale Holocaust-Mahnmal in Berlin und die Gedenkstätte am World Trade Center in New York.

## General | Allgemein

*Jüdische Lebenswelten*, exhib. catalogue, 2 vols.; vol. 1, Andreas Nach-
    ama, Gereon Sievernich, Julius H. Schoeps (eds.), *Katalog*, vol. 2, An-
    dreas Nachama, Julius H. Schoeps, Edward van Voolen (eds.), *Essays*,
    Frankfurt am Main 1991

Cecil Roth (ed.), *Encyclopaedia Judaica*, Jerusalem 1971/72

Julius H. Schoeps (ed.), *Neues Lexikon des Judentums,* Gütersloh 2000

Yosef Haim Yerushalmi, *Zakhor: Jewish History and Jewish Memory*,
    Seattle 1996 (first edition 1982). Deutsche Ausgabe: *Zachor. Er-
    innere Dich! Jüdische Geschichte und Jüdisches Gedächtnis,* Berlin
    1988


## Synagogues, Museums, Memorials
## Synagogen, Museen, Gedenkstätten

*Architectuur en jodendom. Architecture and Judaism, Archis, 7,* 1998

Richard I. Cohen, *Jewish Icons: Art and Society in Modern Europe*,
    Berkeley 1998

Grace Cohen Grossman, *Jewish Museums of the World*, Westport 2003

Aliza Cohen-Mushlin, Isabel Haupt (ed.), *Synagogenarchitektur in
    Deutschland vom Barock zum „Neuen Bauen": Dokumentation zur
    Ausstellung*, exhib. catalogue, Fachgebiet Baugeschichte Braun-
    schweig, Braunschweig 2002

Ruth Ellen Gruber, *Virtually Jewish: Reinventing Jewish Culture in
    Europe*, Berkeley 2003

Samuel D. Gruber, Paul Rocheleau (photographs) and Scott J. Tilden
    (ed.), *American Synagogues*, New York 2003

Hermann Zvi Guttmann, Sophie Remmlinger (ed.) and Klaus Hofmann
    (ed.), *Vom Tempel zum Gemeindezentrum: Synagogen im Nach-
    kriegsdeutschland,* Frankfurt am Main 1989

Harold Hammer-Schenk, *Synagogen in Deutschland: Geschichte einer
    Baugattung im 19. und 20. Jahrhundert,* 2 vols., Hamburg 1981

Thomas Hubka, *Resplendent Synagogue: Architecture and Worship
    in an Eighteenth-Century Polish Community*, Hanover, London 2003

*In einem neuen Geiste: Synagogen von Alfred Jacoby. In a new Spirit:
    The Synagogues of Alfred Jacoby,* exhib. catalogue, Deutsches Archi-
    tektur Museum, Frankfurt am Main 2002

Dominique Jarrassé, *Synagogues: Architecture and Jewish Identity*,
    Paris 2001

Carol Herselle Krinsky, *Synagogues of Europe,* New York, Cambridge/
    Mass. 1985. Deutsche Ausgabe: *Europas Synagogen. Architektur,
    Geschichte, Bedeutung,* Stuttgart 1988

H.A. Meek, *The Synagogue*, London 1995. Deutsche Ausgabe: *Die
    Synagoge*, München 1996

Sabine Offe, *Ausstellungen, Einstellungen, Entstellungen: Jüdische
    Museen in Deutschland und Österreich*, Berlin 2000

Hans-Peter Schwarz (ed.), *Die Architektur der Synagoge,* exhib. cata-
    logue, Deutsches Architektur Museum, Stuttgart 1988

Gabrielle Sed-Rajna (ed.), *Jewish Art,* New York 1997

*Synagogen in Deutschland: Eine virtuelle Rekonstruktion,* exhib. cata-
    logue, Kunst- und Ausstellungshalle der Bundesrepublik Deutsch-
    land, Bonn 2000

Jeshajahu Weinberg, Rina Elieli, *The Holocaust Museum in Washing-
    ton*, New York 1995

Rachel Wischnitzer, *The Architecture of the European Synagogue*,
    Philadelphia 1964

James E. Young, *The Texture of Memory: Holocaust Memorials and
    Meaning,* New Haven and London 1993. Deutsche Ausgabe: *Formen
    des Erinnerns. Gedenkstätten des Holocaust,* Wien 1997

James E. Young (ed.), *The Art of Memory: Holocaust Memorials in
    History,* exhib. catalogue, The Jewish Museum, New York, Munich,
    New York 1994. Deutsche Ausgabe: *Mahnmale des Holocaust. Moti-
    ve, Rituale und Stätten des Gedenkens,* München, New York 1994

James E. Young, *At Memory's Edge. After-Images of the Holocaust in
    Contemporary Art and Architecture,* New Haven and London 2000.
    Deutsche Ausgabe: *Nach-Bilder des Holocaust in zeitgenössischer
    Kunst und Architektur,* Hamburg 2002


## Architects | Architekten

### Ralph Appelbaum

Vincent P. Hauser, "A Room for Reflection", *Texas Architect*, 46, July/
    Aug. 1996

Reed Kroloff, "Dark Remembrance", *Architecture*, 85, Nov. 1996

Barbara Flanagan, "Ralph Appelbaum: Designer of the Year", *Interiors*,
    159, Jan. 2000

### Mario Botta

Luca Molinari, *Mario Botta: öffentliche Bauten 1990–1998*, Mailand
    1998

Mario Botta, *The Cymbalista Synagogue and Jewish Heritage Center*,
    Milan 2001

Irena Sakellaridou, *Mario Botta: architectural poetics,* London 2001

Gabriele Capellato (ed.), *Mario Botta. Luce e gravità, Architetture
    1993–2003*, Bologna 2003

Philip Jodidio, *Mario Botta*, Cologne 2003

### Will Bruder

Aaron Betsky, "Monumenten in de uitdijende stad. Making monu-
    ments in the sprawl", *Archis*, 7, 1996

Francisco Asensio Cerver, *Architects of the World*, Barcelona 1998,
    pp. 6–9

Philip Jodidio, *Building a New Millennium. Bauen im neuen Jahrtau-
    send. Construire un nouveau millénaire*, Cologne 1999, pp. 118–123

## Claus en Kaan

Hans Ibelings (ed.), *Claus en Kaan*, Rotterdam 2001

*beauftragt. Claus en Kaan Architecten*, exhib. catalogue, Aedes, Berlin 2002

Ilka & Andreas Ruby, Angeli Sachs, Philip Ursprung, *Minimal Architecture*, Munich, Berlin, London, New York 2003

## Frank O. Gehry

Francesco Dal Co, *Frank O. Gehry: The Complete Works*, New York 1998

J. Fiona Ragheb (ed.), *Frank Gehry, Architect*, exhib. catalogue, Guggenheim Museum, New York 2001

*Frank O. Gehry: 13 Projects after Bilbao, GA Document*, 68, 2002

*Frank Gehry: de la A a la Z / from A to Z, El Croquis*, 117, 2003

*FOG: Flowing in All Directions*, exhib. catalogue, The Museum of Contemporary Art, Los Angeles 2003

## Zvi Hecker

Kristin Feireiss (ed.), *Zvi Hecker: Die Heinz-Galinski-Schule in Berlin. The Heinz-Galinski-School in Berlin*, Tübingen, Berlin 1995

Meira Yagid-Haimovici (ed.), *Zvi Hecker – Sunflower*, exhib. catalogue, The Tel Aviv Museum of Art, Tel Aviv 1996

Mario Bottero, *scuola ebraica, Berlino*, Torino 1997

Peter Cook, *The House of the Book*, London 1999

## Adolf Krischanitz, Helmut Federle

Edelbert Köb (ed.), *Krischanitz, Federle. Neue Welt Schule*, Kunsthaus Bregenz, archiv kunst architektur, Stuttgart 1994

*Adolf Krischanitz, Architect: Buildings and Projects 1986–1998*, Basel, Boston, Berlin 1998

Ilka & Andreas Ruby, Angeli Sachs, Philip Ursprung, *Minimal Architecture*, Munich, Berlin, London, New York 2003

## Daniel Libeskind

Kristin Feireiss (ed.), *Daniel Libeskind. Erweiterung des Berlin Museums mit Abteilung Jüdisches Museum. Extension to the Berlin Museum with Jewish Museum Department*, Berlin 1992

Alois Martin Müller, *Daniel Libeskind: Radix–Matrix; Works and Writings,* exhib. catalogue, Museum für Gestaltung Zürich, Munich 1994. Deutsche Ausgabe: *Daniel Libeskind. Radix – Matrix. Architekturen und Schriften*, München, New York 1994

Thorsten Rodiek, *Daniel Libeskind – Museum ohne Ausgang: das Felix-Nussbaum-Haus des Kulturgeschichtlichen Museums in Osnabrück*, Tübingen 1998

Elke Dorner, *Daniel Libeskind. Jüdisches Museum Berlin*, Berlin 1999

Daniel Libeskind, Bernhard Schneider, *Jewish Museum Berlin: Between the Lines*, Munich, London, New York 1999. Deutsche Ausgabe: *Daniel Libeskind. Jüdisches Museum Berlin*, München, London, New York 1999

Daniel Libeskind, *Daniel Libeskind: The Space of Encounter*, London 2001

## Al Mansfeld

Anna Teut (ed.), *Al Mansfeld: Architekt in Israel. An Architect in Israel*, Berlin 1998

## Moshe Safdie

Wendy Kohn, *Moshe Safdie*, London 1996

*Moshe Safdie: Museum Architecture 1971–1998*, exhib. catalogue, The Genia Schreiber University Art Gallery, Tel Aviv University, Tel Aviv 1998

## Wandel Hoefer Lorch + Hirsch

Matthias Boeckl, "Wandel Hoefer Lorch Hirsch: Synagoge in Dresden, Deutschland", *architektur aktuell*, 11, 2001

David Cohn, "A complex and tragic history informs Wandel Hoefer Lorch + Hirsch's poetic design for the new Dresden Synagogue", in: *Architectural Record*, vol. 190, issue 6, June 2002

Karin Leydecker, „Neue Synagoge, Dresden. New Synagogue, Dresden", in: Deutsches Architektur Museum, Frankfurt am Main, Ingeborg Flagge, Peter Cachola Schmal and Wolfgang Voigt (eds.), *DAM Jahrbuch 2002: Architektur in Deutschland / Architecture in Germany*, Munich, Berlin, London, New York 2002

Ullrich Schwarz (ed.), *Neue Deutsche Architektur. Eine Reflexive Moderne*, exhib. catalogue, Ostfildern-Ruit 2002

## Mehrdad Yazdani

Joseph Giovanni, "Portfolio: Sinai Temple Akiba Academy", *Architecture*, 9, 1999

# Colophon | Impressum

This book has been published in conjunction with the exhibition |
Dieses Buch erschien anlässlich der Ausstellung
Jewish Identity in Contemporary Architecture
held at the | im Joods Historisch Museum, Amsterdam
from March 26 – August 29, 2004.

Further exhibition venues | Weitere Ausstellungsstationen:
Felix-Nussbaum-Haus, Osnabrück, September 19 – November 14, 2004
Museum of the History of Polish Jews, Warsaw, January 5 – February 20, 2005
Jüdisches Museum Berlin, March 18 – May 29, 2005
Jüdisches Museum Wien, June 22 – September 4, 2005
Münchner Stadtmuseum, Munich, November 4, 2005 – February 5, 2006
Ben Uri Gallery, The London Jewish Museum of Art, April 16 – June 18, 2006

Curators and Editors | Kuratoren und Herausgeber: Angeli Sachs, Edward van Voolen

© Prestel Verlag, München · Berlin · London · New York 2004
© for the artworks, with the architects and artists, their heirs or assigns, with the exception of |
für die abgebildeten Werke bei den Architekten und Künstlern, ihren Erben oder Rechtsnach-
folgern, mit Ausnahme von Barnett Newman with | bei VG Bild-Kunst, Bonn 2004
See Illustration Credits | Bildnachweis, page | Seite 176

Front and back cover | Umschlag: Wandel Hoefer Lorch + Hirsch, New Synagogue Dresden |
Neue Synagoge Dresden, Dresden, Germany | Deutschland,
Photograph by | Fotografie: Roland Halbe
Frontispiece | Frontispiz: Daniel Libeskind, Jewish Museum Berlin | Jüdisches Museum Berlin,
Berlin, Germany | Deutschland, Photograph by | Fotografie: Stefan Müller

Prestel Verlag
Königinstrasse 9, D-80539 Munich | München
Tel. + 49 (89) 38 17 09-0
Fax + 49 (89) 38 17 09-35
www.prestel.de

Prestel Publishing Ltd.
4, Bloomsbury Place, London WC1A 2QA
Tel. +44 (0 20) 73 23-5004
Fax +44 (0 20) 76 36-8004

Prestel Publishing
900 Broadway, Suite 603
New York, N.Y. 10003
Tel. +1 (212) 995-2720
Fax +1 (212) 995-2733
www.prestel.com

Library of Congress Control Number: 2004101173
British Library Cataloguing-in-Publication Data
A catalogue record for this book is available from the British Library.

Die Deutsche Bibliothek verzeichnet diese Publikation in der Deutschen Nationalbibliografie;
detaillierte bibliografische Daten sind im Internet über http://dnb.ddb.de abrufbar.

Prestel books are available worldwide. Please contact your nearest bookseller or one
of the above addresses for information concerning your local distributor.

Translations | Übersetzungen: John Gabriel (German – English),
Bram Opstelten (Dutch – English, Niederländisch – Deutsch),
Annette Wiethüchter (Englisch – Deutsch)

Editorial direction | Projektleitung: Angeli Sachs
Copyedited by | Lektorat: Charles Heard (English), Angeli Sachs (Deutsch)
Editorial assistance and picture research | Lektoratsassistenz und Bildredaktion:
Sabine Schmid
Design and layout | Gestaltung und Herstellung: Cilly Klotz
Origination | Lithografie: Reproline Genceler, München
Printing | Druck: Passavia, Passau
Binding | Bindung: Passavia, Passau

Printed in Germany
on acid-free paper | auf chlorfrei gebleichtem Papier

ISBN 3-7913-3057-8 (hardcover edition | Buchhandelsausgabe)
ISBN 3-7913-6014-0 (paperback edition | Katalogausgabe)

# Illustration Credits | Bildnachweis

All reasonable efforts have been made to obtain copyright permission for the
images in this book. If we have committed an oversight, we will be pleased
to rectify it in a subsequent edition.
Der Verlag hat gewissenhaft versucht, alle Quellen und Urheberrechts-
inhaber zu ermitteln und zu kennzeichnen. Er bittet etwaige
Bildrechtsinhaber, die nicht ausfindig gemacht werden konnten, sich mit
dem Verlag in Verbindung zu setzen.

Numbers refer to pages.
Die Nummern beziehen sich auf Seitenzahlen.
a = all, t = top, b = bottom, l = left, r = right, c = center
a = alle, o = oben, u = unten, l = links, r = rechts, m = Mitte

10/11 Pino Musi, Como; 12, 13, 15 t l | o r, 18, 19 Collection
Jewish Historical Museum Amsterdam; 15 t l | o l © VG Bild-Kunst,
Bonn 2004; 17 Timothy Hursley, Little Rock, AR;
21, 25 c | m, 26, 27, 30 b r | u r Paul Rocheleau, Richmond, MA;
23 Illustrated London News 1866; 24 Ruth Ellen Gruber;
25 l | l Sächsische Landesbibliothek – Staats- und Universitäts-
bibliothek, Abt. Fotothek, Dresden. Lithography | Lithography:
L. Thümeling. Photograph | Fotografie: Heinrich;
25 r | r Stadtarchiv Plauen; 28 Ursula Seitz-Gray, Frankfurt;
29 Archivio Foto Arte, Livorno; 30 t l | o l from | aus: Kristin Feireiss,
Zvi Hecker – Die Heinz-Galinski-Schule in Berlin,
Tübingen/Berlin 1995, p. | S. 31; 33 Leonardo Bezzola;
34 Amiram Harlap; 35 t l | o l Kent Larson; 35 b l | u l Michal
Ronnen Safdie; 35 t r | o r, 38 Moshe & Eli Gross / Keren-Or, Haifa;
37 l | l Leonardo Bezzola; 37 r | r Alfred Berenheim;
40 t | o Amit Giron; 40 b | u Michael Levin, Jerusalem;
42 Timothy Hursley, Little Rock, AR; 43 Stefan Müller, Berlin;
45 Roland Halbe, Stuttgart; 47 Bitter Bredt Fotografie, Berlin;
49, 50 Courtesy of Yad Vashem The Holocaust Martyrs' and Heroes'
Remembrance Authority, Jerusalem; 51 Max Reid, USHMM
Photo Archives, Washington; 52 Alan Gilbert, courtesy of USHMM
Photo Archives, Washington; 53 Julie Cohen 2003, courtesy:
Museum of Jewish Heritage, New York; 54 Tom Powel Imaging, Inc.,
courtesy: Museum of Jewish Heritage – A Living Memorial to the
Holocaust, New York; 56/57 Christian Richters, Münster;
58, 61 t | o, 62/63 Scott Frances / Esto, Marmaroneck NY;
64, 67–71 t | o Christian Richters, Münster; 72–77 Gehry Partners LLP,
Los Angeles. Photographs | Fotografien: Whit Preston;
78, 81 t | o – 85 Stefan Müller, Berlin; 86–91 computer simulations |
Computersimulationen: Miller Hare; 92–97 Collection of Moshe Safdie
and Associates, Somerville, MA. Photographs | Fotografien:
© Ardon Bar Hama; 98–100, 103 t | o, 104–107 Pino Musi, Como;
108, 111–114 t | o, 115 Bill Timmerman; 116, 120–123 Michael
Krüger, Berlin; 118/119 drawings | Zeichnungen: Zvi Hecker.
Photographs | Fotografien: Michael Krüger, Berlin;
124, 127 Norbert Miguletz, Frankfurt; 128–130 t | o Roland Halbe,
Stuttgart; 131 Werner Huthmacher, Berlin; 132–135 Wandel
Hoefer Lorch, Saarbrücken; 136–138, 142, 143 b l, t r, b r | u l, o r, u r
photographs | Fotografien: Christian Richters, Münster;
140 drawing | Zeichnung: Zvi Hecker. Photograph | Fotografie:
Michael Krüger, Berlin; 141 Jüdisches Museum Berlin. Photographer |
Fotograf: Jens Ziehe; 143 t l | o l, 144, 145 Michael Krüger, Berlin;
146, 148–152, 155–157 Margherita Spiluttini, Vienna | Wien;
158, 161 Moshe & Eli Gross / Keren-Or, Haifa;
162, 164–165 t | o Timothy Hursley, Little Rock, AR;
166/167, 173 Stefan Müller, Berlin

© for drawings and plans are held by the respective architects
© für Zeichnungen und Pläne bei den jeweiligen Architekten

720.89924 SAC